S0-BNB-608

HUANG HSING AND THE CHINESE REVOLUTION

STANFORD STUDIES IN HISTORY, ECONOMICS,
AND POLITICAL SCIENCE, XX

HUANG HSING

AND THE

CHINESE REVOLUTION

Chün-tu Hsüeh

———

STANFORD UNIVERSITY PRESS
STANFORD, CALIFORNIA
1961

DS
778
H85
H7

43408

STANFORD UNIVERSITY PRESS
STANFORD, CALIFORNIA

© 1961 BY THE BOARD OF TRUSTEES OF THE
LELAND STANFORD JUNIOR UNIVERSITY

ALL RIGHTS RESERVED

LIBRARY OF CONGRESS CATALOG CARD NUMBER: 61-6531

PRINTED IN THE UNITED STATES OF AMERICA

To my wife
HUANG TE-HUA

PREFACE

This is a study of Huang Hsing, co-founder of the Republic of China. In the Revolution of 1911, which overthrew the Ch'ing dynasty, Huang Hsing and Sun Yat-sen were the two most influential revolutionary leaders in China. Indeed, the dual leadership of Sun and Huang is the key to the understanding of the Chinese revolutionary movement in the decade after 1905.

A meeting between Sun and Huang in 1905 led to the formation of the T'ung Meng Hui, and thereafter most of the military operations of that revolutionary organization were personally directed by Huang Hsing, an intellectual who commanded by the force of his intrepidity and personal courage. Sun, as the ideologist and fund-raiser of the revolutionary movement, and Huang, as its military leader, worked closely together until the overthrow of the Manchu dynasty; and for some time after the establishment of the Republic, most public statements of Kuomintang policy were issued jointly in their names. And yet, for various reasons, much has been written about one of these leaders and very little about the other.

By examining the mass of documents and writings pertaining to the Revolution, including many sources previously unexploited by Western historians and some unpublished even in Chinese, I have tried to establish an accurate and fairly detailed account of the revolutionary events. The emphasis I have given to personalities does not mean that I underestimate the strength of the larger historical forces that made the Revolution possible. Huang Hsing lived at a time when China was threatened by partition from without, and, with the exception of the last five years of his life, was misruled by an alien race from within. The downfall of the Manchu dynasty was brought about by the interplay of foreign impact, imperialism, the unrest of the peasantry, the rise of a Chinese capitalist class, the new intellectual horizons appearing to educated Chinese, and the shift of power from Manchus to Chinese in the government after the Taiping uprising of the mid-nineteenth century. These and other forces were at work to hasten the disintegration of the Empire; but important as they were, they are beyond the scope of this study. My examination of Huang Hsing's career is offered primarily as part of a more general description of the interplay of leadership within the revolutionary movement; this, I hope, will prove to be a worthwhile contribution to further and more comprehensive studies of the revolutionary period.

Throughout the narrative and in most of the quotations I have used the given names of Chinese persons, except for the few of them who are better known by their courtesy, or other, names. The Glossary gives Chinese characters for names mentioned in the text. I have given ages in the Western style rather than the Chinese, by which a man is considered one year old on the day he is born. My romanization follows the Wade-Giles system with most of the diacritical marks omitted; certain well-known geographical names, however, are rendered according to popular usage. Unless otherwise credited, all translations from the Chinese and Japanese are my own.

HSÜEH CHÜN-TU

Stanford, California
March 29, 1961

ACKNOWLEDGMENTS

I should like to extend my sincere thanks to Professors Nathaniel Peffer, C. Martin Wilbur, Franklyn L. Ho, James W. Morley, Alexander Dallin, and other members of the faculty of Columbia University who read the original manuscript and commented on it as it approached final form. Above all, I am greatly indebted to Professor Wilbur, who first suggested that I undertake this study and later offered me a wealth of valuable advice. Professor L. Carrington Goodrich kindly called my attention to several source materials I had overlooked. The Honorable Huang Chen-hua helped clarify for me certain aspects of her father's life, and Professor Huang Wen-shan graciously allowed me to use the private papers and documents in his possession.

My thanks also go out to Professor Vernon Loggins, Mrs. Allen Abbott, Miss Wu Yüeh-ching, Donna and James Taylor, Kenneth W. Furst, Wade A. Doares, Thomas Duddy, and a number of other friends for their occasional assistance and suggestions. I am grateful to Gene W. Tanke of the Stanford University Press for his highly skillful editorial work. I am obliged to Mrs. Shirley Taylor for preparing the index and to the *Journal of Asian Studies* for permission to reproduce (in Chapter Three) part of my article on Sun Yat-sen. Finally, I should like to acknowledge that my association with the Department of Political Science and the Committee on East Asian Studies at Stanford University has greatly facilitated preparation of the manuscript for publication.

C. T. H.

CONTENTS

xi

ONE

THE EARLY LIFE OF HUANG HSING

HUANG HSING was born on October 25, 1874, in Shanhua (now Changsha), Hunan. His given name was Huang Chen and his courtesy name Chin-wu. It was in the underground revolutionary movement that he adopted another name, Hsing (meaning "revival"), and the courtesy name K'o-ch'iang (meaning "strong" or "conqueror of the strong"), by which he was later known.

Hunan is a province in central China lying south of the Yangtze River. It may be considered, however, as one of the regions of the subtropical South in the vast Chinese realms. It is a "land of rice and fish." To the north lies the Yangtze province of Hupeh; to the south is Kwangtung province on the Pearl River. During the Ch'ing dynasty, which began in 1644 when the Manchus captured Peking and established themselves as rulers of China, Hunan and Hupeh were governed as one administrative unit, with a governor of each under a governor-general in charge of the entire area.

In comparison with their neighbors in Kwangtung, the men of Hunan seemed stolid and conservative. And yet many of the first advocates of Western learning in the nineteenth century were Hunanese, among them Wei Yüan, Kuo Sung-tao, and Tseng Chi-tse. Many early Ch'ing nationalist thinkers were also from that province, notably Wang Fu-chih. By contrast, it was the Hunanese Tseng Kuo-fan and Tso Tsung-t'ang, and their Hunan Army, who, in the cause of defending the Confucian tradition, were primarily responsible for putting down the Taiping Rebellion and saving the Manchu dynasty about ten years before Huang Hsing was born.

Huang's father, Hsiao-ts'un, was a schoolteacher of moderate means and held the honorary position of Tu-tsung, or head

1

of a district subdivision. Born in 1842, Huang Hsiao-ts'un married three times during his life of fifty-five years. His first wife died one year after the marriage and left no children. His second wife was from the Lo family of the same village. She was one year older than her husband, and bore him three daughters and two sons, of whom Huang Hsing was the youngest. She died in 1882, when Huang was only eight years old. In the following year, the father married a widow, I Tzu-ju, who bore him no children. The boy's stepmother was considered well-educated for a woman in those days; in 1901, she served as superintendent of a girls' school at Changsha.[1]

Little is known about Huang Hsing's activities as a youth except that he was physically strong and that he developed a fondness for Chinese boxing. He received the normal classical education of young men of his class. In 1892 he married Liao Tan-ju, the nineteen-year-old daughter of Liao Hsing-fang, one of the local gentry. Four sons and two daughters were born as a result of this marriage, but one of the sons died in infancy.[2] In the same year Huang passed the district examination and obtained the first literary degree, *Hsiu-ts'ai*.[3] This opened the way to a career as a scholar-official. His next step would have been to prepare for the provincial examination and then for the metropolitan examination. But times had changed, and the tradition was shaken.

The defeat of China in the war against Japan in 1894-95 was a great shock to the whole nation. The Ch'ing regime had lost its vigor after about 1800, and since the nation had been "opened" by the British in 1842, China had suffered repeated humiliation at the hands of Western powers and had experienced internal disturbances as well. But the greatest humiliation by far was her defeat by Japan. That the tiny kingdom of "dwarf barbarians" could defeat a colossal empire showed the unmistakable material superiority of Western technology, to which Japan had converted after the Meiji Restoration of 1868. The war undermined Chinese complacency and accelerated the growing recognition of China's need to learn from the West. A reform movement was launched by a few progressive officials and farsighted scholars.

Hunan was the most active province in the reform movement. In the fall of 1897 Liang Ch'i-ch'ao, a student of the reform leader K'ang Yu-wei, was invited to Changsha to lecture at the Academy of Current Affairs founded in the provincial capital that year. T'an Ssu-t'ung, chairman of the local reform association, edited the first newspaper of the province. It is likely that Huang Hsing was influenced by the reform agitation in 1897, though we know nothing of his attitude at that time. In 1898, the year that marked the highest point of the reform movement supported by the Kuang-hsü emperor, Huang was studying at the Academy of Hunan and Hupeh (Liang-Hu Shu-yüan) at Wuchang, about 360 miles from his home.[4] His father had died the year before, and he himself, at the age of twenty-four, was now the father of two children.[5]

The Academy was established by Governor-General Chang Chih-tung at the provincial capital of Hupeh. The students were recruited from the two provinces of Hunan and Hupeh, each of which had a quota of one hundred students. They were chosen upon the recommendation of the respective provincial educational authorities from among the most promising young students of the two provinces—students who had received their first degrees and were judged to have displayed "integrity, diligence, introspection, or superior ability." In addition to this student body of two hundred, a quota of forty was reserved for children of tea merchants, men of this trade having originally contributed funds for the establishment of the school. All students were required to live in dormitories, and each was given a government stipend of three dollars a month. In some cases nonresident students and direct applicants for admission without recommendation were permitted; unrecommended students were considered "nonmatriculated" even if they passed the entrance examination.[6] In the official announcement of the establishment of the Academy, dated February 9, 1891, the Governor-General outlined his design for the school as follows:

To encourage scholarship, the Academy will honor those students who achieve distinction in their courses. It will provide a library with numerous books so that the students may be well-read. School regulations will necessarily be strict in order to regulate and control

3

the behavior of the student body. Diaries will be kept by the students and will be constantly examined by the instructors so that each student's accomplishment can be checked. Broad and general knowledge will be balanced by specialized disciplines, and good character will be cultivated. All training is designed in the hope that some day the students will become either prominent officials or famous scholars. . . .

However, if it is discovered that a student loafs, insults the teachers, shows disrespect to government officials, blasphemes Confucius, or criticizes the government, he will be considered to have violated the school regulations and will be immediately expelled.[7]

The curriculum of the Academy in its early stage consisted of six subjects: classics, history, philosophy, literature, mathematics, and political science. Each course was conducted by a specialist in the field, and the students were free to take any number of these courses. Among the teachers who taught there at one time or another were Yang Jui, who was to be known later as one of the "six martyrs" of the reform movement of 1898, and Wang K'ang-nien, one of the pioneers of modern Chinese journalism.[8]

In 1897 and 1898 the Academy of Hunan and Hupeh underwent a change which marked the beginning of another stage in the transitional period from the old Chinese educational system to the modern school system developed after the turn of the century. The curriculum was changed to four courses, and the students were required to study them all: classics, history, geography, and mathematics. The course of study was fixed at five years; only students under twenty-five were eligible for admission. Later astronomy, science, physical education, and military strategy were added to the curriculum. Military drill and target practice with firearms were particularly emphasized.[9]

The educational philosophy underlying the institution was Chang Chih-tung's famous maxim, "Chinese learning for the fundamental principles, Western learning for practical application," according to his memorial to the throne dated May 5, 1898.[10] The Governor-General personally took charge of the final examinations, which were held at the end of the spring and winter sessions. There was but one holiday every ten days. The government stipend for each student was soon increased to four dollars a month, and those who came out first in the monthly examinations were awarded prizes of eight dollars.[11]

In his school days at the Academy Huang Hsing enjoyed writing poems and *tz'u* (metrical compositions). His diary of this time, found in 1933 by his eldest daughter Chen-hua, is full of these literary efforts.[12] His favorite subject was history, and he often sent books to his stepmother after he had finished reading them. He was reportedly a favorite student of Liang Ting-fen, president of the Academy, because "his prose had the style of the writings of Su Tung-p'o, and his calligraphy was excellent in the Northern Wei style."[13] Unfortunately, his opinions on current events are not known, nor can we be certain of his political ideas. It is said, however, that he was a great admirer of T'an Ssu-t'ung and T'ang Ts'ai-ch'ang, two Hunanese leaders of the reform movement.[14]

T'an Ssu-t'ung was one of the "six martyrs" executed after the coup d'état of 1898 which ended the rule of the Kuang-hsü emperor.[15] T'ang Ts'ai-ch'ang was executed for his part in the armed revolt of 1900 by which the reformers, under the leadership of K'ang Yu-wei, attempted to restore the Kuang-hsü emperor to power.[16] Huang probably admired T'an and T'ang as men of action, men who were willing to sacrifice their own lives for a cause.

The failure of this revolt must have left a strong impression on Huang, for a number of its leaders had made their headquarters in the city of Hankow, just across the river from Wuchang, where Huang Hsing was studying; indeed the chief aim of the revolt was to capture Wuchang and Hankow as military bases. The revolt was financed from abroad by K'ang Yu-wei and Liang Ch'i-ch'ao, but it was conducted primarily by men from Hunan, Hupeh, and Anhwei. As a result of its failure, many were executed in those provinces.[17]

The political atmosphere in China changed radically at the turn of the century. From the end of 1899 to the spring of 1900 progressive Chinese were still concerned over the fate of the throne; when the Empress Dowager raised the question whether the emperor should abdicate, she faced strong opposition in the nation, and prominent Shanghai citizens held a meeting of protest against the idea of abdication.[18] But the regime was past saving, and the national humiliation inflicted by the foreign powers as a result of the Boxer catastrophe of 1900 was so great that the masses of people seemed to have lost whatever confidence they might still have had in their government.

During his school days in this turbulent time, Huang Hsing had the reputation of being a quiet and discreet student.[19] Whatever revolutionary ideas he might have had during this period cannot be traced. He probably returned to Hunan to see his family from time to time during vacations. On June 27, 1901, his second son, I-chung, was born. About a month later the family moved from Shanhua to the city of Changsha.[20] In the summer of the following year he was sent by the Hupeh provincial government to Japan to study normal-school education. He arrived in Tokyo in May 1902.[21] According to his friend and biographer Liu K'uei-i, this was the turning point in his life. For it was in Japan that Huang began to realize the nature of the Manchu rule and there that his Western learning made him an advocate of the republican form of government.[22]

One of the reforms undertaken by the Manchu government after the Boxer uprising was the change in the educational system. This began with a series of imperial edicts issued in 1901; by these edicts the "eight-legged" essay was abolished, modern schools were established, and students were encouraged to study abroad. As Japan became the model for the Westernization of China, Tokyo naturally became the center of the Chinese students abroad, having the advantage over other Western capitals of being near China, inexpensive, similar in language, and lenient in the matter of immigration. The anti-Manchu movement of these students in Japan later played a central role in undermining the Ch'ing dynasty.

Before 1900 there were not many Chinese studying in Japan. The earliest Chinese student organization in Japan was the Mutual Encouragement Society (Li Chih Hui), founded in Tokyo in 1900; it was strictly a social club and was dissolved the following year. In the autumn of 1900 the *Translation Magazine* (*I-shu hui-pien*) began to be published. This monthly magazine was the first publication undertaken by Chinese students in Japan. It was devoted entirely to translations of the political writings of Western philosophers, among them Rousseau's *Contrat social,* Montesquieu's *Esprit des lois,* and Mill's *On Liberty* and *Representative Government.* In the same year, another short-lived Chinese magazine, the *New Learning* (*K'ai-chih lu*), was published by Feng Tzu-yu and his friends in Yokohama; it offered articles advocating the ideas of liberty and equality.[23] But the journals that had the greatest influence on Chinese intellectuals were those published by Liang Ch'i-ch'ao in Yokohama, the *Ch'ing-i pao* and later the *Hsin-min ts'ung-pao.* Liang's own essays, which appeared in 1902 and 1903, were particularly influential.[24] His effective criticism of the Ch'ing government, by which he intended only to promote reform, led younger men to become more seriously dissatisfied with the regime.

On May 10, 1901, *The Chinese National* (*Kuo-min pao*) appeared in Japan. This was the first publication by Chinese students in Japan to expound revolutionary ideas. Among the editorial writers was Ch'in Li-shan, a native of Changsha, who had studied at the Academy of Current Affairs and worked for the *Ch'ing-i pao.* He had taken a leading part in the revolt of 1900 and escaped to Japan after its defeat. He blamed K'ang Yu-wei for the failure of the revolt, alleging misuse of funds. He attacked both the political ideas and the personal integrity of K'ang Yu-wei and advocated the overthrow of the Manchu dynasty. He also planned for a time to organize the progressive literati in China and abroad for the revolutionary cause, but he gave up this plan and returned to Shanghai.[25]

With the number of Chinese students abroad increasing rapidly, the Chinese Students Association in Japan was organized early in 1902. In a speech delivered at the first meeting of the Association, Wu Lu-chen, a student from Hupeh studying at a Japanese military school, compared the Association's office to Independence Hall in the United States.

On April 26, 1902, about a month before Huang Hsing's arrival in Tokyo, the Chinese students in Japan planned to commemorate the 242nd anniversary of the Manchu conquest of

China, it having been on that day (the 19th day of the 3rd lunar month) that the last emperor of the Ming dynasty hanged himself on Coal Hill in Peking. A declaration was written by Chang Ping-lin, a scholar from Chekiang province. Although the meeting was forbidden by the Japanese authorities in deference to the Peking government, anti-Manchu feeling mounted.

A few months later some Chinese students quarreled with the Chinese envoy in Japan, Ts'ai Chün, because he reportedly refused to recommend that they be allowed to study in Japanese military schools at their own expense; such recommendations were necessary, for the Peking government prohibited Chinese students from studying in Japanese military academies unless they were sponsored by the government. Wu Chih-hui, a school-teacher from Kiangsu province, after arguing in vain with Ts'ai, refused to leave the Legation unless the envoy granted the students' requests. Ts'ai summoned the Japanese police to arrest him. Wu tried to commit suicide, but was prevented. He subsequently returned to China on August 13, 1902.[26] Incidents of this sort intensified the Chinese students' hatred of the officials of their government.

In the winter of 1902, a few months after Huang Hsing's arrival, some students organized a Young Men's Association, advocating nationalism and violence. Except for the group that published the *Kuo-min pao,* this was probably the first student organization in Japan that harbored definitely revolutionary ideas. Among its founders was Chang Chi, a native of Chihli (Hopeh) province.[27]

Anti-Manchu feeling continued to rise after the New Year. Liu Ch'eng-yü, a native of Hupeh, was expelled from school for his open expression of revolutionary sentiments at a Chinese New Year party held on January 29, 1903, which was attended by more than one thousand persons, including the Chinese envoy, Ts'ai Chün.[28] Many student publications began to appear. It was characteristic that each one was published by a group of students from the same province. In those days fraternal feeling among people from the same province was strong, and there was a sense of "Hunan solidarity" among the Hunanese students in Tokyo regardless of their political beliefs.[29]

8

From 1902 to 1903 Huang studied normal-school education at the Kōbun Institute in Tokyo, an institution established by the Japanese especially to serve the needs of Chinese students. It offered courses in law, physics, political science, and normal-school education. Huang was much interested in Japanese military training. Whenever possible, he watched the Japanese cadets drill, and sometimes he asked Japanese army officers to give him instruction in military strategy. One of his favorite extracurricular interests was target practice; he was a good shot and won many prizes for his skill.[30] According to the recollection of a fellow student, Hu Han-min, "Huang Hsing made no remarkable achievements in the school, but Yang Tu [another Hunanese] was well known for his diligence."[31]

Huang Hsing helped to found the *Hupeh Students' Circle* (*Hu-pei hsüeh-sheng chieh*), a magazine published by Hupeh students in Japan.[32] He was also one of the eight Hunanese who combined to found the Hunan Translation Society (Hu-nan Pien-i She), which published the *Translations by Hunan Students Abroad* (*Yu-hsüeh i-pien*) and many other school textbooks in Tokyo.[33]

Translations by Hunan Students Abroad was a Chinese monthly first published in the fall of 1902 with an introduction by Yang Tu. The magazine offered translations of Western and Japanese works in philosophy, education, military affairs, economics, diplomacy, history, and geography. It also published commentaries on Chinese domestic affairs and world events. The materials chosen for translation were those which the editors thought would be helpful in building a modern China. Essays on Western political institutions, reflections on the French and American Revolutions, and biographies of the Japanese leaders of the Meiji Restoration were translated. The Japanese educational system was studied. The translators remained anonymous, except in the second issue, which indicated the names of the translators in each field. In that issue Huang Hsing translated the works of a Japanese educator on "educational administrative law." This was the first of two articles, and the second one (published in the third issue) was presumably also Huang's work.[34]

9

On April 28, 1903, a Japanese newspaper in Tokyo published the Russian government's new demands concerning the withdrawal of its troops, which had been sent to Manchuria during the Boxer uprising. The Chinese students were aroused.[35] In a meeting held on the following day Huang Hsing and other members of the Young Men's Association proposed the organization of a student volunteer corps to fight the Russians. Of the 500-odd students who attended the meeting, more than 130 volunteered, another fifty or so expressed their willingness to work in the headquarters at Tokyo, and twelve women students signed up for nursing duties. A Student Army was finally organized on May 2, with Lan T'ien-wei as its captain. Two representatives were sent to China to present their views to the government.[36]

The Student Army was immediately disbanded by the Japanese government, acting on the request of the Peking government. In reaction to this, Huang Hsing and the other radical students founded an organization called the Association for Universal Military Education (Chün Kuo-min Chiao-yü Hui). The stated purpose of the Association was "cultivation of military spirit and patriotism."[37] Its real aim, however, was to overthrow the Manchu dynasty. This is clearly stated in the Association's secret declaration of principles, part of which reads as follows:

Why was the Student Army organized? . . . Was it for the defense of our nation's independence? Or was it for the protection of Manchu private property? The aim is so clear that an explanation is unnecessary. All our countrymen agree that more than two hundred years ago the Manchus massacred our ancestors and took our property; that they now oppress our compatriots and cede our lands to foreigners, so that one day we may vanish from the earth; that they are our age-old enemies, and that we should not tolerate them, least of all protect their property.

Why, then, do we resist the Russians? If Russia occupies Manchuria, the other Powers will definitely oppose her, and the result will be war. Regardless of who wins this war, our territories will ultimately be taken away from us. We are not worried about the loss of Manchuria alone, but about the loss of the rest of the nation that will follow it. We are not worried about Russia alone, but about the other Powers who may follow in her footsteps to partition China. Alas! Conquered by the barbarian Manchus alone, our nation can still hope for independence some day; but conquered by the civilized Powers, China will be lost forever. Even if our hopes for the future are doomed to fail, it is better to struggle to the death than to do nothing. This is why we propose to establish the Association for Universal Military Education. . . .

Why, then, did we try to influence the policy of the Manchu government by sending representatives to China? The reason was that in order to send the Student Army to the front, the authorization of the government was necessary. But once our Army was in the North, we could do whatever we deemed fit to serve our real purpose. . . . It was so understood by every one of us . . . and it was for such expediency that we did not explicitly state our nationalistic aims [when the Student Army was organized].

However, the consequence of not having our aim explicitly stated could be disastrous. After the establishment of the Association for Universal Military Education, the response in China will be great; the activities of the proposed association will be watched by the people. Many may follow our example and take similar actions. But if our means to an end is misunderstood as an end in itself, our people will work for the alien regime, to the great harm of China's future. In order to carry out our great task, a proper name must be given to the association so that it will appeal to the people outside it and help our comrades within it to concentrate their efforts for the cause. . . .

Consequently, we propose to have a meeting today, and propose that the principles of the association will be the cultivation of military spirit and the practice of nationalism. . . . The injustice done to our ancestors will be revenged. Civilized Powers that are our enemies will be resisted. If we succeed, we shall become citizens of an independent nation. If we fail, we will be dead heroes in the cause of freedom.[38]

This quotation reveals that in the minds of the revolutionists, overthrowing the Manchu rule was actually conceived as a means of saving China from foreign domination. The revolutionary goal of the Association was kept so well that the organization existed from the day of its establishment in May 1903 to its merging with the T'ung Meng Hui in August 1905 without being discovered by government agents.

11

The Association held no regular meetings and established no offices. For identification, each member was given a round nickel badge as large as a Mexican silver dollar, upon which was shown a portrait of the legendary first emperor of China, Huang Ti, copied from the Tokyo Imperial Library. The Association advocated propaganda, armed revolts, and assassinations as means of revolution. Upon returning to China, each member was to carry out his tasks in his own province. Huang Hsing was among the first to depart. Having graduated from the Kōbun Institute, he left Tokyo for China on June 4, 1903.[39]

TWO

THE HUA HSING HUI AND
THE CHANGSHA REVOLT

A YOUNG HUNANESE student by the name of Chang Shih-chao had joined the Shanghai *Kiangsu Journal* (*Su-pao*) as its chief editorial writer on May 27, 1903. Under his editorship the *Journal* published several violent anti-Manchu articles in May and June. These articles touched off the sensational *Su-pao* case, which resulted in the imprisonment of Chang Ping-lin, the tragic death of Tsou Jung, and the suppression of the newspaper.[1]

The publisher of the *Kiangsu Journal,* Ch'en Fan, was one of the eight Hunanese who, along with Huang Hsing, had founded the Hunan Translation Society, which was publishing *Translations by Hunan Students Abroad* in Tokyo.[2] Early in the year, Ch'en's *Journal* became the general distributor for that magazine and the *Journal* offices became its Chinese headquarters.[3]

Chang Shih-chao was one of forty students who had withdrawn from the Nanking Military Academy in the spring of 1903 after the student strikes. These students came to Shanghai and studied at the Patriotic School; this school had been founded by Ts'ai Yüan-p'ei and other members of the Chinese Educational Society the previous November to accommodate another group of dissident students, those of the Nanyang School in Shanghai, who had left the school in the summer of 1902 after a student strike against the school authorities.[4] (Ts'ai, the chairman of the Chinese Educational Society and a teacher at Nanyang, became its principal.) The students in the Patriotic School organized a "student army" similar to the one established by the Chinese students in Tokyo. A volunteer corps of ninety-six students and faculty members, this "army" later adopted the name of its Tokyo prototype, the Association for Universal Military Education.[5]

The Patriotic School was subsidized by the *Kiangsu Journal*. In turn, the schoolteachers, among them Chang Ping-lin and Wu Chih-hui, were responsible for contributing an editorial to the newspaper every day.[6] Chang Ping-lin, Chang Shih-chao, Chang Chi, and Tsou Jung were four "sworn brothers." Tsou, a native of Szechwan province, had recently returned to Shanghai with Chang Chi after a year's study in Japan; he was then eighteen and the youngest of the "brothers." Chang Chi was not yet twenty-one and a year younger than Chang Shih-chao. Chang Ping-lin was then in his mid-thirties.[7]

Tsou had written a pamphlet called *The Revolutionary Army* (*Ko-ming chün*), the preface of which was dated April 1903. It was probably the most violent and outspoken attack on the Manchus ever written by a Chinese. Tsou asked his compatriots to join in the "overthrow of the barbarian Peking government set up by the Manchus," the "expulsion of all the Manchus now residing in China," and the "killing of the Manchu emperor in order to do away with the dictatorial monarchical system forever." He also advocated, among other things, the "establishment of the Republic of China," freedom of speech, freedom of thought, freedom of the press, and the right to revolt.

Furthermore, the impetuous young author suggested that the United States should serve as a model for organizing the Chinese Republic and that a constitution should be written for it which would approximate the United States Constitution while containing modifications necessary to suit Chinese traditions and conditions. Finally, Tsou attacked one of the most ancient cornerstones of Chinese society: loyalty to the emperor. He argued that one should be loyal not to an individual but to the nation.[8]

On May 27, the *Kiangsu Journal* published Chang Ping-lin's "An Introduction to *The Revolutionary Army*."[9] Four days later the same newspaper published Chang's "Refutation of K'ang Yu-wei's Recent Political Statement," in which Chang criticized the prominent reformer's argument that constitutional monarchy could save China whereas revolution could only bring partition and disaster to the country. In this famous open letter Chang referred to the Kuang-hsü emperor by name and described him as a "low wretch." On June 9 the *Journal* carried a favorable review of Tsou's works, and it later published several other articles reflecting the strong anti-Manchu sentiment of the time. Greatly angered by these articles, the Manchu Court took vigorous steps to suppress the newspaper, which was under the jurisdiction of the International Settlement. Ch'en Fan and other responsible personnel of the *Journal* fled from Shanghai. Chang Ping-lin, who refused to escape, was arrested on June 29, and two days later Tsou Jung surrendered himself.[10] However, the authorities of the International Settlement denied the Manchu government's request for extradition.[11] For the first time a Manchu emperor was involved in a lawsuit against his subjects in a foreign court. It became a sensational case, and thanks also to other circumstances, anti-Manchu sentiment was aroused.

In this eventful month Huang Hsing arrived at Shanghai from Japan. He made contact not only with his fellow provincials in Shanghai but also with educated men from other provinces. Ts'ai Yüan-p'ei has been quoted as having said that prior to the Revolution of 1911 he was often Huang Hsing's host in Shanghai and that his school served as one of Huang's contact places in that city.[12]

Before leaving Shanghai for his native province, Huang apparently attended several services in St. Peter's Episcopal Church. The Chinese minister of St. Peter's introduced him to Huang Chi-t'ing, rector of the Episcopal Church in Changsha. The note of introduction, written on the minister's personal card, reads as follows:

This is to introduce my friend Huang Hsing, whose courtesy name is Chin-wu. He is a native of Shanhua district, Changsha prefecture, Hunan province. He has attended the services of the St. Peter's Church several times, and he is about to register [as a church member]. He is now returning to his native city. I hope that you will have his name listed on your record [as a prospective member].[13]

As one historian has stated, this note may be interpreted in two ways: either Huang was interested in adopting the Christian faith, or he intended to make some use of the church in his revolutionary activities. His friend Ts'ao Ya-po gives the second interpretation.[14]

In this connection one should bear in mind that shortly after the Boxer uprising foreign missionaries enjoyed special rights in China and even the Chinese Christians were in a somewhat privileged position. Government officials were generally very lenient in order to avoid any accusation of "molesting" Christians, a charge that might have serious consequences for them as well as for their country. The clergyman to whom Huang was introduced later saved his life by helping him escape from Changsha.

In Shanghai Huang Hsing met a fellow provincial named Hu Yüan-t'an, who had recently returned from studying in Japan. Hu, now principal of the Ming-te School, had come to Shanghai to recruit teachers for his school, which had been established at Changsha only one semester before. He invited Huang and Chang Chi to teach at Ming-te, and his offer was accepted.[15]

Huang Hsing returned to Changsha by way of Wuchang. Modern steamships ran regularly from Shanghai to Hankow, and he wanted to stop at his former school, the Academy of Hunan and Hupeh, on his way home. He was invited to speak at the Academy, and it is said that he spoke, both in public and in private, on the necessity of establishing a republican form of government.[16] When his activities became known to the provincial authorities, he was ordered by the school officials to leave the Academy. Before his departure, however, he was able to distribute to the army and student circles of Wuchang many copies of *The Revolutionary Army* and other propaganda publications he had brought from Shanghai.[17]

Thus in the fall of 1903 Huang Hsing began to teach at the Ming-te (Illustrious Virtue) School, where he was in charge of the courses in Normal School Education being offered for the first time in the school curriculum.[18] He also taught history, drawing, and other courses, and he sometimes lectured at other schools.

In the following year at Changsha Huang's double life as schoolteacher and revolutionist was busy and exciting. He established a Japanese Language School, where he made full use of every opportunity to convey revolutionary ideas to his students. As his colleague, Chang Chi, recalled many years later:

He was very good at drawing. He drew vegetables and fruit on the blackboard for his daytime class, but he mapped out revolutionary strategy at night. He was alert, quiet, cautious, and courageous. He was respected, even worshiped, by almost every student [he taught] in Hunan. In those days it seemed that anyone who did not advocate revolution was not considered a good student. It had not been easy to create such an atmosphere.[19]

Huang Hsing soon found himself in trouble because of his extracurricular activities. The trouble began when he reprinted and distributed revolutionary propaganda pamphlets written by a young Hunanese student in Japan, Ch'en T'ien-hua. A prominent and conservative member of the local gentry wrote to the provincial governor accusing Huang and his colleagues of fomenting rebellion. For a time the situation looked serious. The governor ordered an investigation. Fortunately for Huang, two of the "trustees" of the school belonged to the influential Lung family, who were related to the principal. One of these men, a former Vice-Minister of Justice in the central government, wrote to the governor praising Huang Hsing highly. An arrangement was also made for Huang to come to the Lung residence to meet a high official of the provincial government. This official later made a favorable report to the governor, describing Huang as "every inch a scholar." After this, the case was dropped.[20] Huang Hsing, however, resigned his position at the school; according to the principal, he did this because he wanted to give all his time to revolutionary activities without involving Ming-te.

Huang Hsing had founded a revolutionary organization called the Hua Hsing Hui (Society for the Revival of China) in December 1903, shortly after his fellow provincial and friend Liu K'uei-i returned to Changsha from Japan.[21] This was the first revolutionary organization to be founded in Hunan. In his founding address, given as the chairman of the society, Huang Hsing is quoted as having said that the key to the success of the revolution was to unite the army, the students, and the secret society members for common action and to seek coordination with other provinces:

One way of starting a revolution is to capture the capital, Peking, so as to command the rest of the nation. The French Revolution broke out in Paris, and the English one in London. But the nature of these revolutions is different from ours. . . . We cannot rely on the ignorant and easy-going Peking populace; nor can we co-operate with the alien palace guards. Therefore, we can only start in one province and hope for simultaneous uprisings in all of the others.

Speaking of Hunan province, there has been a rapid growth of revolutionary ideas among the army and the students, and the people have also gradually accepted such ideas. Furthermore, members of the secret societies who also harbor anti-Manchu ideas have long spread and consolidated their influence, but they dare not start first; they are like a bomb full of gunpowder ready to blow, waiting for us to light the fuse. If we have their cooperation, and when the time comes . . . it will not be difficult to capture Hunan province as a revolutionary base.

However, if the other provinces fail to respond to our initiative, then it will be difficult to conquer the North and to overthrow the Manchu regime; the strength of one province cannot fight the rest of the nation. I hope, therefore, that our comrades will seek cooperation from the people of other provinces whenever possible so that when the time comes, concerted action can be taken.[22]

The Hua Hsing Hui consisted almost exclusively of members of the literati; almost every one of the thirty members active in its early stage had been or later would be a student in Japan. Some of them later played important parts in the revolutionary movement.[23] In order to facilitate his work with the uneducated members of the secret societies, Huang Hsing set up another organization called the T'ung Ch'ou Hui (Society Against the Common Enemy), which was to be affiliated with the Hua Hsing Hui. Liu K'uei-i was a great help to him in gaining connection with the secret societies because Liu had known Ma Fu-i, a secret society leader of Hunan.

On a snowy spring evening in 1904, Huang and Liu set out on foot for a mining camp on a mountain at Hsiangtan, where

18

they had arranged to meet Ma Fu-i. The mountain was about ten miles northwest of Changsha. According to Liu's vivid recollection of this meeting, the three of them talked until dawn, sitting on the ground and warming themselves by a wood fire; with Ma's men on guard through the night, they exchanged ideas on revolutionary strategy, drank wine, and ate chicken. In an excited mood on his way back, Huang composed a poem commemorating the occasion. The last two lines read: "Sealing the alliance with wine / Expelling the Manchus like killing chickens!"[24]

The revolt was planned to take place on the occasion of the seventieth birthday of the Empress Dowager, which fell on the tenth day of the tenth lunar month, or November 16, 1904, by the Western calendar.[25] A bomb was to be hidden in a place where all the provincial officials would be present at a celebration. The capture of the provincial capital, Changsha, was to be the task of the main forces, consisting primarily of soldiers from the local army who had been converted to the cause of revolution. The actual fighting was to be directed by those members of the Hua Hsing Hui who were students at the Wuchang Military Academy. While members of the secret societies were to play a secondary role in capturing Changsha, they were the forces, under the command of members of the Hua Hsing Hui, primarily responsible for the simultaneous uprisings scheduled to take place in five districts of the province.[26]

Huang Hsing organized his men after the pattern of the Japanese army. He assumed the position of commander-in-chief, with Liu K'uei-i and Ma Fu-i as his assistants. He sent two men to make contact with the secret society members in Szechwan province. Ch'en T'ien-hua and others were sent to Kiangsi province to convert an army battalion commander to the revolutionary cause. Chang Shih-chao and Yang Shou-jen were stationed at Shanghai as contact men. In Wuchang Hu Ying and Sung Chiao-jen set up a branch of the Hua Hsing Hui; they were responsible for recruiting members there, especially from the army. Sung Chiao-jen was also in charge of managing the revolt in Changteh, one of the five districts in Hunan where simultaneous uprisings were planned.[27]

Sung, a native of Hunan province, was twenty-two years

old in 1904. His father died when he was about eleven years old, but with some difficulty he managed to continue his studies while his elder brother supported the family. In 1903 he was studying at the School of General Studies (Wen P'u-t'ung Hsüeh-t'ang) in Wuchang. When the Science Study Group (K'o-hsüeh Pu-hsi So) was founded the next year, he was elected as its secretary.

The Science Study Group was the first revolutionary organization to be established in Hupeh province. It was founded in June or early July of 1904 by a group of young students, some of whom had joined the army; the name of the association, of course, was merely a device to mask its real purpose.[28] Although it was dissolved less than six months after its formation, it was the prototype of several later local revolutionary organizations which helped make possible the Wuchang Revolution of 1911.

The relation between Huang Hsing and the young students in Wuchang was quite close. According to the writings of one of its members, the Science Study Group was established for the purpose of carrying out Huang's revolutionary plan.[29] Some of the leading figures of the Science Study Group were also members of the Hua Hsing Hui: Sung Chiao-jen was one, and Hu Ying another.

While still a boy, Hu Ying came to live in Hunan with his father, who was a district magistrate. After both his father and his elder brother died, he was brought up in that province by a friend of the family. When he was about sixteen he studied at one of the schools in Changsha where Huang Hsing taught. Influenced by his teacher, he soon became a radical. When he got into trouble with the local authorities, Huang Hsing helped him escape to Wuchang and introduced him to Wu Lu-chen, a young Japanese-trained army officer. Hu joined the Hupeh New Army, and played a leading role in founding the Science Study Group, serving as its secretary-general.[30] It was he who accompanied the chairman of the Science Study Group, a student at the Wuchang Military Academy, to see Huang Hsing in Changsha.[31]

Huang Hsing arrived at Wuchang in late July or early August of 1904, after making a trip to Shanghai in order to buy ammunition. The Science Study Group held a welcoming party for him, and at the meeting Huang explained his plan for conducting revolt. The Study Group promised him its concerted action in support of the plan.[32]

One writer has said that almost one hundred thousand secret society members joined the Society Against the Common Enemy.[33] This is suggestive, but the number is undoubtedly exaggerated. Another has said that Huang's revolutionary plot was more ambitious than the one conceived by T'ang Ts'ai-ch'ang.[34] Whatever its real extent, the plot was discovered by the Hunan authorities, who sent out intelligence agents posing as revolutionary sympathizers.

Up to this point, the narratives of the revolutionary plot written later by various participants are in substantial agreement on the facts; beyond this, however, they differ from one day to two weeks in fixing the day Huang Hsing began his dramatic flight. The evidence strongly suggests that this occurred on October 24, 1904, the day the government ordered his arrest.[35]

On that day the police surrounded Huang's house, where the family was preparing to celebrate his thirtieth birthday. Finding that he was not at home, the police approached the Japanese Language School. Before they could surround the building, Huang escaped by the back door.[36] He ran to the Ming-te School, where he burst into the principal's office, greatly agitated and carrying a gun. The principal immediately escorted him to the home of the Lung family for hiding.[37]

During the evening of October 24, Ts'ao Ya-po, a member of the Science Study Group in charge of propaganda and a school teacher at Changsha, was writing lecture notes in a dormitory room at the school where he taught. Shortly before midnight a messenger arrived with a letter from Huang Hsing, in which Huang asked Ts'ao to meet him on a matter of great importance. A sedan chair was waiting outside for him. Ts'ao recalled:

I read the letter. I sensed its urgency and knew that the revolutionary plan of K'o-ch'iang [Huang Hsing] must have been discovered. I left my room and locked the door. Then I remembered that I had left my key behind. I re-entered the room by the window and got my key. Then I got into the sedan chair waiting outside

21

the school. All the street gates had been locked. Fortunately, I was wearing Western clothes and was without a queue. The guards apparently thought I was a foreigner, for they woke up and opened the gates for me.

I arrived at the Lung home, where a policeman was guarding the door. I entered the house and passed several anterooms before reaching the living room, where Huang was sitting at a writing desk. He stood up, shook hands with me, and asked my advice about escaping from the police.

I told him not to worry; then I took the same sedan chair to the back door of the Episcopal Church, where Huang Chi-t'ing, the minister, lived. All the street gates were opened for me as before. The clergyman was startled by my urgent knocks at the door. . . . I told him at his bedside what it was all about. He dressed quickly and went out in my sedan chair; I followed him on foot. He came to the Lung family and discussed means of escape with K'o-ch'iang. The minister tried to comfort him first; then he said to Huang's friends who were present . . . that he would guarantee [Huang's] safety but that no one should ever ask his whereabouts.

On the next day [October 25] the situation grew more tense. Two leaders of the secret society . . . who took part in the revolutionary planning were arrested by the police. In the evening, the clergyman went to the Lung family again and told Huang how to leave the house in safety. It was planned that at six o'clock the next evening the minister would come by curtained sedan chair from the South Gate. He would be carried directly into the anteroom of the house before getting out. Then Huang Hsing would get into the same curtained chair and would be carried to the door of a house of prostitution which was located in the street behind the church. There he would alight and enter the back door of the church by a small alley. I was to wait for him at the back door of the church. . . .

The next evening [October 26] I waited. K'o-ch'iang did not arrive in the alley until about fifteen minutes after six. I did not relax until I personally let him in. The man who followed the sedan chair posing as a servant was Chang Chi. It was almost autumn, but Chang was still wearing a blue cotton summer coat. He carried a four-inch gun in his pocket. He said that he had resolved to fight to the death if they came across the police on the way. From then on I respected him as a man. It was the first time in my life I had seen a gun. He left shortly.

Then K'o-ch'iang went to the room upstairs. There was no

furniture except one folding bed, one little desk, and a small chair. I gave him the new cotton mattress which the minister had bought for me in Hankow. I only used one Japanese-made wool blanket. In those youthful days, we were not so afraid of the cold.[38]

With the help of his friend the clergyman, Huang took steps to protect his fellow revolutionists. He sent a telegram and a special emissary to Wuchang to warn the Science Study Group. Thus, when the police raided the offices of that organization on October 28, they found no illegal arms or documentary evidence of revolution. For personal reasons and out of concern for the students, the Wuchang educational authorities were lenient; the extent of their action was to investigate Hu Ying and to expel Sung Chiao-jen and another student from the school.[39] Huang also sent warnings to his comrades in the cities of other provinces. Two of his friends who were employees of the Changsha post office saw to it that his incoming mail did not fall into the hands of the police.

Huang made his escape from the city of Changsha early in November.[40] After shaving off his "Huang-ti" style mustache, he disguised himself as an employee of the customs service; escorted by the clergyman and other friends, he passed through the city gate one evening just before the gate was closed.

After a farewell dinner at the house of the clergyman's friend, a genuine customs employee who lived outside of the city, Huang Hsing sailed at night for Hankow with Chang Chi. When they arrived in Hankow the next evening, they immediately left for Shanghai.[41]

As soon as he arrived in Shanghai Huang made contact with his friends and comrades in order to organize another revolutionary attempt. He set up headquarters in the International Settlement under the cover of a book translation company.[42] But within a few days he found himself in jail.

It happened that on November 19 Wan Fu-hua, who had once studied briefly in Hunan, borrowed a gun from Chang Chi in order to kill a former governor of Kwangsi province. The attempt failed, and Wan was arrested. The next day Chang Shih-chao went to see Wan at the police station and was detained

23

by the police as a suspect in the case. Shortly thereafter, the place where Chang, Huang, and several others were living was raided by the Settlement police.[43] The police found arms and counterfeit money, and Huang Hsing was arrested along with twelve others.*

Among those arrested was a Hunanese by the name of Kuo Jen-chang. Kuo alone did not belong to the rebellious group; he was an army officer on his way to Kwangtung to assume a position as a detachment commander. He had arrived at Shanghai the day before and had happened to make the acquaintance of Huang Hsing and Chang Chi. They invited him to visit them, and all three were arrested when they arrived together at Huang's residence on the evening of November 20.

Of the thirteen persons arrested, none gave his true name except Kuo, the army officer, who was released four days later. Posing as Kuo's traveling companion on official business, Huang Hsing was also released at the same time, as was Chang Chi. Chang Shih-chao and the rest were released much later, when it was found that they were not involved in the attempted murder. The army officer had no idea that his fellow provincial was the revolutionary leader sought by the police. After his release Huang moved into the quarters of the Hupeh Association of Returned Students from Japan, in the French Concession of Shanghai. By this time his identity was known, however, and the Chinese government requested the authorities of the Settlement to arrest him. Hearing of this, Huang fled to Japan.[44]

Some time later, in Japan, he received word that Ma Fu-i, the secret society leader in Hunan, was ready to stage a new revolt. The place chosen for the uprising was Hungchiang, a mountainous area of western Hunan. So Huang Hsing and Liu K'uei-i returned to China, realizing fully that the government had put a price on their heads. They proceeded by sampan

---

* After the abortive Changsha revolt, Huang Hsing and his comrades were desperately in need of money. Huang sent a man to see a Kiangsu district magistrate of the Lung family for financial aid. The magistrate, unable to raise much money, gave Huang's man some confiscated counterfeit money from the treasury of his district. This was the money the police found at the book company. [124], p. 5.

to Hunan after picking up forty-three rifles and some ammunition in Hanyang. On their way they ran into customs inspectors looking for smugglers. A fight started as soon as the first customs man came on board; Huang Hsing threw him into the water and his companions began to fight the others. When soldiers arrived on the scene, Huang abandoned the boat. After a brief exchange of fire, the rebels disappeared into the darkness.

Before reaching Hungchiang, Huang heard that Ma had been arrested. He also learned that the secret cell at Hungchiang had been raided by the police and that there had been some fighting. Huang and Liu were obliged to turn back to Hankow, disguised sometimes as officials and sometimes as merchants. From Hankow, they made a second escape to Japan, where Huang was to meet Sun Yat-sen for the first time.[45]

THREE

SUN YAT-SEN'S ACTIVITIES
BEFORE MEETING HUANG HSING

Sun Yat-sen, whom Huang Hsing was to meet in the summer of 1905, was born to a peasant family on November 12, 1866, in a village in what is now the Chungshan district of Kwangtung province.[1] In 1879 he left his native village for Honolulu, where his older brother Sun Mei kept a general store. He attended an English missionary school there until 1882. In 1883 he returned to China. Two years later he was converted to Christianity and married. In 1892, after five years of uninterrupted study in Hong Kong, he was graduated from the College of Medicine for Chinese. After practicing medicine briefly in Macao and Canton, he went to Shanghai in the spring of 1894. Then, in the summer of that year, he set out for Tientsin with his boyhood friend Lu Hao-tung in an attempt to present his ideas on reform to Li Hung-chang, the Governor-General of Chihli.[2] The gist of the program he presented to Li was set forth in four balanced lines of four ideographs each: the full development of men's abilities; full exploitation of the earth's resources; the full use of material things; and an unhampered flow of commerce.[3] Although he failed to secure an audience, Sun managed to obtain from Li's aides an official endorsement to raise funds abroad for the purpose of establishing an agricultural association.[4] He went to Honolulu in the fall, where he founded the Hsing Chung Hui (Revive China Society); members of the organization began to pay dues on November 24, and this has officially been considered its founding date.[5]

The chairman and other officers of the Hsing Chung Hui were chosen from the local Chinese community. An original record shows that from November 24, 1894, to September 2,

1895, one hundred and twelve Chinese—businessmen, traders, cooks, clerks, tailors, laborers, farmers, and local government employees—joined the organization. Almost all of them were natives of Kwangtung province, and the great majority were from Sun's native district. The total fund raised by September 1895 was $1,388, including the "shares" subscribed by a few "natives" (meaning probably Hawaiians).[6] In January of 1895 Sun Yat-sen returned to Hong Kong, where he soon cooperated with Yang Ch'ü-yün to form the Hong Kong Hsing Chung Hui.[7]

Yang Ch'ü-yün, known as Yeung Ku Wan in his time, was born in Hong Kong on December 16, 1861; his father was a school teacher and government interpreter.[8] At fourteen, Yang was apprenticed to the Hong Kong Naval Dockyard, but his apprenticeship was cut short when he suffered an accident which required the amputation of three fingers on his right hand. He subsequently studied at an English school, and after graduating he taught in a local high school called St. Joseph's College. Later, he became chief shipping clerk in the China Merchants' Steam Navigation Company. In 1891 he met Sun Yat-sen. Although they shared a progressive outlook, they did not immediately establish close relations; when Yang founded the Fu Jen Literary Society (Fu-jen Wen-she) on March 13, 1892, Sun was not among the members.[9]

The motto of the Fu Jen Literary Society was "Ducit Amor Patriae." The organization has been variously characterized as a revolutionary headquarters and a social club. It was probably in the nature of a study group for "new learning" and social activities.[10] Among the sixteen members of the organization was Australian-born Tse Tsan Tai (Hsieh Tsuan-t'ai), a clerk in the Department of Public Works of the Hong Kong government.[11] The other six members whose names can be traced were shipping clerks or worked for shipping companies.

Several of these men joined the Hsing Chung Hui when it was founded in the spring of 1895. Yang Ch'ü-yün, who was then with a British shipping company in Hong Kong (David Sassoon, Sons & Co.), was thirty-five; Sun Yat-sen was twenty-eight, and Tse Tsan Tai twenty-five. Among Sun's close friends who were active in the organization were his schoolmates Cheng Shih-liang and Ch'en Shao-pai, both from Kwangtung province. As a member of the Triads, Cheng was responsible for recruiting members from the secret societies.[12]

There were striking similarities in background, education, interests, and knowledge of the West among Yang Ch'ü-yün, Sun Yat-sen, and their friends. Their joining hands to "revive" China was not an accident. None of them were born into the scholar-official-gentry class, and none of them received the traditional education of the Chinese literati. They obtained their new ideas from travel, foreign schooling, and contact with foreigners; they all witnessed material prosperity in the colonies and discrimination against Chinese by colonial governments. Sun, Yang, and Tse all had ties with overseas Chinese families— in Hawaii, Malaya, and Australia, respectively.

The regulations of the Hong Kong Hsing Chung Hui (located at 13 Staunton Street) were substantially the same as those of the Honolulu branch, although somewhat more elaborate. In both sets of regulations, the avowed aim was not to overthrow the Manchu dynasty but rather to organize progressive elements at home and abroad for the purpose of strengthening China and opposing foreign aggression. Both contained a preamble condemning the corruption and weakness of the Ch'ing government. The Honolulu Hsing Chung Hui regulations consisted of nine articles, which included the following provisions. The membership fee was to be five dollars, with voluntary contributions welcomed. No new member was to be admitted without references from one member in good standing. Meetings, held every Thursday evening, were to be presided over by the chairman or the vice-chairman elected by the members. The thirteen other officers were to include two secretaries and one treasurer; the other officers rotated in routine administrative positions. Decisions were to be made by majority vote. No specific programs were laid down for saving China from the "danger of immediate partition" by foreign powers.

The Hong Kong Hsing Chung Hui regulations consisted of ten articles containing the following provisions. The head office was to be in China, but branches could be established elsewhere with a minimum membership requirement of fifteen. The branch office was not to be used for gambling or social purposes. In addition to the five-dollar membership fee members were invited to buy ten-dollar shares with the prospect that the shares would ultimately be redeemed for one hundred dollars each. New members were to be admitted only upon the recommendations of two members in good standing. Officers, elected once a year, were to consist of a chairman, vice-chairman, Chinese secretary, English secretary, treasurer, and a board of ten directors. Decisions were to be made only after careful consideration by five members and all ten directors. The regulations set forth the following program: to establish newspapers to inform the masses, to establish schools to educate the talented, to develop industry in order to improve the standard of living—indeed, to undertake any project that might promote China's prosperity.[13] What form of government China should have was not indicated. One veteran revolutionary has said that although Sun Yat-sen was working for the overthrow of the Manchu regime, he did not at this time oppose the idea of a monarchy with a Chinese emperor; rather, it was Yang Ch'ü-yün who persistently advocated a republican form of government.[14]

The initial members in Honolulu and Hong Kong are often said to have taken an oath dedicating themselves to the "overthrow of the Manchu dynasty, the restoration of China, and the establishment of a republican form of government."[15] Such a fact cannot at present be established from documents or writings of the participants; it seems likely that the practice of taking such an oath developed gradually, and that historians have given it retroactive effect. At any rate, it is most unlikely that the oath was taken at the founding of the Hsing Chung Hui in Honolulu. The avowed purpose of Sun Yat-sen's trip there was to raise funds with which to establish an agricultural association. Although he may have expressed his real intentions for the organization to a few carefully chosen comrades, many joined the organization without the slightest idea of his plans. This being so, it is almost inconceivable that the founding members should have been asked to take a revolutionary oath.

As a revolutionary party, the organization of the Hsing

Chung Hui left much to be desired. In fact, judging by the letter of its regulations, it can hardly be called a secret revolutionary organization at all; its regulations were political declarations, not revolutionary manifestos. But as the first political society in modern China, the significance of the Hsing Chung Hui hardly needs to be stressed. In practice, perhaps the regulations were never observed. There is little indication that meetings were held according to the procedures prescribed; personality seems to have counted for more than organizational rules.

Taking advantage of the startling defeat of the Ch'ing government in the war against Japan, Sun Yat-sen, Yang Ch'ü-yün, and their friends planned to capture Canton. On March 16, 1895, a month before the Sino-Japanese Treaty of Peace was signed at Shimonoseki, they held a meeting and decided to revolt on the 9th day of the 9th lunar month, which was to be October 26 of that year.[16] On that day of every year, the Chinese, following an immemorial custom, went to the countryside to offer sacrifices before the tombs of their ancestors. This occasion was considered convenient because many strangers would be in the city. Sun Yat-sen was in charge of planning the coup in Canton, while Yang Ch'ü-yün was responsible for raising funds, buying arms, and recruiting men in Hong Kong. Huang Yung-shang, one of Yang's friends, was said to have contributed HK$8,000 to the cause by selling a house.[17]

By August 27, the plans for capturing Canton were completed.[18] On October 10 an election was held in Hong Kong to select the "President of the Provisional Government" in the event of the success of the revolution. The struggle for the "presidency" between Sun Yat-sen and Yang Ch'ü-yün was so intense that their respective supporters were on the verge of calling off the whole endeavor. Sun was finally obliged to give in, and Yang was elected.[19] Thus, although it is well known that Sun Yat-sen founded the Hsing Chung Hui, little notice has been taken of the important role played by Yang Ch'ü-yün, who was the chairman of that organization for almost five years. The general impression that the revolt was financed exclusively by Sun's friends and relatives in Hawaii is also inaccurate.

The fight for the provisional presidency proved unnecessary

in the end. Very shortly before October 26, the revolt was postponed for two days because the preparations in Hong Kong could not be completed in time. On the 27th the plot was discovered by the Canton authorities, and three men were arrested. Sun Yat-sen sent a warning to Hong Kong, but it did not reach Yang Ch'ü-yün until after he had sent men to Canton. On October 28 forty-five rebels were arrested upon arrival in Canton, and two hundred and five revolvers and some eighty boxes of ammunition were confiscated.[20] Sun escaped to Hong Kong, whence he fled to Japan with a price on his head. In the sixteen years that followed before the success of the Wuchang Revolution, he set foot on the Chinese mainland only once—early in December 1907, for an overnight stay on a Kwangsi mountain bordering French Indo-China.[21] In the three years prior to the Wuchang Revolution his nearest domicile to China was probably Malaya.

In August 1897 Sun Yat-sen returned to Yokohama from his first trip to the United States, England, and Canada, on which he seems to have gained a certain intellectual maturity. He was also the beneficiary of much publicity after the famous kidnaping episode in London.[22] He was sought out by Miyazaki Torazō, a Japanese greatly interested in Chinese affairs, who introduced him to a number of Japanese in and out of government.[23] The support of these Japanese was important to Sun's cause at that time, and it also enhanced his position in the revolutionary movement. It was probably their support that enabled him to finance Ch'en Shao-pai's establishment of the *Chung-kuo jih-pao* (*China Journal*) in Hong Kong late in 1899.[24]

By this time Sun Yat-sen had decided to gain undisputed leadership in the revolutionary movement by organizing the Hsing Han Hui (Revive Han Society).* In November 1899 several leaders of the Triads and the Society of the Elders and Brothers were brought to Hong Kong to confer with Ch'en Shao-pai and Miyazaki Torazō. Here they took an unusual

---

* As used in the Society's name, "Han" meant "the Chinese people and the glory of ancient China"; the Han dynasty, traditionally deemed China's imperial age, is notable for long peaceable rule and great artistic achievement.

step which gave formal recognition to Sun's leadership in the new revolutionary organization: a chairman's seal was made, and Miyazaki took it to Yokohama and presented it to Sun.[25] The new party, however, gained little recognition. Its name was dropped when Yang Ch'ü-yün became willing to resign from the chairmanship of the Hsing Chung Hui in favor of Sun Yat-sen. Since Yang could not and would not challenge Sun's leadership, it probably served no purpose for Sun to have a new organization. Besides, the leaders of the Society of the Elders and Brothers soon forsook the revolutionary movement and went over to the reformers' camp organized by T'ang Ts'ai-ch'ang.

Yang Ch'ü-yün's position in the Hsing Chung Hui had been greatly weakened after the abortive revolt of 1895, although he retained his nominal chairmanship of the organization. Since March 1898 he had been living in Yokohama, where he had to make his living by teaching English.[26] In January 1900 he returned to Hong Kong and resigned the chairmanship. Tse Tsan Tai was surprised to learn from Yang that Sun had demanded his resignation. Yang explained it thus:

We were dangerously near being split up into two parties some time ago. Dr. Sun Yat-sen informed me one day that the "Ko Lao Whui" party [Kao Lao Hui, or Society of the Elders and Brothers] of the Yangtze provinces had appointed him "President," and hinted that as there could not be two Presidents, it would be obligatory for me to work independently if I would not recognize him in his new position. I confessed to Sun Yat-sen that I was quite pleased to resign my position, and advised him not to encourage separation. I also informed him that I was always willing to sacrifice my life, let alone my position, for the good of the cause.[27]

Thus, while Yang Ch'ü-yün successfully fought against Sun's leadership in what is now known as the "first revolutionary attempt of Sun Yat-sen," the "second revolutionary attempt" was organized under Sun's undisputed leadership.

The year 1900 saw a great upheaval in China. With the Boxers active in the North, the governor-generals of three southern provinces took concerted action to ignore the imperial decree of June 21, which had declared war against the foreign powers.

During this time of unrest, Hsing Chung Hui members attempted to use the influence of Hong Kong Governor Sir Henry A. Blake to persuade Li Hung-chang, the Governor-General of Kwangtung and Kwangsi, to declare independence from the Empire.[28] When this scheme failed, the revolutionaries intensified their preparations for revolt. The plan for military action was mapped out by Sun Yat-sen, Yang Ch'ü-yün, and their Japanese friends, and was eventually carried out under the command of Cheng Shih-liang. Yang intended to take part personally in the interior, but Sun wanted him to stay in Hong Kong to rally support from local merchants.[29]

The Waichow revolt broke out on October 10, 1900, in the Chinese territory bordering Kowloon opposite Hong Kong. The rebel forces were mainly recruited from the patriotic armed bandits in what is now the Paoan district, Kwangtung province. Members of the Triads played a secondary role.[30] The objective was to capture Waichow, and then advance along the coast of eastern Kwangtung in the direction of Fukien in order to receive military supplies from Taiwan, where Sun Yat-sen was trying to obtain help from the Japanese authorities. But aid did not come, and after some successful skirmishes, Cheng Shih-liang was obliged to disband his troops two weeks later. Thus ended the "second revolutionary attempt of Sun Yat-sen."[31] On January 10, 1901, Yang Ch'ü-yün was assassinated in Hong Kong by agents of the Canton authorities.[32] Cheng Shih-liang died less than a year after the campaign.[33]

The failure of the Waichow revolt ended the first stage of Sun Yat-sen's revolutionary career. During this period almost all of his Chinese associates and supporters were of Kwangtung origin (although Yang Ch'ü-yün's family came from Fukien, he might as well be considered a Cantonese, having been raised in Hong Kong), and none of them belonged to the scholarly elite; they came from the lower strata of Chinese society and from the Chinese communities in Hawaii, Hong Kong, and Japan. Sun's revolutionary leadership in China was confined to Kwangtung province. Unlike the reform movement led by K'ang Yu-wei, which had a tremendous impact upon the nation, the revolutionary movement was hardly noticed by the people of the time.

33

43408

No full account of Sun Yat-sen's activities from 1895 to 1900 would be complete without a thorough examination of his relations with the reformers, especially Liang Ch'i-ch'ao; for the purposes of this study, however, a few brief remarks on the subject must suffice.[34] After the coup d'état of September 21, 1898, which ended the Kuang-hsü emperor's "Hundred Days' Reform," many of Sun's followers abroad went over to the camp of the reformers in exile. Sun and Liang made some attempts to work together, but for a number of reasons their plans were not executed. The official memorials of the Manchu government linked the action of the revolutionaries in Waichow with the armed revolt of the reformers led by T'ang Ts'ai-ch'ang and Lin Kuei in the Yangtze provinces, although there was in fact no coordination between them. Both groups, however, did have a common interest in weakening the regime of the Empress Dowager, and there seem to have been certain understandings between them. The final and complete split between the reformers and the revolutionaries came in 1900, after the failure of their respective military actions. After the execution of T'ang Ts'ai-ch'ang and Lin Kuei, Sun Yat-sen lost the remote connection he had with the antigovernment movement in the Yangtze areas. The man who had served as a contact for him in those provinces was a Hunanese, Pi Yung-nien, whom Sun had come to know in Japan. Pi, who first brought T'ang to see Sun in Japan, was also responsible for bringing several leaders of the Society of the Elders and Brothers to Hong Kong in 1899 in connection with the formation of the Hsing Han Hui. Pi was so disconsolate at the outcome of events in 1900 that he entered the Buddhist priesthood. Sun Yat-sen made every effort to find him, but without avail. With Pi's disappearance Sun lost his "only link" with Hunan and Hupeh provinces; he did not find another until he met Huang Hsing five years later.[35]

The years 1900 to 1905 comprise another stage in Sun's revolutionary career. He had emerged as the undisputed leader of the Hsing Chung Hui by 1900, but he was unable to organize another armed revolt until after he joined Huang Hsing and others to form the T'ung Meng Hui in 1905. With the exception of a trip to Annam in the first seven months of 1903,

CENTRAL LIBRARY
HOLY JUDE COLLEGE

he lived quietly in Yokohama from the end of 1900 to September 1903. Then he left Japan to tour Honolulu, the United States, England, and Europe. He did not return to Japan until July 1905.[36]

Between 1900 and 1905 the growth of the anti-Manchu movement among the Chinese students, both in China and abroad, greatly accelerated. The movement was a spontaneous one: it had several outstanding leaders instead of a single dominant figure, and it had no unified organization. Contrary to the general belief, Sun Yat-sen had no close contact with the intellectual or student leaders in China, and prior to 1905 he was not so closely associated with the Chinese students in Japan as some have believed. It is true that in 1901, while living in obscurity in Yokohama, he was invited to take part in the Kwangtung Independent Association, which had been founded in Japan by students and overseas Chinese of Kwangtung origin who advocated the independence of Kwangtung in view of the chaotic situation in the North. He was also invited to take part in the abortive meeting in the spring of 1902, which was intended to commemorate the 242nd anniversary of the Manchu conquest of China. But these invitations came unsolicited from Chang Ping-lin and a few other students and do not prove that Sun was closely associated with the students in general. In August 1903 Sun helped establish a secret military school at Aoyama for students from his province who were unable to gain admission to the Japanese military academies.[37] But he was absent from Japan in the first seven months of 1903, when anti-Manchu sentiment among the Chinese students was running high.

With the exception of Chang Ping-lin and a few others, then, Sun was primarily associated only with his fellow provincials. From time to time students from other provinces did come to see him, but as a whole they were rather indifferent toward him. As Chang Ping-lin later recalled: "During this time, Sun Yat-sen was living in Yokohama. He was quite well known to the foreigners and Chinese. But, on the whole, the Chinese students in Japan thought he was an uncultured outlaw, hard to get along with, and they did not associate with him."[38]

The reminiscences of Wu Chih-hui also reflect the typical attitude of the Chinese literati toward Sun in those days. Wu recalled that although he had heard of Sun before going to Japan in the summer of 1901, he entertained an impression of Sun as a "tough guy," and a "romantic thief." He was surprised to hear from those who had seen him that Sun was a man of "good appearance and gentle manner." But Wu still declined to see him. "I did not like Sun Yat-sen at first," he explained, "because he was not of the literati, nor did he hold any degree under the old civil examinations. Besides, I suspected him of being illiterate. It was only after I met him [in 1905 in London] that I began to realize that he was very fond of reading."[39]

Sun Yat-sen's trip to Europe from London in the spring of 1905 was the first move which brought him into a closer relationship with the students from other provinces; as such, it deserves more attention than it has received.

Early in 1905 Chu Ho-chung and other Hupeh students studying in Brussels and Berlin received a letter from Liu Ch'eng-yü in San Francisco. As previously mentioned, Liu was the Hupeh student expelled from a Japanese school early in 1903 for his anti-Manchu outburst at a Chinese New Year's party; in 1904 he was recommended by Feng Tzu-yu to edit a Chinese newspaper for Sun's friends in San Francisco.[40] In his letter, Liu informed his fellow provincials that Sun had gone to London from the United States and advised them to get in touch with him there. Upon hearing this, Chu and his fellow students sent some money to Sun and invited him to visit them in Brussels. At the time he received the invitation, Sun had little money and was making little progress in his work; he was overjoyed to find new supporters among the student class.[41]

According to Chu Ho-chung, who played host to Sun Yat-sen in Brussels and Berlin in 1905, Sun then considered the secret societies the only reliable forces for overthrowing the Manchu dynasty. Chu told him what he knew of the revolutionary movement in Hunan and Hupeh, where both the students and the army had played leading roles. Chu argued for the importance of rallying support from these two groups, pointing out that secret society members, who might harbor motives of personal gain, could not be prevented from looting or seizing local power after a successful revolt. After three days of discussion Sun was finally convinced. He admitted that there were too few educated men among his followers, and he agreed that the new literati should play a leading role in the revolutionary movement.[42]

At the end of the informal three-day meeting, Sun urged that each student who favored the revolution should take an oath expressing his determination and devotion to the cause. When Chu read the text of the oath drafted by Sun, he chuckled to himself. Pressed for an explanation, Chu said, "K'ang [Yu-wei] and Liang [Ch'i-ch'ao] have always said that you are illiterate. Now that I have read this statement, so concisely drafted, I know what they say is not true." To this Sun answered proudly, "Why, I have also read a lot of books."[43]

Approximately thirty students took the oath in Brussels. The same procedure was followed later in Berlin and Paris, where only a handful of students were interested in the revolution. The students did not set up a formal organization or elect officers; they became known as the European Branch of the T'ung Meng Hui only after that organization had been established in Tokyo.

In comparison with the number of their fellow students in Japan, the Chinese students in Europe were so few as to be insignificant. Their total number cannot be ascertained, but there were probably no more than one hundred of them in Brussels, Berlin, and Paris. The most active among them came from Hupeh province. Some were former schoolmates of Huang Hsing's in Wuchang. They informed their friends in Tokyo of the latest European developments and urged them to cooperate with Sun when he returned to Japan later in the year.[44] This was the state of the revolutionary movement when Huang Hsing first met Sun Yat-sen.

FOUR

THE T'UNG MENG HUI

THE NUMBER of Chinese students in Japan, which had grown steadily since the turn of the century, increased tremendously in the years 1905–6.[1] This new intelligentsia was a restless group in a restless age, and the educational activities of its members varied greatly: many were not enrolled in regular schools, and many more only attended occasional lectures; some studied for a few days, others for several years. As one of these students, Hu Han-min, recalled:

At that time the Chinese student body in Japan consisted of very diversified elements. Some came strictly for the purpose of seeking government positions or personal gain; others came with noble ambitions. Some, principally students of the natural sciences, studied very diligently, taking no interest in any extracurricular activities; others, primarily students of the social sciences, were very fond of social activities; they were interested in conversations and debates but disliked scholarly work. Some firmly believed that Japan should serve as a model for everything in the future of China; others, not satisfied with the Japanese example, aimed at copying the political institutions and cultures of European countries and of the United States.

The students also greatly varied in their ages, origins, and qualifications. Some were forty or fifty years of age, others were no more than six or seven years old. Some were the children of nobility and wealthy families; others came from the poor and the peasantry. Some were exiled leaders of secret societies; others were already qualified as government officials and came because it was a shortcut to obtaining quick advancement.

However, all these various people may be divided into two groups: revolutionaries and constitutionalists . . . the latter faction being in the majority. . . . There were some who advocated revolution when they first came, but became conservative reformers upon graduation. Thus although this literati class of more than twenty

38

thousand students was full of vitality, it consisted of all sorts of people and was most confusing, complicated, and diversified.[2]

Having escaped to Japan after the abortive Changsha revolt, Huang Hsing became a very popular leader among the Chinese revolutionary literati in Tokyo.[3] Of all the members of the Association for Universal Military Education who had returned to China from Japan, he was the only one who had distinguished himself in action by planning an ambitious revolt. At least one noted Shanghai magazine published the news of his attempt and reported the execution of four conspirators.[4] His house became a well-known meeting place for radical students in Tokyo. At first he lived under a Japanese name, Momowara. Once his real identity became known, Miyazaki Torazō and other Japanese who sympathized with the Chinese revolution lost little time in meeting him, and they soon became good friends.[5]

The Russo-Japanese war, which broke out early in February 1904, was the result of a long power struggle between the two countries over Korea and Manchuria. The war was fought entirely on Chinese territory although China was not party to the struggle, and it was a series of uninterrupted successes for Japan until the Portsmouth Treaty was signed in September of the following year. The war was thus a great stimulus to anti-Manchu sentiment among the Chinese students in Japan; it seemed to them another illustration of the helplessness of the Manchu government.

Late in January 1905, Huang Hsing discovered that Ch'en T'ien-hua, the author of two famous revolutionary pamphlets and a member of the Hua Hsing Hui, had been attracted by Liang Ch'i-ch'ao's writings in support of a constitutional monarchy. Huang persuaded Ch'en to abandon any plan of joining a movement in favor of monarchy.

In the middle of April Huang led a committee set up by Chinese students in Tokyo to investigate the cause of Tsou Jung's death. It was rumored that Tsou had been poisoned by the agents of the Manchu government shortly before his prison term expired. Chang Chi, who was sent back to Shanghai to investigate the matter, later reported that the suspicion was unfounded. On the 7th of May Huang was elected chairman of the Hunan

Students' Association in Japan; for reasons as yet unknown, however, he resolutely declined to accept the position.[6]

Sun Yat-sen had probably heard of Huang Hsing and his activities through the Hupeh students in Europe. But the man who brought them together was their mutual Japanese friend, Miyazaki Torazō. Sung Chiao-jen recorded in his diary on July 19, 1905, that Miyazaki had spoken very highly of Sun, claiming that "no man like him could be found in both the Western and Eastern hemispheres." On the same day that this entry was made, Sun Yat-sen arrived in Yokohama.

Upon arriving in Tokyo, Sun Yat-sen asked Miyazaki if he knew of any outstanding personality among the Chinese students in Japan. Miyazaki told him about Huang Hsing ("a great man") and suggested that the two men meet at Miyazaki's house. But Sun was impatient and wanted to visit Huang right away, so Miyazaki took him to Huang's residence near Kagurazaka in Tokyo. Hearing his name called, Huang Hsing looked out and signaled them to wait outside because he was entertaining visitors at the time. Of what followed Miyazaki recalled:

Huang Hsing, Chang Chi, and Suenaga Setsu came out and took us to a Chinese restaurant called the Feng-lo Yüan. After a brief exchange of greetings, they [Sun and Huang] turned to the subject of revolution, and became as intimate as if they had known each other for a long time. As our knowledge of the Chinese language was limited, we did not know what they were talking about. But we were happy to see these two Chinese heroes getting together. We celebrated this occasion by helping ourselves generously to the wine. For almost two hours, Sun and Huang kept on talking without touching either food or wine. But finally they exclaimed "Hurrah!" and toasted their happy meeting.[7]

Action followed quickly. The first meeting between Sun Yat-sen and Huang Hsing's group was held at the office of the latter's magazine, *Twentieth-century China* (*Erh-shih shih-chi chih Chih-na*), on July 28, 1905. Sung Chiao-jen recorded the event in his diary as follows:

When I arrived at the magazine's offices about two o'clock in the afternoon, Sun Yat-sen and Miyazaki had already arrived. After we exchanged greetings, Sun first inquired how many comrades we had. Before I answered, Ch'en T'ien-hua made a reply. He reported briefly on the attempted Changsha revolt of last year and the way we had worked. Then Sun Yat-sen delivered a lengthy talk on the revolutionary situation and strategy, the gist of which was the necessity of unifying all the revolutionary forces.

Sun said that at the moment China was in no danger of being partitioned by foreign powers, but that the greatest danger lay in revolutionary leaders attempting to act independently in their respective provinces; this, he said, would create the possibility of a struggle for power among themselves, which might repeat the tragic history of the chaotic situation following the overthrow of the Ch'in and the Yüan dynasties. . . . In such a case, argued Sun, China would be lost if the foreign powers took advantage of the situation and intervened. Therefore, the most important thing at the present time should be unification and cooperation. He further said that the strength of the . . . secret societies in Kwangtung and Kwangsi provinces was still great . . . but that they lacked educated men to lead them. If leadership could be found, he believed that the revolution could succeed.[8]

Ever since he had escaped to Japan, Huang Hsing had been contemplating a unification of the various revolutionary groups then existing in China and Japan.[9] Sun Yat-sen's return to Japan encouraged him to pursue this plan. But his friends had various reactions to Sun's talk on the 28th, and on the next day the members of the Hua Hsing Hui held a meeting at Huang's house. Sung Chiao-jen entered this report of the meeting in his diary:

July 29 [1905]: Brought Ch'en T'ien-hua to Huang Hsing's residence in order to discuss Sun Yat-sen's problem. Sun had previously suggested to Huang that he rally the Hunanese revolutionists, and Huang had given him a favorable promise. But some of us did not want to do so. Therefore, a meeting was held today to discuss the matter.

After we had all arrived, Huang Hsing spoke first. He proposed joining hands with Sun Yat-sen in form but preserving the spirit of our party intact. Ch'en T'ien-hua, however, advocated uniting our party with Sun's. Liu K'uei-i opposed joining Sun's organization. Since there were differences of opinion on the subject, I proposed further studies on the merits and consequences of unification or of non-cooperation. Others also enthusiastically expressed their opinions. It was difficult to tell who was right. Finally, it was decided that each should be free to act as he pleased.

Another meeting was set for the following day, July 30. It took place in the Akasaka district of Tokyo at the house of Uchida Ryōhei, which was also an office of the Japanese Black Dragon Society. Kuomintang historians have designated this as the preparatory meeting for the founding of the T'ung Meng Hui.

The meeting was attended by about seventy persons. Sun Yat-sen, who was invited to speak first, talked for about an hour analyzing the revolutionary movement. Then others spoke in turn. When at last Huang Hsing's turn came, he presented his ideas on how to popularize education and develop industry after the success of the revolution; he also touched upon the subjects of domestic politics and foreign affairs under the prospective republican form of government. Finally, he requested those present to sign their names as members of a new revolutionary organization. Miyazaki brought out some papers. There was a pause. Then Ts'ao Ya-po, who had come to Tokyo from Hunan two weeks before, stood up and said that he would be willing to sign first. The rest followed.

For the name of the new organization, Sun Yat-sen suggested Chung-kuo Ko-ming T'ung-meng Hui (The United Revolutionary League of China). Someone suggested a name that would specifically reveal the nature of the organization, such as the United Anti-Manchu League. To this Sun replied that any Manchus sympathetic to the cause should also be allowed to join. Huang Hsing was of the opinion, however, that since the organization was to be secret and underground the word "ko-ming" (revolution) should be deleted. After some discussion, his suggestion was adopted. The name Chung-kuo T'ung Meng Hui (The United League of China) was decided upon; it has generally been called the T'ung Meng Hui for short.

The oath which every member of the T'ung Meng Hui was required to sign was drafted by Sun Yat-sen. Having been approved by Huang Hsing, it was adopted. It reads as follows:

I swear under Heaven that I will do my utmost to work for the expulsion of the Manchus, the restoration of Chinese sovereignty, the establishment of the Republic, and equalization of land rights. I solemnly undertake to be faithful to these principles. If I betray my trust, I am willing to submit to the severest penalties imposed by my comrades.

Prior to the election of officers, all the members' sworn statements were kept by Sun Yat-sen while his own was to be kept by Huang Hsing. Before the meeting came to an end, Huang and seven others were appointed to draft a set of regulations, to be submitted for approval at a formal inaugural meeting.[10]

On August 13 at the Fuji Restaurant in Kōjimachi, Tokyo, a student gathering was held in honor of Sun Yat-sen. It was one of the most enthusiastic student meetings ever held in Japan. More than seven hundred students were said to have attended it, and the street outside the restaurant was thronged with those unable to gain admittance. Among the Japanese guests who spoke were Miyazaki Torazō and Suenaga Setsu. Sun Yat-sen, in his speech, expressed appreciation at being welcomed in Japan as a revolutionary. He was happy, he said, to note that whereas in the past he could find sympathizers among the secret societies but little response from the well-to-do families of society, the necessity of revolution was now recognized by every class of the nation. He disparaged the claim of the reformers that China was suited for a constitutional monarchy but not for a republican form of government.[11]

One week later, at about two o'clock in the afternoon of August 20, the formal inaugural meeting of the T'ung Meng Hui was held at the house of Sakamoto Kinya. This has been officially considered the founding date of the T'ung Meng Hui.[12]

Huang Hsing read the draft regulations, consisting of thirty articles, which were approved after slight modifications.[13] The organization's headquarters were to be in Tokyo. Its purpose was "to work for the overthrow of the Manchu dynasty, the restoration of Chinese sovereignty, the establishment of the Republic, and the equalization of land rights." Some questioned the desirability of equalizing land rights, but they became silent after Sun Yat-sen explained the importance of solving social problems along with political problems.[14]

Following the suggestion of Huang Hsing, it had previously been agreed that Sun Yat-sen was to be the chairman of the T'ung Meng Hui. Huang himself was elected chief of the Executive Department with the title "Shu-wu"; in this position, the second most important in the organization, Huang was authorized to act for the chairman in the latter's absence.[15] Sung Chiao-jen was an officer in the Judicial Department, which was headed by Chang Chi. Hu Ying, Feng Tzu-yu, and later Hu Han-min were officers in the Reviewing Department, which was headed by Wang Ching-wei. Of the thirty-odd officers elected, only two had belonged to Sun Yat-sen's Hsing Chung Hui.[16] Although the T'ung Meng Hui was theoretically based on the principle of a separation of powers among its Executive, Judicial, and Reviewing Departments, joint meetings of the three branches were always held on matters of importance. In fact, for all practical purposes, the Judiciary and Reviewing Departments ceased to function within a year.

According to a record kept at the headquarters of the T'ung Meng Hui and published for the first time in China in 1953, 963 members joined the organization during the years 1905 and 1906. Of this number 863 joined the organization in Tokyo alone, while the rest were recruited from Europe, Malaya, Hanoi, and Hong Kong. The list is incomplete because it was based only on membership oaths received from China or other places outside Japan. It contains, however, almost all the names of those who joined the T'ung Meng Hui in Tokyo in the first two years of its existence: almost all came from the student class of 17 provinces. Kansu was the only Chinese province not represented; there were no members from Tibet, Mongolia, or Manchuria.

Of the 863 members who joined the T'ung Meng Hui in Tokyo in those first two years, 157 were from Huang's home province of Hunan. There were 106 from Hupeh, 112 from Kwangtung, and 43 from Kwangsi. According to the same record, the 18 students who joined the T'ung Meng Hui in Europe all came from Hupeh province.[17]

In terms of education, diversity of background, and contact with China, the membership of the T'ung Meng Hui was quite different from that of Sun Yat-sen's Hsing Chung Hui. It has been estimated that no more than 500 persons joined the Hsing Chung Hui in the eleven years of its existence. Of the 286 members whose names can be traced, only 30 or so were educated; about 176 were overseas Chinese, of whom 137 were from Hawaii alone; in terms of background, 271 were from Kwangtung province.[18]

The founding of the T'ung Meng Hui was a milestone in the history of the Chinese Republican Revolution. For the first time various independent anti-Manchu groups were united in a common cause under the leadership of Sun Yat-sen and Huang Hsing. Sun became convinced that the overthrow of the Manchu dynasty would be accomplished during his lifetime.[19]

At the time the T'ung Meng Hui was established, Sun Yat-sen was almost thirty-nine years old, and Huang Hsing was almost thirty-one; Hu Han-min was twenty-six, Sung Chiao-jen twenty-three, and Wang Ching-wei twenty-one.[20] The great majority of members in the revolutionary organization were enthusiastic youths. Sun Yat-sen was made chairman not only because of his seniority in age and in the revolutionary movement, but also because he was the only member with a firsthand knowledge of the Western world, which the Chinese revolutionaries in those days looked upon with admiration and great respect.

It is significant, however, that no ranking member of the T'ung Meng Hui had ever been a member of Sun's former party. Certainly, no member of the Hsing Chung Hui ever became a national figure in the Republican Revolution. Neither Hu Han-min nor Wang Ching-wei, fellow provincials of Sun's who became his close assistants and played significant roles in the Revolution, had joined the Hsing Chung Hui; Hu Han-min, in fact, did not meet Sun until two months after the formation of the T'ung Meng Hui. After the founding of the T'ung Meng Hui the leadership of the revolutionary movement was undoubtedly in the hands of the new intelligentsia. With few exceptions, the active leading members of the revolutionary alliance had studied in Japan. It is important to bear this in mind when appraising Huang Hsing's influence within the T'ung Meng Hui.

Sun and Huang were the two most powerful men in the organization; they seem to have made every important political and financial decision.[21] Next to former members of Huang's Hua Hsing Hui and Sun's Hsing Chung Hui, the most important group in the T'ung Meng Hui came from the Kuang Fu Hui (Restoration Society). The Restoration Society had its genesis in the activities of Kung Pao-ch'üan, a member of the Association for Universal Military Education in Tokyo. A native of Chekiang province, Kung belonged to a small group within the Association which planned and carried out assassinations. In the fall of 1904 in Shanghai (the time when Huang Hsing was mistakenly jailed by the International Settlement police as a suspect involved in an assassination) Kung's group was reorganized and became known as the Restoration Society, with Ts'ai Yüan-p'ei as its chairman. The new organization was strengthened by the addition of T'ao Ch'eng-chang in the winter of the year.[22]

The early members of the Restoration Society came exclusively from Chekiang and Anhwei provinces. Before its formation Huang Hsing had counted on the support of Ts'ai Yüanp'ei and T'ao Ch'eng-chang in his attempted Changsha revolt; T'ao had planned to stage a coordinated uprising in Chekiang three days after the Changsha revolt was scheduled to take place.[23] It has been said that the Restoration Society consisted solely of intellectuals who had no followers in the masses and that its programs were concerned exclusively with the overthrow of the Manchu dynasty.[24] It should be noted, however, that T'ao had the secret societies in Chekiang well organized and that in reorganizing one of them, the Lung Hua Hui, he had advocated "common ownership of land and the prevention of its monopoly by the rich."[25] It was T'ao's faction that later bitterly attacked the leadership of Sun Yat-sen in the T'ung Meng Hui.

Unlike Sun Yat-sen's Hsing Chung Hui and Huang Hsing's Hua Hsing Hui, the Restoration Society continued to exist after the formation of the T'ung Meng Hui. The famous Anking revolt of 1907 was organized by Hsü Hsi-lin in the name of the Restoration Society. It should be stressed that none of the Society's leaders were present when the T'ung Meng Hui was founded in Tokyo; from the very beginning, Huang's Hua Hsing Hui was the largest and most important single group in the new unified revolutionary organization.

The T'ung Meng Hui planned to organize four bureaus abroad (Europe, the South Seas, the United States, and Honolulu) and five in China (only the South China and Central China bureaus came into existence). Seventeen provincial branches were established, with a chairman selected from each province. Shortly after the Tokyo meeting, Ts'ai Yüan-p'ei joined the Shanghai branch and was elected its chairman.

On September 8, 1905, about two weeks after the formation of the T'ung Meng Hui, Feng Tzu-yu was sent to the British colony of Hong Kong with directions to establish a branch there. This was done by reorganizing the Hong Kong Hsing Chung Hui. The Hong Kong branch later became the most active revolutionary headquarters of the T'ung Meng Hui, serving as a base for launching the organization's military operations, most of which were carried out in Kwangtung.

At first the Hong Kong branch was headed by Ch'en Shaopai, who had been in charge of the *China Journal,* a Chinese revolutionary newspaper in Hong Kong, since late in 1899. In the fall of 1906 Ch'en resigned both positions, which were then taken over by Feng Tzu-yu.[26] Although he had been Sun Yat-sen's closest comrade during the period of the Hsing Chung Hui, Ch'en is seldom mentioned in the records of revolutionary activities after 1906. It was clear by this time that new leadership had taken over the revolutionary movement.

The first branches of the T'ung Meng Hui established abroad were in Europe, where Sun had made several contacts in the spring of 1905. After the founding of the organization in Tokyo, branches were quickly set up in Berlin, Paris, and Brussels, with Brussels as the chief European headquarters. No branch was ever established in any other European capital.

Between 1905 and 1908 branches were established in several of the major cities of Southeast Asia: Saigon (October 1905), Singapore (1906), Hanoi (spring of 1907), Rangoon (spring of 1908), and Bangkok (late fall of 1908). Revolutionary activities in British Malaya and the Dutch East Indies were eventually directed by the South Seas Bureau of the T'ung Meng Hui, which began to operate from Singapore in the fall of 1908 and moved to Penang in the spring of 1909.

Several branches were set up in the United States and Canada after 1909.* None were ever established in Africa, Australia, or South America. It is interesting to note that Sun Yat-sen had a direct hand in the founding of almost all the foreign branches except those in Burma, the Dutch East Indies, and the Philippines (where a Manila branch was founded in 1911); most of the branches abroad were founded after a personal visit by Sun.[27]

Prior to the formation of the T'ung Meng Hui, Huang Hsing and Sung Chiao-jen had founded in Tokyo a Chinese monthly magazine called *Twentieth-century China* (*Erh-shih shih-chi chih Chih-na*). Toward the end of the T'ung Meng Hui's formal inaugural meetings on August 20, 1905, Huang Hsing suggested that since most of the staff members of the magazine had joined the revolutionary organization, the magazine should be given to the T'ung Meng Hui as its organ. This was accepted by all.

However, on August 27 an issue of the magazine was confiscated by the Japanese authorities, who took offense at an article published in it. In the middle of September the leaders of the T'ung Meng Hui decided to give the publication a new name in order to avoid any further complication with the Japanese government; Sung Chiao-jen was informed of this decision by Huang Hsing on the 19th. This was the origin of the famous *People's Journal* (*Min-pao*).[28]

According to Hu Han-min's autobiography, some members favored the appointment of Ch'en T'ien-hua as the magazine's editor. Hu Han-min was finally chosen to handle most of the editorial work, but Chang Chi was given the official title of editor because he was well-versed in the Japanese language and

---

* Branches were established in New York City (1909), Chicago (1909), San Francisco (1910), and Honolulu (1910). Canadian branches were founded in Vancouver and Victoria, B.C., in May 1911; the revolutionary movement had been under way in these cities since the summer of 1910, when Feng Tzu-yu had arrived in Vancouver.

hence better qualified to handle any dealings with the Japanese authorities.[29]

Hu Han-min was the ghost writer of the first editorial in the *People's Journal,* which was signed by Sun Yat-sen.[30] This editorial expounded for the first time Sun's conception of the proper ideological basis for the new China, which later became known as the Three People's Principles.[31] This first issue of the *People's Journal* appeared on November 26, 1905.

The magazine was intended to be a monthly, but it did not come out regularly. It published altogether twenty-six issues, the last of which appeared on February 1, 1910. Chang Chi served as editor of the first five issues. When Chang Ping-lin was released from prison in the summer of 1906, he was immediately escorted by party members from Shanghai to Tokyo, where he assumed the editorship for the next thirteen issues. After this, one issue was published under the editorship of Chang Chi, three under T'ao Ch'eng-chang, and then two more (Nos. 23 and 24) under Chang Ping-lin. It was the 24th issue of the journal, dated October 10, 1908, that was confiscated by the Japanese police on the ground that the views expressed therein were against the public policy of the country. In 1910 Wang Ching-wei managed to publish two more issues.[32]

An article written by Hu Han-min in the third issue (dated April 5, 1906) set forth the magazine's six-point program for China: the overthrow of the Manchu government, the establishment of a republic, the equalization of land rights, the maintenance of world peace, cooperation between the peoples of China and of Japan, and the entreaty of other Powers to act favorably toward the Chinese revolutionary movement. The first three points may be considered the domestic policy and the last three the foreign policy of the T'ung Meng Hui.[33]

On the whole, the magazine's early articles advocated both political and social revolution. But its style and editorial policy changed after T'ao Ch'eng-chang took over the editorship. T'ao put particular stress on stimulating anti-Manchu sentiment and urging overthrow of the alien regime. In part, this changed editorial position reflected T'ao's revolutionary theory, which he had derived primarily from Chinese history and classics. In a greater degree, however, it was probably a reaction to the circumstances of the time. In 1908, after the failure of several revolts, the future began to look gloomy; T'ao probably thought it expedient to emphasize the immediately urgent problem of overthrowing the Manchu dynasty and to shelve the other programs until after the revolution had been accomplished. At least this was the opinion of one of the magazine's editors.[34]

The *People's Journal* did much to bring a larger number of intellectuals into the revolutionary movement, and it successfully opposed the ideas of Liang Ch'i-ch'ao and the reformers who advocated a constitutional monarchy. It became the leading revolutionary publication of the time. It was most popular among the students, just as the writings of Tsou Jung and Ch'en T'ienhua were popular among the less educated. Whereas the writings of the two famous pamphleteers appealed primarily to the emotions, the articles in the magazine were generally calm and theoretical. There is no record that Huang Hsing ever wrote anything for the *People's Journal*.[35]

Since the T'ung Meng Hui was an alliance of different revolutionary organizations, personal conflicts within the rank and file of the party were inevitable. This has been pointed out by many historians, who have usually said either that conflicts took place because of Sun Yat-sen's absence from headquarters or that it was through his leadership that dissenters were finally reconciled.[36] Few seem to have realized that the most serious conflicts were caused, at least in part, by Sun Yat-sen's very leadership. The first of these conflicts, a personal clash between Huang Hsing and Sun Yat-sen, almost wrecked the T'ung Meng Hui.

It happened in February 1907. Owing to the pressure from the Manchu government, the Japanese authorities requested Sun Yat-sen to leave Japan, granting him the right to make a voluntary departure. At that time Huang Hsing also decided to go. It was decided that Wang Ching-wei should go with Huang while Hu Han-min should accompany Sun. Prior to their departure a meeting was held to discuss, among other things, the design of a revolutionary flag. During the meeting, Huang Hsing suggested a flag with the Chinese character "ching" (a well) as a symbol of socialism. (The well-field system of land distribution had been much idealized in China since the Chou dynasty.) Sun Yat-sen objected to this, saying that he considered such a design inartistic and old-fashioned; he insisted on the blue-sky and white-sun flag designed by his friend Lu Hao-tung, who had died in the attempted Canton revolt of 1895. Huang in turn declared that the sky and sun design was ugly and also too similar to the Japanese national flag.[37] The two insisted on their respective designs and neither was willing to give in. For several days they did not speak to each other. It is recorded in Sung Chiao-jen's diary:

February 28 [1907] : I went to the office of the *People's Journal* this evening at seven o'clock in order to talk to Huang Hsing about my resignation. [Sung had been acting in Huang's capacity in the T'ung Meng Hui when the latter was away from Japan.] For a long time he did not answer. Then suddenly he said he wanted to quit the organization and to sever his relationship with it. The reason was that [Sun Yat-sen] had designed a national flag which Huang did not like and had suggested changing. But Sun insisted on his idea and made some offensive remarks. As a result Huang angrily walked out of the meeting. Those who were present tried to mediate, but in vain.

Having given some thought to the matter, I believe that the reason for Huang's anger is deeper than it appears: an indescribable resentment must have accumulated in his heart for a long time before exploding under the present dispute, which was, after all, only a trivial matter; for [Sun Yat-sen] had always been insincere and conceited, and the way he handled things was almost dictatorial and intransigent, sometimes unbearable to others.[38]

Since Sung Chiao-jen was close to Huang Hsing, both personally and politically, we should consider the opinion of those who were close to Sun Yat-sen. To a certain extent, Hu Han-min and Wang Ching-wei shared with Sun Yat-sen the kind of relationship Sung Chiao-jen had with Huang Hsing. Here are Hu Han-min's reflections on the dispute, as stated in his autobiography:

Having failed to win his point on the flag design, K'o-ch'iang [Huang Hsing] was quite unhappy. After we parted, he was still

51

thinking of it and wrote to me saying: "Success need not be attributed to me, nor fame. Moreover, even if success is achieved I lay no claim to it. Why did Sun Yat-sen insist on using the flag of his first revolutionary attempt? It is only for the sake of party unity and for the common cause that I reluctantly accept his opinion at present."

In those days I was devoted to the cause of revolution. I supported the adoption of the revolutionary flag under which some had died already; but both Wang Ching-wei and I were deeply touched by Huang's lofty ideals, such as working for success without claiming credit for it. We both felt that this ideal should not be lost because of the dispute. It should be remembered that in those days we were still idealistic youths. After several entreaties from Ching-wei and me, Huang did not raise the issue again.[39]

This episode suggests the contrast in personality between the two revolutionary leaders. It is not surprising that in the last years of his life Sun Yat-sen should come to think of himself as the sole leader of the revolution. The dispute over the flag was probably the most serious disagreement in the otherwise very harmonious partnership prior to the overthrow of the Manchu dynasty. The dispute was never officially settled by the party, but in later military operations Huang Hsing used the flag desired by Sun. Because of Huang's criticism, however, Sun later made a slight change in the flag by adding red to it.[40] Many later incidents suggest that Sun had a virtual obsession about his flag.[41]

Another internal feud occurred in the summer of 1907. It took the form of an open challenge to Sun Yat-sen's leadership by some of the leading members of the T'ung Meng Hui, who attempted to oust Sun from the organization and put Huang Hsing in his place. This attempt sprang directly from events connected with Sun's departure.

When Sun was requested to leave Japan in February 1907, the Japanese government, as a token of good will, gave him some money for traveling expenses. A sympathetic Japanese stock broker also gave him ten thousand *yen,* part of which he left for the *People's Journal* before his departure.[42] However, Chang Ping-lin, then the editor of the magazine, was furious. He seemed to believe that the chairman should not have left such a small amount of money for the party organ while taking so much for himself. He accused Sun of misappropriating for his personal use funds subscribed by revolutionary sympathizers. He removed the leader's picture from the wall of the magazine's office, and, believing that Sun was in Hong Kong, sent it to the Hong Kong branch of the T'ung Meng Hui with these words: "The picture of Sun Yat-sen, traitor to the *People's Journal,* should be removed."[43]

Opposition to the chairman from within the party increased after the repeated failure of the revolutionary attempts in eastern Kwangtung in May and June of 1907. On June 17, Kayano Nagatomo, a Japanese confidant of the Chinese revolutionary leaders, had left Hong Kong for Japan for the purpose of buying military weapons for the revolutionists.[44] When it was learned that he had bought only old-fashioned guns, Chang Ping-lin immediately accused Sun Yat-sen of unnecessarily and recklessly jeopardizing the lives of the comrades by giving them obsolete weapons.[45] He found many supporters in the headquarters of the revolutionary organization at Tokyo, including Chang Chi and Sung Chiao-jen. They went to Liu K'uei-i, who had assumed Huang Hsing's position in the T'ung Meng Hui while Huang was away, and demanded a special meeting in order to oust Sun Yat-sen and choose Huang Hsing for the chairmanship.[46]

Fortunately for the revolutionary movement, Liu had better judgment. He refused to call a special meeting. This provoked a heated argument in the magazine's office, which also served as the headquarters of the T'ung Meng Hui. Chang Chi, who was always ready to use his strong fists, hit Liu, and the two fought each other in the office. Liu explained his position many years later:

I understood that Sun Yat-sen had given two thousand *yen* for the *People's Journal,* and that the rest of the money he received was for organizing revolts. . . . It was inevitable that he should take a large amount of money with him. Besides, I knew quite well that Huang Hsing was devoted to the cause and not to any title. He and Sun were then organizing a revolt to take place in eastern Kwangtung. Any change of the chairmanship would have seriously affected the future of the party and the relationship of the two leaders; it would be an end to the T'ung Meng Hui. Therefore I was determined in single-handedly opposing the majority.[47]

In an attempt to soothe the feelings of the Tokyo members, Liu wrote to Hu Han-min suggesting that Hu use his influence to induce Sun Yat-sen to send a letter of apology to the comrades in Tokyo. At the same time he informed Huang of the incident through a friend in Hong Kong. Sun refused to apologize. Meanwhile Huang wrote to his friends at headquarters advising them not to put him in an embarrassing position and stressing the importance of avoiding factionalism. The incident was thus closed.[48]

Through the years 1908 and 1909, however, Sun Yat-sen was constantly under fire. The attack came principally from Chang Ping-lin and T'ao Ch'eng-chang, the leaders of the Restoration Society. T'ao joined the T'ung Meng Hui in the late fall of 1906. In the fall of 1907, he cooperated with exiled revolutionaries from India, French Indo-China, and Burma to organize the Pan-Asian Revolutionary United League (Tung-ya Wan-kuo T'ung-meng Hui) in Tokyo with Chang Ping-lin as chairman.[49] In the winter of the same year he joined the Socialism Study Group, which was organized by Chang Chi in Tokyo.[50] He served as editor of the *People's Journal* from April to July 1908, during which time three issues of the magazine were published. Shortly after this he toured Southeast Asia, where he found strong support among the T'ung Meng Hui members in Malaya and the Dutch East Indies.[51] Wang Ching-wei first encountered their hostility on a fund-raising tour in 1908.[52] When Wang managed to publish two more issues of the *People's Journal* early in 1910 after it had been confiscated by the Japanese government, Chang Ping-lin openly denied the "authenticity" of the magazine.[53] In a published statement Chang also charged that Sun had "embezzled" revolutionary funds.[54]

Together with Li Hsieh-ho and others in Malaya and the Dutch East Indies who were dissatisfied with Sun Yat-sen's leadership, T'ao Ch'eng-chang wrote a letter to the Tokyo T'ung Meng Hui headquarters requesting that Sun be replaced by Huang Hsing as chairman of the organization.[55] An anonymous joint statement, issued in the name of the "T'ung Meng Hui members of seven provinces," ridiculed Sun's leadership. T'ao was reportedly the principal author of this document, which reads in part as follows:

At the time the T'ung Meng Hui was established, we comrades supported him [Sun Yat-sen] as the chairman merely because we believed in his boast . . . that he had many organizations in Southeast Asia and that he could easily raise a great deal of money from the overseas Chinese communities. That was exactly what we had dreamed of. We sincerely recognized him as the leader and worked wholeheartedly to build up his position for the common cause. . . . As a result, his prestige suddenly became great. In turn, he made use of the revolutionary students' support and the propaganda of the *People's Journal* to increase the honors of his position.[56]

The editors of the *People's Journal* were in dire need of money, and they were angry because Sun did not give them financial aid. They probably believed that he had a huge amount of money at his disposal. As a Chinese writer commented in the Paris *Le Siècle Nouveau* (*Hsin shih-chi*) of November 13, 1909:

They [the accusers] wanted huge funds. That was why the first thing of which they accused Mr. Sun was the embezzlement of two hundred thousand dollars. They did not seem to realize that even Mr. Sun's traveling expenses had been contributed by poor students.

T'ao Ch'eng-chang subsequently went to Tokyo to see Huang Hsing, but Huang refused to have the "joint statement" circulated or to summon a meeting to discuss the matter. Instead he wrote a letter to Li Hsieh-ho defending Sun Yat-sen.[57] He also made a trip to Semarang, Java, in order to break down the opposition of the comrades in the Dutch East Indies. There he wrote a letter to Sun Yat-sen, which was to be signed by all the leading comrades in reaffirmation of their support.[58] Huang's defense of Sun, in the words of Hu Han-min, was made "not only on behalf of Mr. Sun himself but also for the sake of the revolution."[59] These unjustified attacks on Sun Yat-sen sprang only from petty factional jealousy and personal resentment; they had nothing to do with the basic aims or ideology of the revolutionary organization.[60]

FIVE

STRUGGLES AGAINST THE MANCHUS

OF SUN YAT-SEN'S "ten unsuccessful revolutionary attempts," two took place in Kwangtung province before the formation of the T'ung Meng Hui; these were the Canton attempt of 1895 (which was planned but not carried out) and the Waichow revolt of 1900 (a military effort led by Cheng Shih-liang). The remaining eight occurred between 1907 and 1911 in south and southwest China: one each in Kwangsi and Yunnan provinces and six in Kwangtung. Most of these eight military operations were personally led by Huang Hsing; only once was Sun Yat-sen briefly present at an actual revolt.

In terms of military activity the years 1906 through 1908 were the most active; six major revolts took place in that period, and there were at least three more uprisings which were not initiated by the T'ung Meng Hui, although some of its members played important roles in them. The year 1909 was quiet from the military standpoint, and only one attempt was made in 1910. The most daring and sensational campaign was the Canton Revolution of 1911, which shook the entire country.

Since the attacks on the Manchu regime were organized outside China, the military strategy of the T'ung Meng Hui was to capture a province (Kwangtung, Kwangsi, or Yunnan) near either British Hong Kong or French Indo-China, both of which were operational bases for the revolutionists. It was believed that the border provinces could be more easily infiltrated than the interior of China; supplies could be more easily obtained from abroad in case of success, and sanctuaries could more readily be found for refuge in case of defeat. It was the result of a deliberate strategy, therefore, that practically all of the T'ung Meng Hui's eight revolts were staged in these three border provinces. After repeated failure, however, this strategy became unpopular with some members from the Yangtze provinces. Consequently, on July 31, 1911, the Central China Bureau of the T'ung Meng Hui was founded in Shanghai for the purpose of intensifying revolutionary activities in the region of the Yangtze River.

The T'ung Meng Hui had no army of its own. Huang Hsing realized that without effective military support, secret society members alone were not strong enough to carry out a successful revolt, for they lacked both training and arms.[1] He constantly pondered ways of winning over the army of the Manchu government to the revolutionary cause. Between 1906 and 1908 he was in fairly close contact with Kuo Jen-chang, the army officer he had met in the fall of 1904 in Shanghai when the two of them had been arrested on the mistaken charge of connection with an attempted assassination.

Until 1910 the armed revolts of the T'ung Meng Hui were conducted primarily by secret society members. After that time the infusion of revolutionary ideas into the army became so successful that the revolutionary leaders began to concentrate their efforts in that direction. The army later played the leading role in the October revolution at Wuchang, which finally led to the overthrow of the Manchu dynasty.

Having laid down some basic programs for their revolutionary organization, both Sun Yat-sen and Huang Hsing decided to leave Japan for action. Sun left for Saigon on October 7, 1905, to start a fund-raising campaign.[2] Huang left for China shortly after and arrived in Hong Kong before the end of the year.[3] Under an assumed name, he then proceeded to Kweilin in Kwangsi province in order to talk with Kuo Jen-chang. By this time Kuo had been transferred to Kweilin as Detachment Commander of the Provincial Forces, and Huang hoped to persuade him to lead an armed revolt.

The commander was friendly to Huang, but he refused to take any overt action; he said that he was not on good terms with his colleague Ts'ai O, Superintendent of the Primary Military School, and therefore did not feel free to act. Ts'ai, a Hunanese military student educated in Japan, happened to be an old friend of Huang's. Huang tried to mediate between the two, but in vain. However, he did succeed in winning over to the side of the revolution certain faculty members and students at the school, many of them Hunanese.[4]

In late February or early March of 1906 Huang Hsing traveled to Singapore; he probably arrived in June. The comrades there had been requested by Sun Yat-sen to receive him "as if he were Sun himself."[5] Chang Yung-fu, chairman of the Singapore Branch of the T'ung Meng Hui, later recalled his first impression of Huang:

I had notified all the comrades to meet Huang. He spoke with a Hunanese accent, and we had some difficulty understanding him. He was a diligent reader, physically powerful and commanding, but also calm and quiet. Although he got along well with us and was quite agreeable, he was silent and deep. We therefore refrained from asking impertinent questions, realizing that he had secret military missions. After a few days he left for Hanoi via Saigon.[6]

After this trip Huang returned to Hong Kong, where a representative of the Society for the Daily Increase of Knowledge (Jih Chih Hui) had been waiting to see him.

The Society for the Daily Increase of Knowledge was originally the name of the browsing room of the American Church Mission at Wuchang. Later several former members of the Science Study Group used the place for advocating revolutionary ideas under cover of the regular Sunday meetings. Almost all the former members of the Science Study Group joined the Society after it became formally organized in late January 1906. It was soon a front for the Hupeh branch of the T'ung Meng Hui.[7] In the summer of 1906 it sent a member to Hong Kong to ask Huang Hsing for instructions. Huang advised the Hupeh comrades to bide their time until more funds could be raised from abroad.[8]

On September 11 Huang Hsing returned to Tokyo. His activities during the previous nine months must have been dangerous and exciting; Sung Chiao-jen recorded in his diary that upon hearing Huang describe his travels, he concluded that Huang had been too reckless and tried, without apparent success, to persuade him to be more careful in the future.[9]

During Huang Hsing's absence the T'ung Meng Hui members in Japan quarreled among themselves over the new Japanese regulations concerning Chinese students. Announced by the Japanese Ministry of Education in November 1905, these regulations provided for more rigid control of private schools that admitted Chinese students; only certain schools would be approved by the government and students would be required to live in places selected and supervised by Japanese authorities. According to Hu Han-min, then a student leader, these measures were taken partly because of pressure from the Manchu government, which was worried about the revolutionary leanings of the Chinese students in Japan, and partly because the facilities in many schools were in poor condition. Apparently the aim of these institutions was to make profit; some were said to have sold certificates and diplomas.[10]

The pride of the Chinese students in Japan was further hurt by certain adverse and insulting editorial comments from the Japanese newspapers. Several thousand Chinese students of all political persuasions organized a strike in various schools and colleges to protest the action of the Japanese authorities.[11] On December 8, in the midst of the unrest and excitement, Ch'en T'ien-hua committed suicide by drowning himself in the waters off Ōmori Beach in Tokyo. He left behind an open letter to his fellow students in which he expressed the hope that his death would open their eyes to the "ugly realities" of their existence and remind them constantly to act with diligence and patriotism.[12]

Within the T'ung Meng Hui opinion was split: a majority, led by Hu Ying, T'ien T'ung, and Sung Chiao-jen, argued that all the Chinese students in Japan should return to China, where they could establish schools of their own or take up revolutionary work; the minority, led by Hu Han-min and Wang Ching-wei, argued that despite the present humiliation, it would be better for the students to remain in Japan in order to complete their education. Since both Huang Hsing and Sun Yat-sen were ab-

59

sent from Tokyo, no decision was made in the name of the party, for the two groups were unable to reach any agreement.[13] However, after the vigorous protests of the Chinese student body, the Japanese government did not insist on enforcing the new regulations, and as time passed the students became less emotional. The proposal for a mass exodus to China was dropped.

The growth of the T'ung Meng Hui had been very encouraging. On December 2, 1906, the party held a meeting in Tokyo to celebrate the first anniversary of the publication of the *People's Journal*. Five thousand students were said to have attended the meeting, which was presided over by Huang Hsing.[14] After Chang Ping-lin had recited an ode he had written in classical Chinese, there followed a speech by Sun Yat-sen, who had returned to Japan from Saigon less than two months before. In this speech Sun elaborated what came to be known as the "Three People's Principles" and expounded for the first time his theory of the "five-power constitution."[15] Six Japanese guests were invited to speak. Then Huang Hsing spoke. He said he was sure that the students present were sympathetic to what they had heard, but added that he hoped they were not merely sympathetic onlookers. After analyzing the students' role in the European revolutionary movement and in the Meiji Restoration of Japan, Huang urged those present to fulfill their duty as students by taking part in revolutionary work.[16] He was interrupted five times by applause during his brief speech. The meeting lasted from eight o'clock in the morning until two o'clock in the afternoon. Before it came to an end, 181 students contributed 780 *yen* toward the support of the magazine.[17]

The success of the meeting reflected to some extent the students' enthusiasm for revolution and their common attitude toward the Manchu government, which was then preparing to adopt a constitution and was initiating a reform of its own administration. Two days after the meeting mass uprisings broke out in Pingsiang of Kiangsi province and Liling of Hunan province; on December 7 a similar revolt began in Liuyang, Hunan.[18] The uprisings lasted for more than a month and were crushed only by the joint government forces of four provinces.[19]

The "Ping-Liu-Li" uprisings were not organized by the

T'ung Meng Hui in Tokyo. Some had revolted in the name of the "Republic," others in the name of the "New Chinese Empire." The T'ung Meng Hui members who took part were acting on their own initiative. In fact, the party headquarters knew nothing about the revolts until they were reported by the Japanese newspapers. As soon as it was known, however, members were sent back to various Yangtze provinces. Huang Hsing himself went to Kwangtung early in January 1907, but he had to return in the middle of February because of the alerting of the local government. He found it difficult even to stay in Hong Kong.[20]

On December 14, 1906, the Society for the Daily Increase of Knowledge was banned by the Manchu government.[21] The arrest of one of the Society's leading members caused the American Church Mission at Wuchang to demand that the Chinese authorities have the church's name cleared. The Mission also attempted to intervene on behalf of the Christians among those who were arrested.[22]

While open fighting was confined to the border areas of Hunan and Kiangsi, the uprisings actually involved four provinces. Various plots were discovered, and many revolutionists were either arrested or executed. Hu Ying was arrested in Hupeh on January 8, 1907.[23]

In Hunan Liu Tao-i was executed for plotting with the army in Changsha, and his brother, Liu K'uei-i, was deprived of his status as a government student. Huang Hsing composed an elegy on Liu's death which can still be found in some collections of revolutionary literature.[24] In Nanking Sun Yü-yün was arrested along with several others. Sun was related to the prominent family of Sun Chia-nai, Grand Secretary of the Manchu government, and he had served as acting vice-chairman of the T'ung Meng Hui when Huang Hsing was away from the Tokyo headquarters. Mass arrests and executions also took place in Shanghai and other cities in Kiangsu and Kiangsi provinces. As a result of such measures the T'ung Meng Hui in the Yangtze River areas was considerably weakened, and it was not able to recover its influence for some time.[25]

Ts'en Ch'un-hsüan, the governor of Hunan, inquired of the

Chinese Legation in Tokyo whether Huang Hsing was still studying in Japan, and requested that he be expelled if so. The authorities in Shanghai and all the coastal provinces were also notified to arrest Huang if he should be found entering China.[26] Governor-General Chang Chih-tung offered five hundred taels each for the arrest of Huang Hsing and other "Hunan bandit chiefs" who were reported to have come to Hupeh to organize insurrections.[27]

Another important revolt which was not organized by the T'ung Meng Hui took place in the summer of 1907 in Anhwei province. It was planned by Hsü Hsi-lin, a native of Chekiang and a leader of the Restoration Society.

Hsü Hsi-lin, who was related to Yü Lien-san, a former governor of Hunan, gained prominence soon after his return from Japan, which was probably in April 1906. He became a protégé of En Ming, the Manchu governor of Anhwei, and in the spring of 1907 he was appointed Associate Chief of Police of the provincial capital, Anking. On July 6, in the presence of all the officials assembled for the graduation ceremony of the police academy, he shot the governor in cold blood. He failed to arrest all the other officials present, however, and he was soon captured and executed.[28]

The failure of the Anking revolt led to the arrest of Ch'iu Chin a week later in Chekiang. A Japanese-educated woman from Chekiang, Ch'iu was born in Fukien province and had spent a number of years in Hunan. She and Liu Tao-i had belonged to a small secret revolutionary group called the "Group of Ten." Most of the members of this group were Hunanese.

Ch'iu had been among the first to join the T'ung Meng Hui in Tokyo in 1905, and she was one of the students who worked in a bomb-making organization established by Huang Hsing in Yokohama. After she returned to China, Hsü Hsi-lin invited her to join the Restoration Society, and she was put in charge of organizing revolts in Chekiang. She once sent a man to Japan to ask Huang for help in this task, but Huang was away at the time. Ch'iu was probably the first educated Chinese woman to die for the revolutionary cause.[29]

Shortly after his return to Japan in mid-February of 1907,

Huang Hsing became involved in the controversy with Sun Yat-sen over the choice of a revolutionary flag; on March 1, Sung Chiao-jen noted in his diary that a reconciliation had not been reached. On March 4 Sun Yat-sen and Hu Han-min left Japan for Hanoi (via Hong Kong, Singapore, and Saigon).[30] Of the various conflicting accounts of Huang Hsing's subsequent activities during this period the diary of Sung Chiao-jen is the most reliable; it places Huang in Japan from the middle of February through the month of March.[31] The following extracts from Sung Chiao-jen's diary for the month of March give a rare record of Huang Hsing's day-to-day activities, including his plans for a revolt in Manchuria:

March 6 [1907]. Huang Hsing and I discussed the matter of going to Manchuria. It was decided that Furukawa and I will make the trip.

March 7. Went to see plum blossoms this morning at Ōmori Beach. . . . On our way back, we met Huang Hsing, Suenaga Setsu, and Furukawa. They were also coming to see the plum blossoms, and they invited us to come along and see them again. So we followed. . . . We stayed there overnight.

March 8. After breakfast Huang Hsing and Furukawa played Japanese chess. Having stood by watching the game for a long while, I thought I knew how to play it. So I played with Furukawa, but he beat me several times.

March 9. Miyazaki [Torazō] invited Huang Hsing, Chang Chi, Chang Ping-lin, and me to lunch at the Feng-lo Yüan, a Chinese restaurant.

March 11. Planned to borrow money from banks for the purpose of going to Manchuria.

March 12. Gave up the plan of borrowing money from banks because I had no security to offer. Huang Hsing told me that the Russian revolutionaries also planned to take action in Manchuria but needed our cooperation. Huang said he was going to Yokohama in a few days to confer with them.

March 13. Called on Huang Hsing this evening.

March 17. Huang Hsing said that I should leave for Manchuria before the 22nd of this month. I told him that it would depend upon whether I could raise enough money by that time.

March 19. Went to the Chinese Legation for the purpose of collecting my stipend [for government-sponsored students] without success. On my way to the Legation, I met Pai Ch'u-hsiang [a native of Hupeh and a member of the T'ung Meng Hui], who told me that he had about two thousand-odd dollars, a trust fund from his native district to help students of that district now studying in Japan. He said that he wanted to put the money to some other good use and asked what I thought about that. I fully approved, and told him of the Manchuria project. Happily, he wanted to come along.

March 20. In the morning Huang Hsing and Pai Ch'u-hsiang talked about the Manchuria trip. After a lengthy discussion, they decided to meet again at noon in order to talk it over with Suenaga and Furukawa at the Feng-lo Yüan. Shortly after we had arrived at the restaurant, Huang and his company also arrived. It was decided that three of us—Pai, Furukawa, and I—shall leave for Shimonoseki on the 23rd and then go to Pusan by boat. From there we shall proceed to North Korea by train. We shall cross the Yalu River to the Manchurian border and reach Antung district, which will be our destination. The plan after reaching Manchuria is to get in touch with the "mounted bandits" to rob the treasury of Tunghua district. Then we shall organize a large-scale uprising. In the afternoon, Pai told me that it would be better for him to leave Tokyo tomorrow. So it was decided that he should go to Shimonoseki first and wait for me there. I tried to borrow some money from some other friends. In the afternoon I met Miyazaki Tamizō, elder brother of Miyazaki Torazō. Tamizō told me that his younger brother was going to invite Huang Hsing, Chang Ping-lin, me, and others to have dinner at Torazō's house. Later, Chang and the rest went to the party. I did not go because I had to pack. In the evening, I hurriedly wrote a biographical sketch of Huang Hsing and sent it to Miyazaki Torazō as requested [the Miyazaki brothers were publishing a magazine called the *Revolutionary Review* (Kakumei Hyōron)]. Pai came at eight with his luggage, saying that he was leaving for Shimonoseki right away. He gave me three hundred and seventy-five *yen* and left at ten o'clock.

March 22. Invited Huang Hsing, Chang Chi, and Mr. and Mrs. Miyazaki Torazō to lunch at the Feng-lo Yüan.

Sung Chiao-jen and his Japanese friend left Tokyo on the morning of the 23rd and arrived at Shimonoseki two days later, where they were joined by Pai. On April 1 they crossed the Yalu River, arriving at Antung the same afternoon. They soon got in touch with the "mounted bandit" chiefs, but their mission failed: Pai was arrested by Manchu agents, and Sung returned to Japan. Thus ended the Manchuria adventure.

Shortly after the failure of the plans for a revolt in Manchuria, two insurrections organized by Sun Yat-sen at Hanoi took place in eastern Kwangtung: one broke out on May 22 at Huangkang, about 30 miles from the city of Chaochow, and the other occurred on June 2 at Chinuhu, about seven miles from the city of Waichow. These were very small uprisings led by local leaders. The Huangkang revolt was suppressed by local government troops within six days; the revolt at Chinuhu lasted about ten days. Sun Yat-sen called these his third and fourth unsuccessful revolutionary attempts.[32]

By this time Huang Hsing had joined Sun Yat-sen at Hanoi, which became the operational base for the next four unsuccessful revolutionary attempts: two in southwestern Kwangtung, one in southern Kwangsi, and one in southeastern Yunnan—all areas bordering on French Indo-China.

The first of these four military operations, which took place in the Chinchow area of southwestern Kwangtung, broke out on September 1, 1907. In the spring of that year peasant riots protesting an increase in taxes took place in the districts of Chinchow bordering on Kwangsi and Annam; these riots were suppressed by the Manchu forces in May. Taking advantage of the local unrest, the revolutionary leaders attempted to organize the armed peasants into a revolutionary army. At that time the Manchu military officers in charge of this part of Kwangtung were Kuo Jen-chang and Chao Sheng; Kuo was the Detachment Commander stationed at Chinchow and Chao was a Regiment Commander stationed in the neighboring area of Lienchow. Late in May 1907, Huang Hsing went to see Kuo, and Hu Hanmin's brother went to visit Chao, in attempts to convert the military officers to the side of the revolution. On June 17 Kayano Nagatomo sailed from Hong Kong for Japan, where he was to purchase arms for the revolutionists. Then, as mentioned in the last chapter, the campaign against Sun Yat-sen started in the headquarters of the T'ung Meng Hui in Tokyo. Contrary to Sun Yat-sen's account, however, it was not this rift that prevented delivery of the "obsolete" arms; the revolutionists in China were unable to receive the weapons for other reasons.[33]

The rebels, led by local leaders, struck on September 1. On September 4 they captured the district city of Fangcheng and executed its magistrate.[34] The revolutionary forces then marched toward Chinchow, where Huang Hsing had been staying with Kuo Jen-chang's army. Kuo, however, was still unwilling to join in the revolt, and with less than five hundred untrained soldiers the rebels had little hope of capturing a city defended by several thousand government troops. Giving up the idea of a frontal attack, they planned to capture the city by surprise by opening the city gate from within at midnight on September 10, but this plan was thwarted by alert city officials. The partisans then attacked Lingshan in the hope that Chao Sheng would throw his troops into the action. But after seeing that Kuo did not revolt, Chao, whose position and forces were much inferior to Kuo's, dared not act. With little support from the outside, the revolutionary forces were obliged to disband; some of them retreated to the border between Kwangtung and Kwangsi.[35] This revolt, which Sun Yat-sen called his fifth unsuccessful attempt, is generally dated as having ended on September 17.

After the failure of the Chinchow revolt, Huang Hsing returned to Hanoi. The next target was Chengnankuan, which literally means the "frontier pass that guards the South." Chengnankuan is located in southwestern Kwangsi near the border of French Indo-China; it was an important strategic stronghold, being only a few miles from the last station on the Annam-Kwangsi Railway. About the Chengnankuan campaign, Sun Yat-sen had this to say:

> After the failure in the Chinchow and Lienchow districts, I personally led Huang Hsing, Hu Han-min, and more than one hundred revolutionaries in French Indo-China, and with the help of some French officers, seized Chengnankuan, and occupied three strategic points. . . . So a little over a hundred of our troops had to fight with several thousands of our enemy's troops. . . . We kept on fighting for three days continuously, and finally we had to retreat to French Indo-China.[36]

In point of fact, the frontier pass had been captured before the revolutionary leaders arrived on the scene. At midnight on December 1, 1907, about 100 men led by a local guerrilla leader took three mountain fortresses of Chengnankuan by surprise.[37] This group had been planning the attack for some months and had several men serving as agents inside the fortresses. The revolutionary leaders at Hanoi received the news of the capture the next day. On the morning of December 3, Huang Hsing, Sun Yat-sen, Hu Han-min, Ike Kyōkichi, a retired opium-smoking French artillery captain, and a few others took a train from Hanoi to the Annam-Kwangsi border. From there they walked to a Chinese village, where they found a local leader who furnished a dozen men as guides to the fortress. Accompanied by these guides, who carried no weapons except knives, the revolutionary leaders began to climb the mountain at about five o'clock in the afternoon. Hu Han-min, whose health had always been poor, fainted on the way up. They did not reach the fortresses until after ten at night.

At dawn the next day the French captain, after taking his opium, examined the weapons in the fortress. He soon discovered that the range finder on the only big gun which was still useful was out of order; but using his own judgment on the distance, he succeeded in bombarding the government troops for a short time. The fortresses were good for defense but not for offensive actions; seeing that no purpose could be served by staying in the mountains, the revolutionary leaders decided to return to Hanoi in order to raise funds and get supplies for the men in the fortresses. They also hoped to send for the men who had retreated to the Kwangtung-Kwangsi borderland in the last revolt. On the evening of December 4 they set out for Hanoi. On December 8, only three days after Sun, Huang, and their comrades had returned to Hanoi, the fortresses were recaptured by government reinforcements.[38] Sun Yat-sen listed this as his sixth revolutionary attempt. It was also the only time in his revolutionary career that he witnessed fighting, and he was deeply moved at seeing his motherland again after twelve years.[39]

On his way back to Hanoi Sun Yat-sen was recognized by

a French policeman at a railway station in the French territory and was expelled from French Indo-China. He left Hanoi for Singapore in March 1908.[40] Huang Hsing and Hu Han-min remained to carry on the work.

On January 28, 1908, Huang had made a trip to the headquarters of Kuo Jen-chang in order to obtain military supplies from the Hunanese commander. T'an Jen-feng, a Hunanese member of the T'ung Meng Hui, had accompanied him because he had also known Kuo. They arrived at Kuo's headquarters the following midnight. The commander was quite friendly at first, but his attitude changed the next day when he received word from Canton that he had been given back the command he had wanted.[41] Huang Hsing therefore hurried back to the French territory before anything could happen to him.[42] T'an, however, remained behind. An episode recalled by T'an reveals the scheme of the revolutionary leaders for winning the support of the commander:

Kuo . . . asked me the amount of the [revolutionary] military funds available in Annam. I said, "Only a few million [dollars]." Kuo became genuinely interested again. . . . The next day he sent his nephew . . . to Annam with me. Whenever I saw our comrades, I introduced him as Commander Kuo's nephew. They all understood what I had in mind. When he inquired about the revolutionary forces and financial sources, they grossly exaggerated our strength. In the evening, K'o-ch'iang [Huang Hsing] invited him to dinner. Arrangements had been made for Huang to receive four reports during the course of the dinner. Two of these purported to describe military preparations for the capture of Lungchow [in Kwangsi]. They appeared to have been sent by the First and Second Armies respectively, and had official seals. The other two messages were in French, reporting (as explained by an interpreter) that thousands of dollars had been received from certain places. Kuo's nephew was very excited and believed us wholeheartedly. On the following day he invited me to accompany him back and made the most favorable report to his uncle. Consequently, Kuo agreed to supply arms and ammunition without further persuasion from me. A place for transferring the arms was decided upon. However, when I returned [to Hanoi] K'o-ch'iang had already gone into the Chinese interior.[43]

68

Upon returning to Hanoi from Kuo's headquarters, Huang had organized a force of 200 men, half of them equipped with rifles and the other half with Mauser pistols. On March 27 he led this force from Tunghsing (just across a river from French territory) into southwestern Kwangtung, whence he fought his way to the southeast part of Kwangsi province.[44] Sun Yat-sen later stated in his autobiography:

Huang K'o-ch'iang [Huang Hsing], leading only a handful of two hundred men, walked about the Chinchow and Lienchow districts as he pleased, capturing towns and taking cities. For several months, the Manchu soldiers did not dare to approach him. Although the exhaustion of his ammunition eventually forced Huang to retreat to French Indo-China, he was already known throughout China as a gallant fighter.[45]

The campaign lasted only forty days. The territory in which Huang was fighting was under the military jurisdiction of Kuo Jen-chang, and it had been agreed that Kuo would supply arms and ammunition to Huang's men. But when Huang and his troops arrived at the spot agreed upon for receiving the equipment, Kuo's men had already left. It is not clear whether this was a trick by Kuo or simply bad luck for the revolutionary forces.[46]

Despite whatever understanding they might have had, the armed rebels and the government troops were bound to clash. One day Kuo's men came across the revolutionary forces and, mistaking their identity, opened fire. In the skirmish that followed, Huang Hsing shot a battalion commander from his horse, and Kuo's men were defeated.[47] Later on Huang sent a man to return the army flag to Kuo with an apology; but the commander was so angry that he broke with Huang. Kuo Jen-chang's flirtation with the revolutionists had come to an end.[48]

Huang Hsing's forces had expanded to 600 well-disciplined men. At first they seemed to have the support and cooperation of the local peasants. But fearing reprisals from the government troops, the people grew steadily less enthusiastic about the revolutionary army, and eventually the morale of the troops deteriorated. When its ammunition ran out the army was finally obliged to disband and begin a retreat.[49] This campaign was listed by Sun Yat-sen as his seventh unsuccessful revolutionary attempt.[50]

For a while Hu Han-min, who was in charge of supply at Hanoi, thought Huang was lost; but although many of the comrades became ill and suffered from skin disease, Huang Hsing returned to Hanoi on May 5 in good health and spirits.[51] Hu Han-min was overjoyed to see Huang Hsing, not only because Huang was safe but also because a revolt had broken out at Hokow, Yunnan, and the rebels there were desperately in need of an experienced revolutionary leader.

The city of Hokow, a strategic stronghold in Yunnan province, was separated from the French territory, Laokai, by the Namti River. Besides police forces, the Manchu government had four battalions stationed there; there were 659 men in each, according to the system of the time. The "people's army" had only about three hundred men, but thanks to the defection of one government battalion commander, Hokow was captured in less than a day after the partisans, led by a secret society leader, struck at midnight on April 29, 1908. The regional military commissioner was killed, and the rank and file of the other battalions in the vicinity surrendered. This sudden success brought more than three thousand soldiers to the side of the revolution. There had never been a brighter moment; it appeared that all of Yunnan province could be taken as a revolutionary base.

But the army had to be fed and paid. At Hanoi Hu Han-min was desperately in need of funds. He wrote frantic letters to Sun Yat-sen in Singapore, who in turn wrote to other comrades. Wang Ching-wei was sent to the Dutch East Indies for fundraising. Since the revolutionary troops in Yunnan were also in need of an able commander to direct them, Hu Han-min was overjoyed to receive a telegram from Huang Hsing on May 3. Huang had just retreated to the French territory from his Kwangtung campaign. On May 5 Huang arrived at Hanoi on a night train from Haiphong, and within a day or two he set out for Yunnan to take up the command.[52]

In those days it took about twelve hours by train to travel from Hanoi to Hokow. Upon arriving in Hokow, Huang Hsing found that the revolutionary forces there lacked fighting spirit. His strategy was to attack Mengtsz, the gateway to Kunming, the provincial capital of Yunnan, but he found the soldiers very reluctant to move.

After a few days in Hokow, Huang realized the necessity of having his own personal army equipped with superior arms in order to command the other troops. He also planned to summon his former comrades-in-arms from the previous Kwangtung campaign. Therefore, he returned to Hanoi for a day to discuss these plans with Hu Han-min. On May 11 he returned to the front by train.[53] Before he reached the Chinese border, however, he was questioned by a suspicious policeman at Laokai. Huang claimed to be Cantonese, but he spoke the dialect with a strong accent. His identity was soon discovered, and the Hanoi French authorities expelled him from the territory. Consequently, he departed for Singapore.

The loss of Huang Hsing was disastrous for the Hokow campaign. Without a chief commander, the rebels soon disintegrated and were defeated by reinforcements sent by the Manchu government. Hu Han-min was unable to find a suitable man to take Huang's place; he was also unable to send supplies to the front because of the sudden alertness of the French authorities along the railroad from Hanoi to Laokai.[54] The revolt had ended in failure by May 26.[55] Sun Yat-sen called this his eighth unsuccessful attempt.[56]

From a modern historical perspective it is hard to believe that the amateurish rebellions just described were intended to defeat the coordinated military and governmental system of the Empire. The revolutionary plan to invade the southern provinces of China and march northward to the Yangtze Valley seems a naïvely ambitious project, considering the tiny force of amateurs who were to undertake it. As Lyon Sharman has observed:

When we think of the great bulk of China stretching northward over fourteen hundred miles to Peking, we wonder what these men could have been thinking of, when, gathering a hundred or two zealots together, they went forth to storm some stronghold or to beat out a few months in border warfare. It seems the very wooing of futility.[57]

But these abortive revolts should not be judged solely as military operations. They were also in the nature of political demonstrations against the Manchu regime. As bold and dramatic actions by the revolutionary party, they helped sustain the faith in revolutionary ideas; and even from repeated failure, the revolutionists gained valuable experience.

In terms of military activity, the year and a half that followed the failure of the Hokow campaign was uneventful. The only notable action was the Anking revolt of November 19, 1908, led by a young army officer, Hsiung Ch'eng-chi. After six unsuccessful revolutionary attempts within a year, the T'ung Meng Hui was financially exhausted and its members greatly discouraged.

The military operations of the T'ung Meng Hui during this period were financed by overseas Chinese, primarily from British Malaya and French Indo-China. Sun Yat-sen devoted himself wholeheartedly to fund-raising.[58] He sent Wang Ching-wei on a fund-raising tour of French Indo-China, British Malaya, Burma, and the Dutch East Indies, which lasted from the fall of 1907 until January 1909.[59] Late in October 1908 Sun himself set out from Singapore on a fund-raising tour to Malaya, accompanied by Hu Han-min and Wang Ching-wei.[60] From Penang, Wang left for Rangoon on November 8; Sun and Hu proceeded to Siam and then returned to Singapore on December 14. Wang did not return to the British colony until early in January 1909.[61] The result of these travels was far from satisfactory.[62]

In the middle of November 1908, only a day or two before the death of the aged Empress Dowager, the Kuang-hsü emperor had died of mysterious causes. With the state temporarily disorganized, the time seemed favorable for revolution. But funds were low, so Sun decided to sail for Paris in the hope of raising some money. However, he was unable to leave until May 19, 1909, because the traveling expenses promised by a Chinese merchant in Siam did not arrive on time.[63] Whatever Sun's reasons for believing that he could raise money in Paris, he failed completely. He left Paris for London in August, and then proceeded to the United States in late October. He found little support from the overseas Chinese in the United States.[64]

As for Huang Hsing, he did not stay in Singapore long after his expulsion from French Indo-China in May 1908. By August of that year, he had gone to Japan, where he stayed with Chang Ping-lin, who was again in charge of the *People's Journal,* and T'ang Tseng-pi, the new assistant editor.[65] Discouraged by the repeated failures of the T'ung Meng Hui and influenced by the Russian revolution of 1905, T'ang Tseng-pi (Man-hua) wrote an article entitled "The Psychology of Revolution," which advocated assassination as a revolutionary technique. This article, published in the *People's Journal* of October 10, 1908, reflected the current sentiments of the revolutionists; it also gave the Japanese government a good excuse for confiscating the magazine.[66]

The Paris *Le Siècle Nouveau* (*Hsin shih-chi*) of December 26, 1908, gives some details about the confiscation case, which were probably supplied by the comrades in Tokyo. According to the Paris weekly, on October 19 the Japanese police confiscated the October 10 issue of the *People's Journal* and ordered the *Journal* to cease publication. Four days later Chang Ping-lin wrote to the Japanese Home Minister refusing to accept the order, but his strong language had no effect on the action of the Japanese government. In a meeting on October 25, Huang Hsing and his comrades in Tokyo discussed the possibility of continuing publication of the magazine in the United States. Meanwhile Chang Ping-lin and Sung Chiao-jen tried to secure a court hearing of the case. They did not succeed, however, and for some reason they also abandoned the plan of having the journal published in the United States.[67]

It was about this time that the Japanese police offered to pay Miyazaki Torazō to spy on the revolutionary leaders. In spite of his great financial need, Miyazaki strongly rebuked the police. Hearing of this, Huang Hsing wrote to Sun Yat-sen suggesting that Sun send a note of appreciation to their mutual friend thanking him for his loyalty. Sun accordingly sent such a letter (dated March 2, 1909); after offering thanks to Miyazaki, Sun expressed regret at being unable to help him financially because he himself was having difficulty obtaining enough money to travel from Singapore to Europe.[68]

Huang himself was constantly in debt in the spring of 1909.

After publication of the *People's Journal* was suppressed by the Japanese government, he summoned the chairmen of the provincial branches to a meeting for the purpose of establishing a new party headquarters. To support the headquarters, they agreed to resume collecting monthly dues from their respective branch members—a regulation which apparently had not been enforced for some time. Consequently, Huang rented a house to serve as the headquarters and named it the Ch'in-hsüeh She (Diligent Study Club). T'an Jen-feng suggested that he invite some "legal experts" to live there in order to draft a constitution and laws for the future republic. The suggestion was not accepted because Huang felt that such an act was too important to be undertaken by a few comrades alone; he thought the writing of a draft should be postponed until all the most talented men in the nation would have an opportunity to participate.[69] This decision suggests that Huang was not by temperament a theorist, but rather a pragmatic and unpretentious man of action.

The initial enthusiasm for supporting a new headquarters soon cooled, and the collection of dues did not last long. Huang managed to maintain the headquarters house into the winter of 1909 by taking out loans at usurious rates of interest. At one time he had to live at Miyazaki's home for two months in order to avoid creditors.[70] He re-established an "athletic society" for the purpose of giving the T'ung Meng Hui members physical and military training. A few Japanese officers were invited to give instruction.[71]

In 1909 Sun Chu-tan, a member of the T'ung Meng Hui, secured from the General Staff of the Japanese army some reputedly secret and valuable military documents concerning Manchuria. The revolutionists believed that the Russians might be interested in having the information; accordingly, Hsiung Ch'eng-chi (who had been introduced to Huang in Japan after escaping from the Anking revolt in November 1908) was sent to Manchuria to seek a Russian buyer. The money they hoped to obtain by selling these allegedly confidential documents was to be used to alleviate the party's acute financial difficulties. The revolutionists also seemed to believe that friction between Japan and Russia over Manchuria might lead to another war, and they were quite willing to fish in troubled waters.[72] However, Hsiung was betrayed by a friend. He was arrested on January 10, 1910, at Harbin, and was subsequently executed by the Manchu government. He was then in his early twenties.

Discouraged by their repeated failures, the revolutionists became increasingly interested in assassination and terrorist activities. There was great enthusiasm among the T'ung Meng Hui members for making bombs. Huang Hsing personally did not like assassination as a revolutionary tactic, but he hoped that it would prove effective if his comrades insisted on using it. He set up a secret cell in Tokyo for bomb-making experiments.[73]

Assassinations were not new at this stage in the history of the Chinese Revolution. As early as October 1900 Shih Chien-ju had made an attempt on the life of Te Shou, the Manchu governor in Canton. In Shanghai in November 1904 Wan Fu-hua attempted to kill Wang Chih-ch'un, a former governor of Kwangsi. In September 1905 at the Peking railway station Wu Yüeh attempted to throw a bomb at the five imperial commissioners, who were setting out for a tour of Western countries to observe governmental systems. All these noteworthy attempts ended in failure. Probably the most sensational effort was Wang Ching-wei's plan to assassinate the Manchu Regent, Tsai Feng, in April 1910; like many others before him, Wang failed, but his motives exemplify the kind of desperate frustration which had overtaken many revolutionists by 1909.

Like most other members of the T'ung Meng Hui, Wang had grown pessimistic after the failure of the Hokow revolt. He was also irritated by the ridicule heaped on Sun Yat-sen and his Cantonese associates by reformers outside China, who were fond of remarking that the revolutionary leaders seemed to let others fight the battles while they themselves traveled abroad in safety. Wang doubtless wanted to refute such malicious charges by some heroic action.[74] Furthermore, he deplored the constant friction within his own party (such as the previously described attacks on Sun Yat-sen by Chang Ping-lin and others). He believed that only some sensational action could restore the morale and unity of the party and destroy any false hopes the Chinese people might have for the constitutional reform then being undertaken by the Manchu government.[75]

When the South China Bureau of the T'ung Meng Hui was set up in the fall of 1909 at Hong Kong, Wang was elected secretary. But he took little interest in the Bureau's work and instead worked constantly on his assassination plan. A telegram jointly signed by Huang Hsing and Sun Yat-sen had once before succeeded in stopping him from taking such a drastic and reckless step. But this time he was determined to carry out his plan regardless of their reasoning.[76] But his plot was discovered, and on April 10, 1910, the Peking police arrested him along with his accomplice, Huang Fu-sheng. Both were sentenced to life imprisonment.

The T'ung Meng Hui's South China Bureau, headed by Hu Han-min, took over most of the important activities previously exercised by the Hong Kong branch of the party, leaving the branch's jurisdiction confined to Hong Kong. The first important task that confronted the new bureau was the organization of an army coup d'état in Canton.

The situation in Canton in the fall of 1909 was favorable to subversion. Three regiments, each equipped with modern weapons, were there, and the revolutionists believed they could secure the cooperation of a majority of the troops. Chao Sheng, a Regiment Commander whose support Huang Hsing had courted in the Chinchow revolt of 1907, had been transferred to Canton and then deprived of his rank because he was suspected of being sympathetic to the revolutionary cause. After his demotion, he came to Hong Kong and worked actively with the revolutionists in planning a coup d'état. The man who was actually in charge of subversive activities in Canton was I Ying-tien, a native of Anhwei province and a former minor army officer in Canton. His work was so successful that by the end of 1909 more than two thousand men, most of them soldiers, were said to have joined the T'ung Meng Hui in Canton and Hong Kong.[77]

When the preparations for the coup were well under way, Huang Hsing was urged to come to Hong Kong to plan and lead the military operation. After borrowing 500 *yen* from a Japanese stockbroker, he hurriedly left Tokyo on January 23, 1910, and arrived in Hong Kong on January 29.[78] A Hong Kong businessman made a contribution of HK$20,000 toward the expenses of organizing the revolt. A telegram requesting funds was sent to Sun Yat-sen, who had recently arrived in New York. Sun immediately cabled Huang a promise to send HK$20,000 within two months, as requested.[79]

During his next four and one-half months in the United States, Sun Yat-sen organized T'ung Meng Hui branches in New York, Chicago, and San Francisco; the sum of money raised by him from the Chinese communities in these cities amounted to HK$9,000. This was the second time the Chinese in the United States had contributed substantial amounts to the party in Hong Kong for financing military operations (the first time having been in the spring of 1908, when they sent HK$800).[80]

The army revolt was tentatively scheduled for late February 1910, when the holiday spirit attendant upon the Chinese New Year would prevail. However, on the afternoon of February 9 several soldiers clashed with policemen over a trivial matter in the city. Both sides were excited, and it seemed for a while that an armed conflict might break out between the army and the police. The revolutionists, however, were not ready to take advantage of such a situation, and hoped to avoid it at all costs. In the moment of crisis, I Ying-tien rushed to Hong Kong to consult with the party leaders. In an all-night conference it was decided that the coup should be rescheduled for the 15th of the month and that Huang Hsing and Chao Sheng should come to Canton then to direct the fighting.

I Ying-tien returned to Canton in the early morning of February 12 as soon as the conference ended. But the soldiers of the First Regiment had started a riot during his absence. Carried away by the situation, which was already uncontrollable, I Ying-tien went to the base of the First Regiment that afternoon and led more than one thousand soldiers in an attack; he was among the first to be killed by government troops loyal to the regime. The other regiments were unable to move, for their ammunition had been impounded by the army authorities as a precautionary measure. The rebellious soldiers were defeated within a day or two.[81] Thus ended what Sun Yat-sen called the "ninth revolutionary attempt of my party."

SIX

THE REVOLUTION OF
MARCH TWENTY-NINTH

THE ATTEMPTED Canton army coup of 1910 was by far the most disappointing military failure yet experienced by the revolutionary leaders. It had been the first real opportunity for them to fulfill their long-cherished hope of turning government troops against the government itself. But although the revolt had been crushed, the revolutionary work in the army was not completely uprooted. After another year of intensive preparation, Huang Hsing led what proved to be the most sensational unsuccessful armed revolt in the history of the Republican Revolution: the Canton revolution of March 29, 1911.[1]

In order to raise money after the "ninth revolutionary attempt" in Canton, Huang Hsing, Chao Sheng, and Hu Hanmin traveled together to Singapore on March 28, 1910. Shortly after their arrival, they received the news from Hong Kong that Wang Ching-wei and his accomplice had been arrested in Peking for plotting assassination. Shocked and grieved, Hu Hanmin went to Penang to consult with comrades there about finding a way to save his friends.

In Singapore Chao Sheng's attempts to raise money met with no success. A temperamental and impatient military man, Chao found it difficult to get along with the local Chinese, who did not offer donations as freely as he wished. After a few days of soliciting he returned to Hong Kong in disgust.[2]

Huang Hsing also found reasons for hurrying back to Hong Kong. Miyazaki Torazō had wired from Japan asking Huang to meet him in Hong Kong on a matter of importance. At about the same time, he had received a cable from the Hong Kong comrades, who stated that they had an important message for him from Sun Yat-sen.

When Miyazaki came to Hong Kong, he brought with him a man by the name of Kodama Yūji. According to Huang Hsing's letter of May 13 to Sun Yat-sen, Miyazaki had been magnifying the Chinese revolutionary strength in talks with General Hasegawa Yoshimichi, who passed on the information to Terauchi Masatake, the Resident-General of Korea. Fearing that the Chinese revolutionists might succeed, and that their future republican government might not be friendly to Japan, Terauchi decided to send one of his men to collect firsthand information on the strength of the movement. This, Huang thought, explained Kodama's presence with Miyazaki. The two Japanese stayed in Hong Kong for one week and then left. When he talked with them, Huang tried to impress the Japanese agent by exaggerating the growing sympathy of the French and American people toward the Chinese revolution.[3]

The letter Sun Yat-sen wrote to Huang on March 28 cannot be found, but Huang's reply of May 13 suggests that it dealt primarily with a plan for finding a base for training partisans and storing arms imported from abroad. The plan had been suggested by an "army man"—probably the hunchbacked American military theoretician Homer Lea—and Sun Yat-sen asked Huang whether he considered the plan feasible.

In his reply Huang stated that the French-leased territory of Kwangchowwan in southern Kwangtung could be used for storing arms and gathering men; a place had been found there where several thousand men could be disguised as farmers. But he politely rejected as impractical the "army man's" idea of inviting foreign army officers and technicians to train troops in Kwangchowwan. He said it would be difficult to find a place where training could be carried on and that even if a place could be found, as in Kwangchowwan, the activities in it would inevitably arouse the attention of the Manchu government. However, Huang added, he would welcome the help of foreign sympathizers after the outbreak of revolution.

This letter of May 13, 1910, is one of the most important documents on the Republican Revolution because, in the words of Hu Han-min, "it outlined the steps and laid down the strategy of the subsequent revolutionary actions."[4] In this letter Huang stated that the best force for overthrowing the Manchu government was its own army. In analyzing the Kwangtung situation as it stood after the abortive coup, he asserted that despite the setback in February, Canton remained a better place to start a revolt than any remote border area of the province, in part because the revolutionary organization in the Canton army had not been completely destroyed.

Huang believed, according to the letter, that Kwangtung could be taken by capturing Canton, and that the capture of Canton would still depend on the conversion of the army. Although the First Regiment and certain other forces had been disbanded after the earlier coup, the Second and Third Regiments remained, and they were unlikely to be transferred (as it had been rumored) to another part of the province in the foreseeable future. Many of the 3000 soldiers in the Circuit Battalions (Provincial Reserve Forces) were sympathetic to the revolution.

Furthermore, Huang pointed out that the Kwangtung authorities were going to recruit 1000 troops from Hunan province, and he predicted that these new troops could easily be converted to the side of revolution, especially by Hunanese revolutionists. Huang argued that this could be done if there were enough money on hand; the soldiers of the reserve forces could be easily won over to a righteous cause, especially if there were some prospect of gain.

As to the other provinces, Huang Hsing reported that there were several scores of comrades among the officers of the Kwangsi army. Many officers in the armies of Kiangsu, Chekiang, and Kiangsi provinces were also revolutionists. In the Hupeh army revolutionary work done by a certain Sun Wu was reportedly successful, and in Hunan the revolutionary strength in the army equaled that in any other province. In Yunnan members of the T'ung Meng Hui had made such inroads into the army that they might venture to start a revolt without waiting for cooperation from the other provinces. The secret societies of the Yangtze Valley could be mobilized as auxiliary forces; those in Chekiang province were especially useful.

With respect to North China, Huang told Sun Yat-sen that

in the previous year Kayano Nagatomo had brought several important coastal pirates of the Yellow Sea and some notorious Manchurian "mounted bandits" to see him in Japan. Given financial aid, they could organize an uprising that could at least hamper troop movements in the North. In summarizing, Huang predicted that once revolution broke out in one province it would be taken up in all the others, "like one cry in a ravine, echoed from all the mountain sides."

With regard to obtaining comrades for the "central organization" (a matter apparently discussed in earlier correspondence, for the T'ung Meng Hui had no headquarters after the short-lived Diligent Study Club), Huang suggested selecting them on a geographical basis in order to ensure a future harmonious relationship among provinces. He suggested persons from various provinces whom he considered capable of taking greater responsibility when the revolution approached. Among the Hunanese mentioned were Liu K'uei-i, Sung Chiao-jen, and Yang Shou-jen. Huang's comments on these persons are especially interesting because some of them have become famous.

"Yang Shou-jen," Huang wrote, "is now majoring in science in England. When you have money, you must send for him. Like [Wang] Ching-wei, he is a thoughtful person, and his literary refinement and personal character are also equal to Wang's. Ts'ai Yüan-p'ei is now in Germany. Although he is not a broad-minded person, he is a thinker of great ability. . . . Wu Chih-hui has great prestige; but he is rather idealistic and lacks efficiency in practical matters. However, he has many excellent ideas."

After listing some of the capable comrades then residing in China, Huang Hsing stated that as soon as he had money, he would go to Japan and summon a meeting of those who were capable of revolutionary action, after which he would send them back to China to start revolutions in various provinces. Those who were well-educated or who could not return to China should remain in Japan or Hong Kong to work for the "central organization." Significantly, Huang added: "If we are modest and willing to listen to the opinions of others without prejudice, there is no one who would not be happy to work with us."

Finally, Huang Hsing reported in his letter that Chao Sheng was very eager to act. He recommended that Chao should be given the command of any revolt in Kwangtung because of his close relationship with the army at Canton. Huang then suggested that a meeting be held in order to plan a revolt in Kwangtung. This was the origin of the famous Penang Conference, held later in the year, at which the "tenth revolutionary attempt" was decided upon.

Shortly after writing this letter, Huang Hsing left Hong Kong for Japan. He met Sun Yat-sen in Yokohama on June 15, 1910, just after Sun had returned from Hawaii.[5] Kayano Nagatomo's later account of this meeting is interesting for its description of the comradeship of the two revolutionary leaders and their attitude toward money:

Huang Hsing was wanted by the Japanese police. . . . I hid him and waited anxiously for Sun Yat-sen, who was returning from America. . . . One night on the Ginza we eluded a detective and thereafter I hid Huang at the Fukuzumi Hotel in Hakone. . . .

The day before Sun Yat-sen was to arrive at Yokohama, I went to the hotel . . . by a two-puller rickshaw. . . . The next day Huang Hsing and I took a rickshaw and came down to Kozu, where we secretly entered a hotel . . . that was in front of the Yokohama station. . . .

As soon as Sun Yat-sen's ship from the United States docked in the port, Huang Hsing jumped aboard it. The two men, who were meeting for the first time in a long while, said little about personal matters but very hurriedly discussed the situation of the movement. . . . We went to Sun Yat-sen's hotel. There for about two hours Sun and Huang exchanged ideas on various important subjects and agreed upon various policies for the future. . . .

When the time finally came for Huang to leave, he said to Sun: "Oh yes, money. Do you have money?" Sun answered, "Yes, I have," and showed him a whole trunk filled with money. Sun had just returned from a trip to the United States, where he had solicited funds from the overseas Chinese.

Huang Hsing took the trunk without even estimating the amount of money in it and prepared to leave. Then, as if suddenly remembering something, he said, "Oh yes, I had better leave you some, in case you should need it." Without even pausing to count them, he gave several rolls of bills to Sun and left. He left for his own country the same day. . . .

I was watching all this as it happened and was greatly impressed. Both the giver and the receiver of the money seemed completely indifferent to the amount. Throughout their lives these two leaders shared a feeling that cannot simply be described as "comradeship," and their attitude toward money was always just like this.[6]

Huang Hsing's next destination was Yunnan, but we find him first in Burma. It appears that in the summer of 1910 Yunnan revolutionists and businessmen in Burma planned to instigate a revolt in the western part of their native province. Lü Chih-i, a Yunnanese newspaperman in Burma, cabled Huang Hsing for assistance. After arriving at Rangoon, Huang went with Lü to Lashio to meet a rich merchant who was said to be willing to finance the revolt. But before the plan was well organized it had to be abandoned because of a border incident that led the Burmese authorities to confiscate the arms which the revolutionists had intended to ship to Yunnan.[7] In the next few months, Huang apparently remained in Burma. In the fall he set out for Malaya, where the hierarchy of the T'ung Meng Hui was to hold a conference.

Sun Yat-sen had been in Malaya since midsummer. Upon arriving at Yokohama in the middle of June, he had been advised by the Japanese police to leave; two weeks later he had left for Malaya and had arrived at Singapore on July 11.[8] After a short time in Singapore he moved to Penang, where he directed the reorganization of the Malayan branches of the T'ung Meng Hui.[9] By October Sun Yat-sen was definitely considering a conference in order to organize another Canton revolt, as suggested earlier by Huang Hsing.[10] On November 13 Huang arrived in Penang from Rangoon.[11] Among others who came to the conference were Chao-Sheng, Hu Han-min, Teng Tse-ju, and several leaders of the Chinese community in Malaya.

The revolutionary leaders decided at the conference to make a massive effort to capture Canton. The principal forces to be relied on would be sympathetic troops of the government army, but the initiative would be taken by 500 members of a "Dare-to-

Die Corps" recruited from the rank and file of the T'ung Meng Hui. The leaders decided to raise a large amount of money before taking military action, having learned from previous experience that funds were often exhausted as soon as revolts began. The publicly stated aim of the fund-raising campaign was to be the promotion of Chinese education. It was planned to raise HK$130,000 among the overseas Chinese: $50,000 in British Malaya, the same amount in the Dutch East Indies, and $30,000 in Siam and French Indo-China together. No quota was set for the Americas, probably because the possible contribution from there was considered insignificant or unpredictable. This was an ambitious project under the circumstances, for the revolutionary leaders were then finding it difficult even to provide for themselves.

After the conference the revolutionary leaders parted. Huang Hsing went to Burma, and he seems to have returned to Singapore some time in December.[12] Chao Sheng was the first to return to Hong Kong to make preparations for the revolt. Sun Yat-sen left for Europe on December 6.[13] He arrived in New York on February 17 of the following year to begin a fund-raising tour of North America.[14] For the same purpose Hu Han-min made two trips to Saigon and at least one trip to Siam during the first two months of 1911.[15]

Upon his return to Singapore from Rangoon, Huang Hsing was greatly distressed to hear from Hu Han-min that only HK$10,000 had been raised so far in Malaya. At that moment prospects in the Dutch East Indies were also discouraging. In desperation, Huang tried to find Teng Tse-ju, who was on a fund-raising tour of the Peninsula. Huang Hsing narrowly missed Teng several times in various towns, but finally located him in his home town of Ipoh on December 31.

Teng was deeply touched by Huang's distress over the result of the fund drive. He suggested that they make one more effort, and asked Huang to appeal with him in person to the revolutionary sympathizers in Malaya. Although his son had just been born and he had been home for only one day after an absence of 40 days, Teng left his family and set out immediately with Huang Hsing on another fund-raising tour of Malaya.

The next day was New Year's Day, 1911. Huang and Teng summoned their comrades at Seremban. During the meeting, which was attended by about 30 persons from that town, Huang stressed the urgency of the situation and appealed for more financial subscriptions. As a result, a businessman who had previously promised to contribute HK$1,000 now raised the amount to HK$5,000. The response from the others was also enthusiastic.

On the following day, January 2, 1911, the pair went to Kuala Lumpur, but they had little success there. The wealthy Chinese, as usual, were very cautious in dealing with the revolutionists, and were not enthusiastic about the cause. That evening Huang and his companions stopped for the night at an old-fashioned schoolhouse near a town called Lungpan; finding it impossible to sleep because of the mosquitoes, however, they sat on the students' bench and talked until dawn.

On the third day they arrived at Ipoh. During a dinner party given by local Chinese community leaders, more than HK$5,000 was raised. Huang and his friends were constantly on the move during the next few days and by January 7 the total amount subscribed was not far from the original goal of HK$50,000. The week of intensive effort had been very rewarding, and Huang Hsing was both grateful and touched.[16] On the 9th of the month he returned to Singapore, whence he sailed for Hong Kong three days later.[17] The day before he left Singapore he wrote to the comrades in Siam, explaining why another revolt was being organized and urging them to do their part by contributing funds. The first part of this letter, dated January 11, 1911, reads as follows:

Japan has annexed Korea and has reached an agreement with Russia. Manchuria and Mongolia are in great danger. England has sent troops to Tibet and has fortified the Burma border. The time will soon come when western China will be lost. The German railway areas in Shantung and the French ones in Yunnan are no longer our territory. The United States, having no territorial ambitions in China, has therefore pledged to maintain Chinese independence and integrity in order to monopolize foreign loans. The Manchu government, unaware of this danger, and caring little about it, welcomes the

American policy and passively consents to the demands of the other nations. Meanwhile the Manchu rulers try to deceive the people by declaring their willingness to adopt a constitution; but their real intention is to deprive the people of their rights and to increase the centralization of power. The present situation in China is such that if she is not conquered by partition, she will be lost in invisible financial control by foreign powers. How can we possibly tolerate this! . . . Therefore we decided to make an all-out effort to strike. . . . We hope that you will do your part by contributing generously to support this coming revolt. . . .[18]

The total sum of money raised by the revolutionists approached HK$190,000, far more than the original goal. It was subscribed solely by overseas Chinese, principally those in Southeast Asia. The contribution of the Chinese in the United States was relatively insignificant; it amounted to HK$14,000, $10,000 of which was collected in San Francisco, with $2,000 each coming from Honolulu and New York. The contribution of the Chinese in Canada, however, surpassed all expectations: the Hung League in Victoria alone contributed HK$33,000 by mortgaging its properties; Vancouver contributed $19,000 and Montreal, $11,000. The following table shows the approximate amounts, in Hong Kong dollars, contributed by the various Chinese communities abroad.[19]

British Malaya	HK$47,660.00
Canada	63,000.00
Dutch East Indies	32,550.00
French Indo-China and Siam	30,000.00
United States	14,000.00
Total	HK$187,210.00

Huang Hsing arrived in Hong Kong from Singapore on January 18. At 35 Happy Valley Road he set up an elaborate General Staff with himself as the chief of staff and Chao Sheng as his assistant. Hu Han-min was put in charge of the secretariat, but since he did not return to Hong Kong until late February or early March, Ch'en Ch'iung-ming served as acting chief of the secretariat.

It had been planned that once the revolution had succeeded in Kwangtung, Huang Hsing would lead one army marching northward to attack Hunan and Hupeh. In order to coordinate action in those two provinces and other Yangtze areas, Huang sent T'an Jen-feng to central China in February with $2,000 for the purpose of financing the local revolutionists, who had been quite active for some time.*

In Canton the revolutionists set up more than forty secret cells. In order to avoid involvement in case of discovery by the police, each cell was generally kept ignorant of the others. One difficulty the revolutionists had to overcome in setting up secret places was meeting the common renting conditions. Tenants were required to give references, and landlords were usually reluctant to rent houses to single men. Consequently, the rebels set up two rice shops in the city to serve as guarantors and references. (Rice bags were also convenient for hiding arms.) Some female comrades posed as wives; since there were few of them, they had to appear as housewives in several places. Many "marriages" took place among the "families" thus established, because the marriage ceremony afforded a convenient way of transferring arms. It was customary in China for the groom to wait in his own house for the coming of his bride, who was always carried to him in a curtained sedan chair. Trunks which contained dowries also changed hands on such occasions. Guns were easily hidden under the chairs and in the trunks.

Weapons were purchased abroad, principally in Japan and Saigon, but also in Siam and Hong Kong. Bombs were made by comrades in Hong Kong. These arms from abroad were first shipped to Hong Kong and then smuggled into Canton by various methods. Bullets were hidden in wigs (and for this purpose two stores selling wigs were established in Canton, and one in Hong Kong), or in tin cans supposedly containing dyes. These were usually sent to Canton as cargo, but sometimes they were carried into Canton by the comrades themselves.

The revolution had been tentatively scheduled to take place

---

* Certain unexpected results of this trip had a direct bearing on the Wuchang Revolution and will be discussed in the following chapter.

on April 13, 1911. But on April 8 a comrade from Malaya, without revealing his intention to anyone, shot a Manchu general in broad daylight. Because the provincial authorities became alert after this assassination, and also because both a shipment of arms from Japan and the remittance of funds from America and the Dutch East Indies were delayed, the revolt was postponed until the end of the month. However, the revolutionists had to strike before the end of April because it was rumored that the Second Regiment of the Canton army would be demobilized early in May. It became indeed ironic that the success of the revolution depended upon the government troops.

For a moment the outlook was good. A new brigade commander and a new regiment commander were both old friends of Huang Hsing's.[20] The brigade commander had been among the first to join the T'ung Meng Hui in Tokyo.[21] Intensive propaganda and organizational work had been done among the soldiers. Each one who joined the revolutionary organization was given a dollar and had his photograph taken. The soldiers were told that their pictures would be sent to the General Staff in Hong Kong in order to make their pledges unequivocal; but actually the pictures were destroyed immediately so that they could never fall into the hands of the police.

Besides the Canton army, the revolutionists also tried to convert the Provincial Reserve Forces, or Circuit Battalions as they were then called. The militia in the countryside near Canton was also organized. It had been decided at the Penang conference that the action initiating the revolt was to be taken by the 500 members of the "Dare-to-Die Corps." This number was found insufficient, however, and the corps was expanded to 800 and divided into ten groups each numbering between fifty and one hundred.

The members of the "Dare-to-Die Corps" were recruited from various provinces. Those from Szechwan, Fukien, and Southeast Asia were under the command of Huang Hsing. Chao Sheng's men were almost exclusively from Kiangsu and Anhwei. Most of them had reached Hong Kong by the middle of April, and they began to pour into Canton.

On the evening of April 23 Huang Hsing left Hong Kong for Canton to take charge of the imminent military action. Before leaving he wrote several letters to his friends in Malaya who were in charge of the fund-raising campaigns. The one to Teng Tse-ju reads as follows:

I am sorry that I have been unable to write you more often because I have been so busy. I am leaving today for the battlefield. I am determined to lead my men to wipe out the enemy, and I shall not fail your expectations. All the funds, even the smallest amount, that we received and spent for this revolt are recorded. The account will be sent to your town, then to the Dutch East Indies, and then to America so that regardless of the outcome of the revolution, it will be known that every penny was spent for the cause. We are much to blame if owing to our limited ability the preparations prove defective and some of the money not well spent. But we hope that the Chinese race is not lost forever and that we may succeed by one blow; otherwise my own death will not atone for the mistakes. But my conscience is clear and I would have these be my last words.[22]

The Kwangtung authorities were not unaware of the rebels' plan. After the intensive fund drives, the plan to revolt became an open secret in Singapore, and the Manchu agents there had sent warnings to their government. On the same day that the Manchu general was murdered at Canton, several conspirators were arrested in the city for carrying arms. On April 23 a Chinese journal in Shanghai published a report by the Governor-General of Kwangtung and Kwangsi to the Ministry of War stating that the provincial authorities had taken every precaution against the rebels. The only thing the provincial authorities did not know was the date set for the attempt.

The rebels at Canton had tentatively decided to revolt on April 26. After his arrival at Canton, Huang Hsing postponed the outbreak for one day because arms from Japan and French Indo-China could not reach Hong Kong until the 26th of the month. Meanwhile, he stopped the remaining revolutionary troops in Hong Kong from coming to Canton (they were scheduled to come on the 24th and the 25th) by wiring the following message to Hu Han-min: "Epidemic has broken out in the city. Don't send children home yet."

On the 25th Huang learned that two of the Circuit Battalions had been called back to Canton by the government to strengthen the defenses of the city. He realized that his plan had probably leaked out and that there might be counter-revolutionary agents working among his men. After several comrades suggested postponing the revolt temporarily, Huang Hsing reluctantly acquiesced and sent some of Chao Sheng's men back to Hong Kong. But later in the day, when he heard that the police were about to make a house-to-house search for revolutionary conspirators, he began to think that any postponement might mean no revolt at all. Huang thus decided it would be better to rally his men to attack the Governor-General's office rather than disband without a fight.

On the following day, the 26th, the men responsible for instilling revolutionary ideas in the army and the reserve forces reported that of the ten officers in the Circuit Battalions recently transferred to the city, eight were revolutionary sympathizers, one was neutral, and one was opposed to the revolution. This encouraged Huang to think that success was still possible and he decided to carry out the original plan of revolt on the 27th, as scheduled.

Huang Hsing's reasons for deciding to carry out the revolt against such heavy odds were not so much military as political. The intensive and highly successful fund-raising campaign had made it possible for the revolutionists to organize what was potentially their most powerful offensive. Postponing the attack could only make later action difficult, or even impossible; and Huang believed that unless he took action, he would be betraying the trust placed in him by the overseas Chinese who were the revolution's main financial backers. He was determined to justify their trust so that they would not cease to support the revolution.[23] Huang's devotion to the future of the revolution and his willingness to keep his word even at the risk of his life were in the best Chinese tradition.

In order to get all available men and arms sent to Canton immediately, Huang wired to Hu Han-min: "Mother is getting better. Bring medicine here at once." His telegram confirming the 27th as the date for revolt did not reach Hong Kong until ten o'clock on the evening of the 26th. There were more than three hundred men and two hundred guns still in Hong Kong, but the last night boat for Canton had already departed. Chao

Sheng suggested that all the men with weapons should sail together by morning boat and be prepared to begin fighting at the Canton harbor in case they should meet resistance. But Hu Hanmin and T'an Jen-feng cautioned against such a move. They were of the opinion that some of the men should take the morning boat but that most of them should sail in the evening. (In those days only one ship sailed from Hong Kong to Canton in the morning, but more ships went in the afternoon and evening.)

Consequently, a telegram requesting that action be postponed until the 28th was immediately sent to Huang Hsing. T'an Jen-feng, who had returned to Hong Kong from the Yangtze areas, was sent to Canton early in the morning to explain the situation to Huang; among those who went in the morning were Huang's eldest son, I-ou, and other comrades. Chao Sheng and Hu Hanmin were to take an evening boat. But it was too late to change Huang's plan. By the time T'an arrived at the Canton headquarters, Huang and his men were ready for action. T'an failed to persuade Huang to postpone the revolt.

By about four o'clock in the afternoon of the 27th, Huang Hsing's men had gathered at his headquarters. Each was then given a weapon, ammunition, and one dollar; they wore rubber shoes and each had a white handkerchief on his arm as a sign to be recognized by other comrades. T'an, already beyond middle age, asked to join the "Dare-to-Die Corps," but Huang Hsing refused his request. When T'an insisted, Huang gave him a gun but quickly grabbed it back when T'an accidentally fired it. At five-thirty the rebels started to move. Thus began the famous Canton Revolution of March 29.

The original plan had called for a ten-route offensive by the 800 members of the "Dare-to-Die Corps," but it was changed to a four-route attack because many of the men were still in Hong Kong. Huang Hsing led one group to attack the Governor-General's office. Another group was to attack the north gate of the city and let in the government troops which had been converted to the cause. The third group was to guard the south gate, and the fourth was to seize the police school so that its 200 students might come over to the side of the rebels. It turned out later, however, that only the group led by Huang Hsing had carried out its attack as planned; the other three groups took no organized part in the fighting when they realized the heavy odds against them.

Huang Hsing marched to the Governor-General's office with 130 men. After a brief skirmish he succeeded in capturing the office. The Governor-General had fled, and no official of any importance appeared to be there, so Huang set fire to the building and left.

Back in the street he encountered government soldiers. One of Huang's men stepped forward to call for their defection by shouting, "Chinese don't fight against Chinese!" He was immediately killed by the enemy. Huang himself had a narrow escape; two fingers on his right hand were shot off.

Huang's men then split into three groups, each taking a different route of attack. The battle soon raged all over Canton. On his way to the south gate with ten men, Huang encountered government forces. Fighting ensued, and the rebels were defeated. Huang escaped to a deserted drygoods store and managed to change his clothes. In disguise, he then made his way to a secret cell in the countryside south of the Pearl River, where Hsü Tsung-han, a widow who had been active in T'ung Meng Hui since 1908, bandaged his wound and kept him safely hidden. Three days later, on April 30, he escaped to Hong Kong with Hsü Tsung-han, who later became his wife.[24]

When Chao Sheng, Hu Han-min, and several other comrades arrived in Canton on the morning of April 28, the revolt had ended in defeat on the previous day. They returned to Hong Kong the same day. Some of the scheduled concerted uprisings took place in the countryside and the neighboring districts, but they were suppressed by government troops within a few days.

The T'ung Meng Hui had pooled all its resources and mobilized its maximum power for this revolt. The inability of the revolutionists to concentrate their power because of the three changes in the date of the revolt was one of the main reasons for their failure. Whether parts of the government army would have joined the revolt if the rebels had concentrated their strength and scored an initial success is a moot question. It was always known that without the army's cooperation, the revolt was doomed. Years later Hu Han-min commented on the Canton revolt as follows:

Prompted by their righteous cause, the revolutionists acted regardless of the outcome of the revolt. They were willing to die, and they died with conviction. The great spirit of selflessness in the revolutionary party thus became well known to the nation. It was a moving event at the time; years have passed, and it is still a touching memory even today. As a result of it the Manchu court was shaken and the people were electrified. It precipitated the Wuchang Revolution, to the first shot of which the whole nation echoed. Therefore, it may be considered as a conclusive appraisal that although the Revolution of March 29 failed, its effect was one hundred times greater than the capture of one city.[25]

This "tenth revolutionary attempt of our party," as Sun Yat-sen put it, was certainly the most daring of all the revolutionary military operations. Unlike the previous revolts, which took place in small towns or villages in remote areas, it broke out in the center of a provincial capital, one of the most important cities in China. Among the members of the "Dare-to-Die Corps" who sacrificed their lives in Canton were some of the best-educated students recently returned from Japan: they were the flower of the party, and the courage revealed in the letters they left for wives and parents is moving.[26]

In 1918, six years after the establishment of the Republic, a magnificent memorial was built on the site of Huanghuakang (Yellow Flower Mound) in the northern suburb of Canton, where the bodies of the 72 rebels who died in the revolt were buried shortly after its failure. Although it was discovered years later that at least 85 rebels had died, the phrase "seventy-two martyrs" had already acquired nationwide currency.[27] Because the revolt occurred on the 29th day of the 3rd lunar month by the old-style calendar used in pre-Republic days, March 29 has become the national memorial day instead of its equivalent in Western style, April 27. The story of the "Huanghuakang Revolution of March 29" has repeatedly been shown on the stage and in films. Huanghuakang became, in the words of Wu Chih-hui, the "Holy Land of the Republic of China."[28] And Huang Hsing's name seems to have been more commonly identified with the "Huanghuakang Revolution" than with any other role he played in the revolutionary movement of China.

SEVEN

THE WUCHANG REVOLUTION

THE WUCHANG REVOLUTION of October 10, 1911, came only after a decade of growing discontent. The Empress Dowager's return to power after the coup d'état of 1898 introduced a period of reaction which brought on the Boxer uprising of 1900. The Boxer catastrophe aroused the country and signaled the beginning of a basic shift in the Chinese attitude toward the alien regime. A general demand for reform arose throughout the country, and the government found it difficult to ignore. In the following decade the Manchu government undertook a series of reforms. For the first time in the history of the dynasty, Manchuria was opened to Chinese immigration; the ban on intermarriage between the two races was lifted; certain special privileges of the Manchus were eliminated; the educational system was changed; constitutional government was promised, and provincial assemblies were formed. Although a good number of reforms were instituted and many more promised, many Chinese came to see the whole reform movement as nothing more than a political expedient for avoiding internal upheaval; they considered the regime too self-seeking to promote any fundamental changes. As the plight of the masses grew worse, numerous "rice riots" took place, the most notable one being the Changsha riot of 1910. The refusal of peasants to pay taxes became commonplace throughout the country. In 1911 anti-government sentiment was intensified by the government's plan to nationalize the railways.

In May 1911 Sheng Hsüan-huai, Minister of Posts and Communications, secured a four-power loan from British, French, German, and American financial syndicates to build railways from Hankow to Canton and Szechwan; on hearing of this, the people and the gentry of Kwangtung, Hunan, and Szechwan rose up against the policy. The strongest protests came from the Szechwan gentry, who had already organized their own railway company to build railways in Szechwan province. These men had no intention of promoting the overthrow of the government, but when threatened with the loss of their investment they soon reached a state of acute exasperation and began to stage organized protests. They held meetings, circulated petitions, closed their shops, and refused to pay taxes. Through August and September the disturbances spread. When the situation reached a grave state, the government attempted to suppress the riots by force, causing an even more violent reaction.

Within the revolutionary movement, two important organizations existed in Hupeh in 1911, and they had made great progress. One was the Common Advancement Society (Kung Chin Hui); the other was the Literary Society (Wen Hsüeh Hui). Some historians have given the Literary Society full credit for initiating the Wuchang Revolution, whereas others—notably, certain official historians of the Kuomintang—have tended to minimize its contributions.[1] It may thus be fitting here to summarize the revolutionary activities in Hupeh up to the eve of the Wuchang Revolution and the part played in them by leaders of the T'ung Meng Hui.

Between 1904 and 1911 a number of local revolutionary organizations existed in Hupeh province, and more than six of them attracted sizable followings. One rose as another fell. It was characteristic of these organizations that they were all founded by both students and soldiers but eventually run by the soldiers.

As we have noted, the Science Study Group was the first revolutionary organization in Hupeh. It was affiliated with Huang Hsing's Hua Hsing Hui until it was dissolved for taking part in the abortive Changsha revolt of 1904. Its successor, the Society for the Daily Increase of Knowledge, was a front organization for the Hupeh branch of the T'ung Meng Hui. It was likewise banned by the government when its members were found to have taken part in the uprisings in Pingsiang, Liling, and Liuyang in the winter of 1906. For a year and a half after this, the movement in Hupeh lay dormant.

In the summer of 1908 the former members of the Society for the Daily Increase of Knowledge became active again. In the middle of December the Society of Self-Government Studies (Ch'ün-chih Hsüeh-hui) was established. The declared purpose of this organization was to improve the education and the self-governing ability of its members, who were recruited exclusively from the army. There were almost no officers among its members, because they were distrusted by the soldiers.[2]

Following the Changsha rice riot of April 1910, in which a mob of starving peasants and others burned down the provincial governor's office, the Hupeh revolutionists attempted to organize a revolt in Hunan and Hupeh. But the Hupeh authorities discovered the conspiracy, and the leaders of it fled the province.

In the late summer of 1910 some members of the Society for Self-Government Studies decided to form a new organization. Called the Military Study Society (Ch'eng-wu Hsüeh-she), it was formally established at the Chinese Mid-Autumn Festival on the 15th day of the 8th lunar month, which happened to be September 18 of that year. Within a month it had 240 members; all of these were soldiers in the New Army, and each one was responsible for recruiting a new member every month. Before long, however, some of the leading members of the society, including its Hunanese chairman, were expelled from the government army for suspected subversive activities. This interrupted the activities of the Military Study Society.[3]

On January 30, 1911—Chinese New Year's Day—the Military Study Society was reorganized as the Literary Society, with Chiang I-wu as the chairman.[4] Chiang had had some education in his native province of Hunan, but had been expelled from school because of his alleged revolutionary activities (reputed to have some connection with Huang Hsing's Changsha revolt in 1904).[5] In about 1906 he planned to go to Japan but fell ill at Shanghai, where he attended a school for a short time after his recovery. Later a fellow provincial invited him to join the T'ung Meng Hui and to work for a Shanghai newspaper.[6] In the fall of 1909, this same friend brought him to Hupeh, where Chiang joined the government army. He was then in his mid-twenties.

When the leaders of the Military Study Society were dismissed from the army, Chiang was chosen to lead the society. In reorganizing the society and carrying out its work, he often sought the advice of the imprisoned Hu Ying, and much credit has been given to Hu Ying for the success of the Literary Society.[7] Thus the Literary Society's leadership had some contact with the T'ung Meng Hui, and especially with Huang Hsing's group in the party.

As to the Common Advancement Society, its origin, aims, and regulations have been variously described by several of its former members. However, two facts are certain: the organization had its genesis in Tokyo, and it was affiliated with the T'ung Meng Hui. It seems that in the spring of 1907, Liu K'uei-i, the acting vice-chairman of the T'ung Meng Hui during Huang Hsing's absence from Tokyo, planned to make a new effort to recruit secret society members as well as revolutionists of various provinces. The project hung fire, however, because Lü Chih-i, who was supposed to direct it, failed to show up at the appropriate party meeting. Those who were interested in the project later took it up by forming the Common Advancement Society.[8] According to one of its founders, the Society was formally established in August 1907.[9]

The Common Advancement Society declared that it would seek the cooperation of other revolutionists in the common cause of overthrowing the Manchu dynasty. Its purposes were about the same as those of the T'ung Meng Hui, but it substituted the "equalization of human rights" for the "equalization of land rights." According to one member of the Society, the "equalization of human rights" referred to the relation between the Manchus and the Chinese.[10] According to another, however, the phrase was intended to appeal to the secret society members, who were traditionally looked down on by the people.[11]

The most active members of the Common Advancement Society were from Szechwan, Hunan, and Hupeh. They did not relinquish their T'ung Meng Hui membership. For example, Chiao Ta-feng, who was a department head in the Society, took part in the military training courses organized by Huang Hsing in Tokyo in the latter part of 1908. Huang is said to have expressed displeasure to Chiao about the founding of the Society; he feared that it might create factions within the revolutionary camp. But he reluctantly acquiesced when, upon returning to Tokyo, he was informed of the establishment of the Society.[12] According to one of its founders, the Common Advancement Society was meant to be not a rival of the T'ung Meng Hui, but rather an extension of it.[13] The Society members in China eventually came to support the chairman of the T'ung Meng Hui as the head of their organization in order to avoid friction between the two parties.[14] And at one time, T'an Jen-feng, a leading T'ung Meng Hui member, was listed along with the Society's chairman as being an administrator of the sworn statements of the Society members.[15]

The activities of the Common Advancement Society in Hupeh began after Sun Wu and Chiao Ta-feng returned from Japan in late 1908 and early 1909, respectively. A native of Hupeh province, Sun Wu had been a member of the Science Study Group. He was graduated from a military academy in Wuchang and had served as an army officer in both Hunan and Hupeh before he went to Japan in 1905 to take naval training. Having taken a leading part in the previously described Chinese student strike against the Japanese government, he returned to Wuchang and then traveled to Manchuria. In 1908 he planned to join Huang Hsing in Yunnan, but by the time he reached Hong Kong on his way to that province, the revolt there had ended in defeat and Huang had left. So he went to Japan, joined the Common Advancement Society, and was chosen to head its military department. Shortly afterward he returned to Hupeh, being followed by Chiao Ta-feng a few months later. In the late fall of 1909 he made a trip to Hong Kong, where he joined the T'ung Meng Hui. In the summer of 1910 he returned to Hupeh, and made great progress with revolutionary work in that province.[16]

When Huang Hsing was organizing the Canton Revolution early in 1911, he sent for T'an Jen-feng to assist him. When T'an arrived in Hong Kong from Japan on February 4, Huang gave him two thousand dollars to make a trip to Hunan and

• Hupeh for the purpose of organizing uprisings there which would coordinate with those planned to take place in the south. T'an arrived in Hankow on the 23rd of February, having left Hong Kong on February 5.[17] Through Chü Cheng he conferred with the leaders of the Common Advancement Society and through Hu Ying he met the leaders of the Literary Society.

Chü Cheng had recently returned from Japan to his native town in Hupeh. Before T'an's arrival, he had received a message from Huang Hsing asking him to instigate an uprising in Hupeh which would coordinate with the one in Canton. Having been away from the province for a long time, Chü was not familiar with the local situation, so he immediately went to his friends in the Common Advancement Society, which had named him a department head while he was in Japan. Thus when T'an arrived in Hankow, Chü was able to bring Sun Wu and other leaders of the society to confer with him.[18]

T'an gave six hundred dollars to Chü and two hundred dollars to Sun.[19] With this money they set up secret cells in the Hankow French Concession and in Wuchang. Later a headquarters was established in the Hankow Russian Concession.[20] It was there that Sun Wu accidentally set off the bomb which precipitated the Wuchang Revolution.

T'an Jen-feng's meeting with Chiang I-wu and other leaders of the Literary Society was held in Hu Ying's prison cell in Wuchang. Although serving a sentence of life imprisonment, Hu was not out of touch with the revolutionary movement. A brilliant man of great personal charm, he had quickly won over the wardens, who let him enjoy certain liberties that were denied to other prisoners. He was permitted to receive visitors and to correspond with the outside world. His connection with the T'ung Meng Hui in general and with Huang Hsing in particular enhanced his importance in the eyes of the local leaders, who were eager to seek his advice.[21] T'an did not at first have much respect for the local leaders of the Literary Society, but after talking with Hu Ying he overcame this prejudice.[22] Thus the cooperation between the Literary Society and the T'ung Meng Hui was made possible.

Inspired by the courageous actions of their comrades in Canton, the Hupeh revolutionaries were eager to strike. Some members of the T'ung Meng Hui had been advocating revolution in the Yangtze areas. It may be recalled that in the latter part of 1910 there was much informal discussion in Tokyo among T'an Jen-feng, Sung Chiao-jen, Chao Sheng, Chü Cheng, and others on the desirability of instigating revolution in the Yangtze regions.[23] This was partly because they were critical of Sun Yat-sen's leadership.[24] They blamed Sun for neglecting the revolutionary movement in central China, and accused him of withholding funds from comrades who planned to work in areas other than Kwangtung.[25] They decided to set up a Central China Bureau, which was one of the five bureaus originally planned by the T'ung Meng Hui. T'an Jen-feng went to Hong Kong to present this plan to Huang Hsing. Huang agreed that the plan should be carried out, but only if funds were available. Hu Han-min, however, opposed it on the ground that it might create problems within the party leadership. T'an was so furious that he broke relations with Hu after a heated argument.[26]

After the failure of the Canton Revolution, T'an Jen-feng, Sung Chiao-jen, and others began to focus their attention on the Yangtze regions, and especially on Wuhan, which includes the cities of Wuchang, Hankow, and Hanyang. They wanted a local organization through which to act because at that time the central leadership of the party seemed incapable of action: Chao Sheng had died of illness after the Canton revolt; Huang Hsing and Hu Han-min were discouraged, and had made themselves virtually inaccessible; Sun Yat-sen, as usual, was abroad.

The Central China Bureau was founded on July 13, 1911, with headquarters in Shanghai; its main purpose was to instigate revolution in the Yangtze area. Although it was intended to be a branch within the framework of the T'ung Meng Hui, similar to the South China Bureau, it was organized under collective leadership, and its chairmanship was deliberately left open for some future "eligible person."[27] T'an Jen-feng, Sung Chiao-jen, Ch'en Ch'i-mei, and two others were elected as the five executive officers. Chü Cheng was put in charge of the movement in Hupeh, and Chiao Ta-feng was to direct activities in Hunan.

The executive officers kept Huang Hsing informed of recent developments and often asked for his advice.[28]

Remembering his own experience, Huang Hsing suggested to his comrades that they watch each member closely in order to avoid infiltration by government agents. He questioned the democratic principle upon which the Bureau had been organized, and advocated iron discipline. In a letter to the five executive officers of the Bureau, dated October 6, 1911, he wrote:

One of the reasons for the failure of the Canton Revolution was our blind admiration of the democratic principles upon which the General Staff was organized. This allowed indecision to prevail. For example, the revolutionary forces were disbanded on the 27th [day of the 3rd lunar month (April 25, 1911)] only to be assembled again on the following day. We did not realize that in instigating revolution, dictatorship is imperative. Once a dissenting voice is permitted the revolution is bound to fail. Napoleon once remarked that it is better to have one bad commander in an army than to have two good ones. This is because although the commander may be bad, at least his orders are absolute. If two commanders have different ideas, conflict will prevail. . . . In instigating revolution, our party must be organized by strict army discipline. One way to correct the faults of dictatorship is to have many advisers or staff members, who can contribute to careful planning. Once a decision is made, it should be carried out without any question or doubt. . . . This is also the way it should be in the early stage of the military government after the success of the revolution.[29]

With the formation of the Central China Bureau, revolutionary work in the Yangtze areas became more intensive than ever. In Hupeh Chü Cheng and Sun Wu had been working fervently, but by the middle of April they had exhausted the money T'an Jen-feng had given them. In desperation, Chü and Chiao Ta-feng planned to enter a popular temple in the area and steal a Buddha which was alleged to be made of solid gold.[30] This scheme apparently failed. One comrade tried robbing his rich aunt, and when that also failed he kidnaped his nephew and held him for a ransom of eight hundred dollars.[31]

The acute financial situation was remedied temporarily by

101

the arrival of Liu Kung, the chairman of the Common Advancement Society. Liu had joined the T'ung Meng Hui in Japan when he was a student there, and he had taken a leading part in the formation of the Common Advancement Society in Tokyo. In the fall of 1910 he returned to his home town in northwestern Hupeh. When he appeared in the provincial capital the following summer, he brought with him a large amount of money given to him by his father for the purpose of buying an official position in the Manchu government. His comrades successfully persuaded him to contribute $5000 of it to help the party.[32]

By this time a unification of the two revolutionary groups in Hupeh had come to be considered imperative. The first moves toward unification were not easy to make, however, because there was a struggle for leadership between the two organizations. Although some members of the Common Advancement Society also belonged to the Literary Society, the chief figures of the two groups were men of quite different caliber and background.

The leaders of the Common Advancement Society had all been students in Japan. They were also members of the T'ung Meng Hui and worked very closely with its members of Yangtze origin. Indeed, it is often hard to discover, in given cases, whether they were working in the name of the Common Advancement Society or in that of the T'ung Meng Hui.

In the Literary Society, however, both the leadership and the members were provincial. Although Chiang I-wu, the Hunanese chairman, was reputed to have joined the T'ung Meng Hui, neither he nor his colleagues had ever been abroad. Hu Ying served as perhaps their only important link with the revolutionary movement in the country. The rank and file of the Literary Society were almost exclusively soldiers recruited from the New Army in Hupeh. Some of them were educated, but no one of them could have provided the able leadership that could be supplied by the T'ung Meng Hui.

In terms of real strength, the Literary Society surpassed the Common Advancement Society, for its members were to be found in practically every regiment or unit of the New Army in Hupeh. But the leaders of the Common Advancement Society had more prestige, and Chiang I-wu had misgivings about joining hands with them.[33]

The problem of unification was discussed in a meeting held by the leaders of the two groups on May 11, 1911. Yang Yü-ju, a leader of the Common Advancement Society, suggested giving financial aid to the Literary Society if Sun Wu could be made its chairman. This proposal was unacceptable to the Literary Society.[34]

On June 1 cooperation with the Common Advancement Society was formally proposed and approved by the Literary Society.[35] But the two groups did not reach an accord until the Common Advancement Society found an acceptable formula of compromise on the 14th of September. It was then informally agreed by both sides that in the coming revolt Chiang I-wu, chairman of the Literary Society, should be the provisional chief commander while Sun Wu, head of the Military Department of the Common Advancement Society, should be the chief of staff. Chü Cheng was sent to Shanghai on the 16th for the purpose of inviting Huang Hsing, Sung Chiao-jen, and T'an Jen-feng to come to Wuchang to take charge of the revolution.[36]

The compromise formula on the matter of leadership was formally proposed and confirmed in a joint meeting of the two societies held on September 24. The meeting was attended by more than 60 representatives and was presided over by Sun Wu in Chiang I-wu's absence. October 6 was established as the tentative date for a revolt in Wuchang. Chiao Ta-feng was notified of this decision in the hope that he could organize a simultaneous uprising in Hunan. The date scheduled for revolt was later postponed.[37]

Chü Cheng arrived at Shanghai on September 25 and immediately got in touch with the leaders of the Central China Bureau of the T'ung Meng Hui.[38] At the same time he sent an emissary to Hong Kong to report to Huang Hsing on the latest developments in Hupeh.

The emissary, Lü Chih-i of Yunnan, arrived at Hong Kong from Shanghai on September 29, carrying a letter from the Central China Bureau and also a personal letter from its leaders.[39] Because of the precautions Huang Hsing had taken after the failure of the Canton Revolution, Lü was unable to meet him until three days later, October 2.[40]

Sun Yat-sen had taken no part, either direct or indirect, in organizing the Wuchang Revolution. Indeed, it caught him by surprise. Even Huang Hsing apparently did not realize the tremendous progress of the revolutionary movement in Hupeh until the arrival of Chü's emissary.[41] After the failure of the Canton revolt, he was determined to assassinate some top-ranking officials at Canton to avenge the death of his comrades.[42] And in late September he was still thinking of the possibility of instigating another revolt in Yunnan; he had sent some money to T'an Jen-feng and wired him to come to Hong Kong so that they could travel together to that province.[43] However, he abandoned this plan as soon as he received the report from Lü Chih-i.

Huang Hsing's analysis of the revolutionary situation on the eve of the October revolution at Wuchang is best revealed in his letter to Feng Tzu-yu, who was then in Vancouver. The second part of the letter was written on October 5, 1911, three days after he had met Lü Chih-i and five days before the outbreak of the revolution. It reads:

According to the emissary sent here from Shanghai by Chü Cheng, the representative of Hupeh, who was in charge of organizing a coordinated uprising in that province when the last Canton Revolution was being undertaken, the revolutionary movement in [Hupeh] has made tremendous progress. . . .

We now have about two thousand men there, many of them low-ranking officers. As to the soldiers, only those of the best caliber have been recruited. . . . With such good soldiers on hand, the situation in Hupeh seems to look better than it does in Kwangtung. Since the railway riot in Szechwan has taken a grave turn, the comrades in Hupeh have advocated immediate action. Revolt is imminent.

Incidentally, Hu Ying had also sent emissaries here. Although in prison, Hu is still in close touch with the army circle. I wrote to him last year, asking him to organize a revolt there in order to respond to our action in Canton. Since then his work in that direction has made great progress. He has about a thousand men; some of his men also belong to the group under Mr. Chü. The two groups plan to take unified action in the near future. If we take advantage of the Szechwan situation, more will join our side later.

The army men in Hupeh have long been subject to suppression. On the surface they did not seem to have the qualifications for taking the initiative. But actually they have that potential. The comrades there have long been subjected to criticism and ridicule by their fellow revolutionists, and they want to answer with action. With enthusiasm running high and revolutionary spirit aroused, there is a great possibility of their taking the initiative. This is indeed a rare opportunity. If we suppress it, try to stop it, or let it break out without the help of our leadership, the revolution may fail. That would be a great pity.

From the military point of view, Wuhan is not really a good place for defensive purposes. But it can be used well by a good commander. Hu Lin-i, the traitor and general of the army of the Manchu government, was once able to use the place as a stronghold for the government even after being thoroughly defeated [by the Taiping army]. This was because he knew how to defend it.

Now if we can take the Hanyang Arsenal, we shall not be in want of ammunition. Our military strength may be a match for the [government troops of the] North. The Yangtze areas east of Hupeh may accordingly fall into our hands. We may conveniently launch an expedition marching toward the north along the Peking-Hankow railway line. From the geographical standpoint, therefore, Wuhan also has its advantages. Heretofore, we have concentrated on Kwangtung and Kwangsi provinces merely because it is not easy for us to infiltrate into the Yangtze areas. Besides, we were not sure that the army would be on our side and that supplies could be conveniently obtained. This is why we have not previously attempted to start a revolution there.

Now that we have such formidable forces there, we can use Wuchang as the center and Hunan and Kwangtung as the rear, coordinated with simultaneous uprisings in Nanking, Anhwei, Shensi, . . . and Szechwan. Thus to overthrow the Manchu dynasty at one blow may not be difficult. We must make use of this opportunity to stride forward bravely. The chance of success is much better there than in Kwangtung. The problem of military expenditures can be easily solved. It is estimated that two hundred thousand dollars or so will be enough for overall preparations in all areas. In Hupeh alone the revolution can be initiated with forty or fifty thousand dollars.

At any rate, according to Chü, the Hupeh revolution will definitely be carried out as planned even without financial aid from outside. If necessary, the comrades in Hupeh are determined to manage by raising funds themselves. The situation is like riding a tiger.

You cannot dismount but must hang on. We must realize and appreciate the hardship of the comrades who are instigating revolution in the interior, and help them with large funds so that the revolt will not fail because of a shortage of money. I appeal to you with all my heart to do something about this.

I had intended personally to carry out assassinations instead of attempting another revolt which might cost the lives of more comrades. But such action is hardly different from suicide. Now that a last attempt is being ventured in Hupeh, it is better to die this way. Therefore I have promised my comrades in Hupeh to work for them, and I am going to the Yangtze in the near future. Please wire to Chung-shan [Sun Yat-sen] for me. I am sure that you will do your best to help, upon receiving this letter. . . . I shall leave here as soon as I hear from you.[44]

When the letter was finally forwarded to Feng Tzu-yu, he was in San Francisco, and it was three weeks after the outbreak of the Wuchang Revolution.[45] Nor was Sun Yat-sen able to help. In an often-quoted passage of his autobiography, Sun recalled:

While the Wuchang Revolution was taking place, I arrived at Denver, Colorado. About a fortnight before, I had received a telegram from Huang K'o-ch'iang [Huang Hsing] in Hong Kong. Because my secret code book was in my trunk, which had already gone to Denver, I had no way of translating it on the way. That night, on arriving in Denver, I took out the secret code and decoded the telegram from K'o-ch'iang, which read: "[representative of] Chü Cheng arrived at Hong Kong from Wuchang, reporting [sympathizers in] the New Army are determined to move. Please remit funds at once," etc.

I was then in Denver, and I could think of no way to get funds. I was thinking of wiring an answer, "Do not move," but it was late at night, and I was extremely tired from the day's tedious traveling, and I was confused in my thoughts. I thought I would have a good night's rest first, and then would answer him next day after giving the matter some more thought. However, I slept until eleven o'clock the next morning. When I got up, I was hungry. I went to a cafeteria to get my breakfast. On passing a newsstand in the lobby, I bought a newspaper which opened with the news, "Wuchang occupied by the revolutionists." All the difficulties involved in answering Huang's telegram were completely removed. Consequently, I sent a telegram to him, explaining how my reply was delayed and telling him my plan. I immediately left for the eastern part of the United States.[46]

Events in Hupeh had moved rapidly. Since the end of September the authorities of the Wuhan cities had known that revolutionary agitation was being carried on; the cities were full of rumors that revolution was imminent. Several different dates have been given as the tentative date set for the revolt, but these had originated only in informal discussions. By the account of Hsiung Ping-k'un, who was reported to have fired the first shot in Wuchang, no deadline was actually set while the Hupeh comrades were waiting for the return of Chü Cheng and the arrival of Huang Hsing.[47]

On the morning of October 9, Chiang I-wu, who had been away from Wuchang on military duties, returned to the city. He learned from his comrades that Chü Cheng was still in Shanghai and that Huang Hsing had suggested postponing the revolution until the end of October in order to gain time for organizing simultaneous uprisings in other provinces. He was also informed that Huang was definitely coming to Shanghai. Consequently, Chiang summoned his comrades to a meeting and explained that it would be better to wait for further developments before taking action in Hupeh.[48]

It was then the news reached Chiang that a bomb had accidentally exploded that morning in the revolutionary headquarters in the Hankow Russian Concession.[49] After the accident, in which Sun Wu was injured, the police searched the headquarters, captured several rebels, and seized a number of seals, proclamations, and revolutionary documents. The case was immediately turned over to the Chinese authorities in Wuchang. Chiang I-wu was forced by the circumstances to reverse his earlier decision. At five o'clock in the afternoon he issued an order calling for military action at midnight.[50]

Midnight came, but the signal to begin the revolt was not given; for some reason, the comrade entrusted with this task had failed. That night the Hupeh authorities raided several revolutionary cells in Wuchang. Thirty-two persons were arrested, and arms, ammunition, and explosives for making bombs were seized. Chiang I-wu had a narrow escape and fled from the city. Three of the arrested revolutionists were beheaded early the next morning. The rumor was widespread that the police had captured the lists naming the soldiers who had joined the revolutionary organizations. Feeling themselves in imminent danger the soldiers could wait no longer, and it was decided to take action that evening. Thus began the Wuchang Revolution of October 10.[51]

About twenty-five government battalions were stationed in the city of Wuchang and its environs. The number of troops was estimated at from fifteen to eighteen thousand men. Many soldiers who were sympathetic to the revolution had been transferred to Szechwan because of the railway riots there. Five battalions, totaling about two thousand men, composed the entire revolutionary force.

Sun Yat-sen later called the success of the revolution a "sheer accident." He believed that had Governor-General Jui Cheng stayed after the outbreak, the military commander would not have fled and the government would have kept the situation under control.[52] This view has been criticized by Chang Nan-hsien as an underestimation of both the revolutionary strength and the popular sentiment of the time.[53] Li Lien-fang also argues that while the time and the manner in which the revolution broke out were certainly accidental, the success of the revolution cannot be called an accident. Extrapolating from what is known about the fighting on the evening of October 10, Li maintains that after the first shot was fired the revolutionary soldiers in fact carried out the orders given for the previous afternoon; otherwise, he argues, they could not have moved and attacked in ways so similar to those set forth in their previous orders.[54]

At any rate, before noon of the next day the revolutionists had taken Wuchang. In the moment of victory, however, they were leaderless—or as the Chinese put it, "dragons without heads." Sun Wu was wounded, Chiang I-wu had fled, and Liu Kung was away, as were the other T'ung Meng Hui leaders. In a desperate attempt to find a person to head the newly proclaimed revolutionary military government of Hupeh, the soldiers seized upon a brigade commander by the name of Li Yüan-hung. They literally forced him to assume the governorship. In the first few days he was a political prisoner of the revolutionists, who constantly guarded him in order to prevent his escape. He refused to sign any official papers or declarations issued in his name as the Military Governor of Hupeh, so the comrades had to sign for him.[55] It is one of history's ironies that he later became a factor to be reckoned with by the revolutionists and was given more credit and honor than he deserved.[56]

On October 12 Hanyang and Hankow fell to the revolutionists, whose numbers had swelled after their initial success. On the same day Liu Kung and Chiang I-wu returned to Wuchang. But neither was given a position in the military government, which was reorganized on the 17th. Hu Ying, however, headed the Department of Foreign Affairs, and Sun Wu the Department of Military Affairs.[57] The neutral position adopted on October 18 by the foreign consular body at Hankow was a decisive diplomatic victory for the revolutionary government. Any foreign intervention at this stage might have led to a great setback. Meanwhile, cables had repeatedly been sent to Shanghai by the Hupeh military government requesting the presence of the leaders of the Central China Bureau of the T'ung Meng Hui and urging Huang Hsing to come to Wuchang.[58]

Despite the general inexperience of their officers and men, the revolutionary forces scored a victory over the government troops on October 18 and 19. The revolutionary army drove the enemy seven miles outside of the city of Hankow and thus preserved the initial success of the coup. The war became a stalemate until the 27th, when the army of the Manchu government, helped by naval forces, launched a counterattack. When Huang Hsing arrived at Hankow the next day, fighting had already broken out in the streets and the revolutionary leaders at Wuchang were desperate. Huang's arrival greatly heartened the comrades and the troops; it is said the soldiers received him as "a general from heaven."[59]

Huang Hsing had planned to raise some money before going into the interior, and he was waiting for news from abroad when the revolution broke out. He then rushed to the scene as quickly as he could. He arrived in Shanghai from Hong Kong on October 24, accompanied by Hsü Tsung-han.[60] All the ports of the Yangtze River under Manchu control had been alerted by the government, and at first it seemed almost impossible for him to proceed safely to Hankow.

However, Hsü knew a woman doctor who was then practicing in Shanghai. Disguised as a member of the local Red Cross, which had been organized by the woman doctor, Huang left Shanghai for Hankow on the 25th, accompanied by Liu K'uei-i, Sung Chiao-jen, and others. Hsü also made the trip disguised as a nurse.[61] The date of Huang Hsing's arrival at Hankow is uncertain, but the evidence seems to support Chang Nan-hsien's conclusion that it was October 28. At any rate, as Chang comments, "Although the differences are of only a few days, the significance is that once Huang Hsing arrived on the scene, he immediately assumed the leadership of the revolution and became its central figure."[62]

As soon as Huang Hsing arrived in Hankow, he crossed the river to Wuchang. Li Yüan-hung's representatives were waiting for him at the river bank with military bands and honor guards. He was immediately escorted to meet the Military Governor, who expressed great admiration for him and requested that he take charge of the war in Hankow. Huang accepted without hesitation.[63] Li then sent a few cavalry to parade through the Wuhan cities with a sign reading "Huang Hsing has arrived in Hupeh," in order to calm the populace.[64]

Huang Hsing assumed the position of Commander-in-Chief and set up his headquarters at Hankow on the following day. Meanwhile, the offensive by the Manchu government forces continued through the 28th and the 29th, and during these two days more than two thousand revolutionary soldiers were killed or wounded. Huang Hsing found on the morning of the 30th that there were only about six thousand soldiers under his command in Hankow. They fought well, but the outcome of the battle was a foregone conclusion. The revolutionary army was made up of new and hastily trained recruits. Their morale was high, but they were also exhausted, and they were without machine guns to face their well-equipped and well-trained opponents. By November 1 the situation was hopeless. The next day Huang Hsing retreated to Wuchang, and Hankow fell.[65]

With the battle of Hankow ended, the battle of Hanyang began. On the evening of November 2, the military government held an emergency meeting to hear Huang Hsing's report on the front and to discuss measures for safeguarding Wuchang and Hanyang. It was decided that Huang should take charge of the defense of Hanyang and that urgent appeals for help should be sent out again to those provinces which had declared their independence.

By this time five provinces had seceded from the Empire. Hunan was the first province to be captured by the revolutionists after the outbreak of the Wuchang Revolution. Changsha, the provincial capital and Huang Hsing's home town, fell into the hands of the revolutionists on October 22; Chiao Ta-feng then became the Military Governor of Hunan.[66] Kiukiang, the important port city of Kiangsi province lying along the Yangtze River southeast of Wuchang, was taken on the next day. The capture of these two cities by the revolutionary underground of the respective provinces was important in the early days of the Wuchang Revolution. Both Changsha and Kiukiang were in strategic positions for safeguarding the three cities of Wuhan, and the news of their capture elevated the morale of the Hupeh comrades who had begun the revolution alone.

In the midst of the gloomy and critical military situation on the evening of November 2 following the fall of Hankow, two brigades of troops from Hunan arrived at Wuchang. These reinforcements were highly disciplined New Army troops, quite different from the shabbily clothed and ill-equipped new recruits fighting at the front. Their appearance inspired the Wuchang garrison with new confidence. Huang Hsing was overjoyed. Meanwhile certain members of the T'ung Meng Hui then present in Wuchang were discussing the idea of having Li Yüan-hung replaced by Huang Hsing as head of the revolutionary military government of Hupeh. There is some controversy as to what actually happened in the course of their discussion on the evening of November 2.

111

According to Ts'ao Ya-po (who was not present in Wu-chang at that time), after the emergency meeting was over Chü Cheng summoned a secret meeting at which he suggested electing Huang Hsing as the Military Governor-General of Hunan and Hupeh. The proposal was enthusiastically received by several members. The wisdom of such a move was questioned, however, by Wu Chao-lin, a former army officer now serving as the Assistant Chief of Staff of the military government.

Wu, like Li Yüan-hung, had been forced into the revolutionary camp. He opposed the suggestion on the ground that such a change might create friction within the revolutionary government. Claiming that he personally had no objection to making Huang Hsing the Governor-General, he argued that since Huang was a well-known revolutionary leader, loved and respected by all, it was unnecessary at the moment for him to take over a local government because he would certainly be made the leader of the central government when it came into existence. Furthermore, Wu argued, although Li Yüan-hung was not a revolutionist, nevertheless he had gained the support of the Hupeh army since he had sided with the revolution. Besides, it was in his name that the military government had notified the foreign powers of its existence, and any change of the head of the government might throw doubt in the minds of foreign countries as to the stability of the revolutionary regime. Wu contended that although Li himself might not mind being put under Huang's authority, the army officers who had come over to the side of the revolution might feel uneasy about it. And if those who were close to Li should become a jealous faction, Wu warned, there might be a repetition of the kind of tragic power struggle which had undone the initial success of the Taiping Rebellion.

According to Ts'ao, there followed a heated debate, with the T'ung Meng Hui members insisting that the new situation did not affect Li's position since he would remain the Military Governor of Hupeh and Wu repeatedly calling for caution. Finally, Sung Chiao-jen suggested dropping the whole idea. He said that the proposal had been made only because it seemed that Huang Hsing, with his long standing and prestige in the revolutionary movement, might be more popular and thus enhance the chances for the success of the revolution. But, continued Sung, the comrades had no intention of pressing for action on their proposal if it might complicate the situation.[67]

According to Li Lien-fang, then the Chief Secretary of the military government, no heated argument took place. The informal discussion between the revolutionary leaders and high officials of the military government took place by moonlight in the courtyard of the government office and was undertaken in an atmosphere of comradeship. Neither Huang Hsing nor Li Yüan-hung knew about the meeting. According to Li, the T'ung Meng Hui members preferred electing Huang to be the "Commander-in-Chief of the Southern People's Army," thus conferring upon him power over all the revolutionary armies of the South (as opposed to the government army of the North). The officials of the military government who supported Li Yüan-hung, however, preferred giving Huang the title "Wartime Commander-in-Chief of the People's Army"; in that position he would be technically subject to the authority of the Military Governor. Realizing that the military situation was critical, the T'ung Meng Hui comrades did not insist on their plan. Li Lien-fang concludes that the subsequent rumors of friction between Huang and Li, as well as the charge that Huang deliberately threw the burden of the fighting upon the Hupeh troops instead of on the Hunan reinforcements, were fabrications contrived later to smear Huang Hsing for political reasons.[68]

Li Lien-fang's account is probably more reliable than Ts'ao Ya-po's. But whatever the nature of the discussion, it was most unfortunate for the cause of the revolution that Huang Hsing's followers failed to replace Li Yüan-hung, for although Li was only a figurehead in the beginning, he was later able to exercise real power in the position he held. Because the revolutionists failed to take over the Wuchang government either upon Huang Hsing's first arrival or during the later period under discussion (which was probably the last opportunity they had), the fate of Hupeh was later dictated by Li Yüan-hung. Far from having any revolutionary connections, Li and his opportunistic associates had strong sentimental attachments to the old order, which they had never actually renounced. Conflicts of interest were bound to occur between them and the revolutionists. Thus two years later, when war broke out between Yüan Shih-k'ai and the Kuomintang, which succeeded the T'ung Meng Hui, Li Yüan-hung sided with the conservative North. The province in which the revolution had begun was never again a stronghold of the revolutionists.

It is of course debatable what would have happened if the revolutionary old guard had removed Li Yüan-hung when his services to the revolution were no longer needed. Some have argued that such a move would have weakened the Hupeh army and created internal friction among the revolutionists. On the other hand, it might be argued that no serious complications would have followed. After all, the revolutionary governorship of Kiangsi was changed three times within a month after Kiukiang gained independence, and the same thing happened in other provinces without repercussions. Still, the case in Hupeh was different: it was there that the Manchu government had concentrated its best forces and there that the only major battles of the revolution were fought.

While Huang Hsing's followers did not insist on carrying out their original ideas, they arranged, with Li Yüan-hung's consent, to make a special ceremony of Huang's appointment as Wartime Commander-in-Chief of the People's Army, a position to which he was technically appointed by the Military Governor. It was believed that such a ceremony, besides being a testament of respect, would give an "official" character to Huang Hsing's authority over the rank and file of the army. Heretofore he had in fact commanded the army by virtue of his prestige in the revolutionary movement and not as a regular army commander. It is interesting to note how the idea of "legality" was still at work in the minds of some who were then conducting a revolution.

On the morning of November 3 the special ceremony was held. Both Huang Hsing and Li Yüan-hung rode abreast before the rank and file of the army, and both delivered brief speeches during the ceremony.[69] In the afternoon Huang set out with his staff to establish headquarters across the river in Hanyang.

For the next ten days the front was quiet except for sporadic artillery engagements. After the Hankow fighting, the troops on both sides found time to rest and regroup. The Manchu government had ordered the army to halt its advance after capturing Hankow, hoping to settle their differences with the revolutionists by negotiation. Huang Hsing took advantage of this lull to organize his troops and map out his strategy for the defense of Hanyang.

Huang's troops at Hanyang consisted of three brigades and one regiment of infantry, one artillery battalion, one engineers' corps, and two brigades of the Hunan army. According to an estimate by the Manchu military authorities, the total force in Hanyang amounted to thirteen or fourteen thousand men. In his military report, the commander of the government army expressed surprise at the remarkable defense works put up by the rebels, who had recruited thousands of civilians and coolies for digging trenches.[70]

By the middle of November the revolutionary forces were ready for action. On the 14th Huang Hsing held a staff conference and decided to make preparations for recapturing Hankow. During the afternoon of the 16th his troops stood ready for the attack. That evening they crossed the Hsiang River and succeeded in establishing a beachhead. But they met with strong opposition, and after almost twenty-four hours of continuous fighting, the revolutionary troops could hold out no longer. In the afternoon of the 17th they began to retreat to Hanyang. Their casualties were great: 75 officers and 792 soldiers were either killed or wounded.[71] Huang Hsing himself was very nearly killed in the retreat. As an enemy soldier was preparing to shoot him from behind at very close range, Kayano Nagatomo shouted a warning and Huang turned and killed the enemy with one stroke of his sword.[72]

After this engagement, Huang adopted a defensive strategy. The Imperial forces began preparing to drive the revolutionists out of Hanyang, and by the 20th of the month their offensive preparations were completed. The main force to be used in the attack was the Fourth Division of the Northern Army under the command of Feng Kuo-chang, which totaled about ten thousand men. Counting the continued flow of reinforcements into the neighboring areas, the total forces which the Manchu government had mobilized in the Wuhan area amounted to roughly thirty thousand troops, the best in the Northern Army.[73] At no other place in the country had the government concentrated such a formidable military force.

On November 20 and 21 the two sides prepared for the last week of fighting. When it began, the revolutionary troops could not match the superior forces of the Manchu government. The situation became critical on the 25th, and Huang Hsing ordered the ammunition and machines of the Hanyang Arsenal to be moved to Wuchang in order to prevent them from falling into the hands of the enemy. By the 26th the revolutionists were beaten out of their strategic strongholds, and at midnight Huang Hsing, looking desperately tired and discouraged, ordered a retreat to Wuchang. By the morning of November 27 Hanyang was lost. In the nine days of fighting, 137 revolutionary officers died and 85 were wounded; of the soldiers, 2,693 were killed and more than 400 wounded.[74] The total dead and wounded on both sides during this time has been estimated at 10,000 men.[75]

The battles at Hankow and Hanyang were the two major conflicts of the revolution. In commenting on the battle of Hanyang, which was full of heroic episodes on the part of many individual revolutionists, Chinese historians have generally agreed that in view of the tremendous odds against him, Huang Hsing did all that was humanly possible.[76] During the Hankow battles, five provinces seceded from the Empire, and while Huang Hsing was holding out at Hanyang, ten more provinces declared their independence. Of Huang Hsing's leadership in Hanyang, Chü Cheng has written:

Because K'o-ch'iang [Huang Hsing] was holding out in Hanyang, [the revolutionists in] other provinces gained the time they needed to organize other revolts. Thus one province after another seceded from the Empire and the revolutionary forces were greatly strengthened. The credit for this must go to Huang Hsing, because without him it is questionable whether Hanyang could have been defended at that time. Besides, the former officials and generals of the Manchu government were unscrupulous and unprincipled men without any sincere revolutionary convictions. They might declare independence

116

one day, only to reaffirm their loyalty to the Empire the next. The action of Sun Pao-ch'i in Shantung province is a case in point. Therefore, Huang Hsing's contribution was not that he defended the besieged city of Hanyang, but that he resisted fearlessly the well-trained Northern troops of Feng Kuo-chang with untrained recruits. As a result the Wuchang situation was stabilized, and the other provinces were able to secede. . . . In each province, as a rule, once revolution started the officials and generals escaped or surrendered without a fight. . . . While the public demands for the Republic and the lack of popular support for the Empire might account for the sudden collapse of the Manchu regime, the other provinces could not possibly have gained time to respond to the Wuchang Revolution if the revolution had been crushed by the government shortly after it had started. Therefore, Huang Hsing deserves great credit for defending Hanyang against overwhelming odds.[77]

Feng Tzu-yu had this to say:

The fact that he [Huang Hsing] was able to hold out in Hanyang until the revolutionaries of other provinces gained time to revolt was a decisive factor in the creation of the Republic. Although the city was eventually lost, it was not his fault. For a month he fought valiantly and tenaciously. . . . He and Sun [Yat-sen] have been called the two founders of the Republic. Huang certainly deserves that honor.[78]

EIGHT

THE ESTABLISHMENT OF THE REPUBLIC

MANY CHINESE historians have claimed that during the meeting of the Hupeh military government on November 27, after the fall of Hanyang, Huang Hsing suggested abandoning Wuchang so that the troops garrisoned there could be used for an attack on Nanking. In one account it is even said that Sun Wu and Li Yüan-hung agreed to this plan but were strongly opposed by others.[1] That Huang Hsing, or indeed any revolutionary leader, could have made such a suggestion is inconceivable. In addition to the great distance between the two cities, the lack of both supplies and means of transport to sustain such a march, as well as the danger of enemy troops attacking along the route, made such a plan unfeasible. According to Li Lien-fang, this story, like the one about Huang's alleged attempt to replace Li Yüan-hung as the highest authority in Hupeh, was deliberately fabricated later by certain Hupeh leaders who wanted to stir up ill feeling against Huang for political reasons.[2] The facts that they twisted to suit their story are given in this account by Li Lien-fang:

After Huang Hsing retreated to Wuchang, Military Governor Li [Yüan-hung] summoned a meeting. In sorrow and exasperation, Huang had little to say. He stated with deep regret that he was responsible for the loss of Hanyang and expressed his intention of going to Shanghai in order to help the comrades there to take Nanking, which would release the [Imperial military] pressure on Wuchang. At that time many comrades expressed their opinions on the situation; all maintained that Wuchang should be defended and that, from a geographical standpoint, it could be defended. Huang Hsing remained silent. Since the fall of Hanyang had relieved him of his duty to defend it, there was little to be gained by his staying in

Hupeh. Consequently, he sailed on the following day [the 28th]. . . .
Chang Chien, T'ang Shou-ch'ien, and other leaders in Shanghai
had previously sent a representative to Wuhan . . . suggesting to
Huang Hsing that he come to Shanghai in order to organize a central
government there. This was another reason for Huang's leaving for
Shanghai. There was little he could do then in the defense of Wuchang [which was under the command of Military Governor Li
Yüan-hung], and his going to Shanghai would better serve the revolutionary cause.[3]

Wuchang was in chaos after the fall of Hanyang. The Imperial troops occasionally shelled the city from across the river.
On December 1 a shell hit the military government's office, and
this prompted Li Yüan-hung to flee the city. From a military
standpoint, Wuchang was difficult to defend without the shield
of its two sister cities. The authorities of the Hupeh government were thus overjoyed when they learned that the British
consul-general at Hankow was to mediate a three-day cease-
fire. A truce was readily agreed upon and was then repeatedly
renewed and extended to the other parts of the country. On
December 1 Huang Hsing arrived in Shanghai, which (along
with its suburbs) had been captured in early November by the
joint efforts of Ch'en Ch'i-mei, Li Hsieh-ho, and others.[4]
    On the following day Nanking was captured by the revolu-
tionists after a brief battle. The capture of Nanking only four
days after the loss of Hanyang offset the major defeat of the
rebels and added to their prestige. It also shifted the center of
revolutionary power away from the besieged Wuchang. It was
in Nanking that the revolutionists finally organized a provisional
central government and began conducting the negotiations with
the Peking government which led to the downfall of the Manchu
dynasty.
    As more and more provinces seceded from the Empire, the
revolutionists became aware of the need to organize a provisional
government. On November 7 Li Yüan-hung sent a telegram
to all provincial revolutionary authorities asking their opinions.
It was clear to everyone that in order to seek the recognition
of foreign powers and to join the seceded provinces in united
action, such a step should not be delayed. Two days later Li,

119

in his capacity as Military Governor of Hupeh, formally cabled all provincial revolutionary authorities to send delegates to Wuchang for the purpose of organizing a provisional government.[5]

The Shanghai group, however, soon tried to capture the privileged position which Wuchang enjoyed as the revolutionary center. In a joint telegram sent to Shanghai Military Governor Ch'en Ch'i-mei on November 11, 1911, the Military Governors of Kiangsu and of Chekiang, Ch'eng Te-ch'üan and T'ang Shou-ch'ien, suggested following "the example of the Continental Congress held by the thirteen colonies during the early days of the American Revolution." They proposed that the military government and former provincial assembly of each province send one representative to Shanghai, that meetings begin as soon as representatives of more than two provinces arrived, and that the meetings be held in Shanghai because it was "a communication center and the most important port city of the country immune to the scourge of war." Ch'en Ch'i-mei readily welcomed the proposal.[6]

Li Yüan-hung, however, rejoined that the representatives could not conveniently meet in Shanghai because five other provincial governments had already agreed to send delegates to Hupeh, and also because there was no suitable person whom the Hupeh government could send to Shanghai at the moment ("Huang Hsing is now in charge of important military affairs here and cannot leave Hupeh, and T'an Jen-feng and Sung Chiao-jen are away").[7] On November 14 Kiangsu Military Governor Ch'eng Te-ch'üan cabled to other revolutionary provincial authorities suggesting that they request the return of Sun Yat-sen for the organization of a provisional government.[8] This was probably a countermove and its reception is not clear; later, when Huang Hsing was available in Shanghai, the proposal was dropped.

On November 15 the representatives held their first meeting and organized the Provincial Representative Council.[9] Five days later Sung Chiao-jen (the Hunan representative) and the representatives of five other provinces cabled Li Yüan-hung and Huang Hsing from Shanghai offering their recognition of the Hupeh military government as the Central Military Govern-

120

ment of the Republic.[10] Three days later Chü Cheng arrived in Shanghai and urged the representatives of various provinces who had gathered there to hold their meetings in Wuchang. The representatives soon left for Wuchang, leaving behind one representative from each province for consultation and contact.[11]

While the delegates were on their way, the military situation in Hupeh was undergoing a drastic change. By the time they arrived there for their first meeting on November 30, Hanyang had been lost to the Imperial army and Wuchang was in great danger. The meeting had to be held in the British Concession at Hankow. T'an Jen-feng was elected chairman of the Provincial Representative Council.

The position of the Wuchang group was weakened, and the Shanghai group relatively strengthened, by the capture of Nanking and Huang Hsing's presence in Shanghai. On December 4, three days after the arrival of Huang Hsing and the capture of Nanking, the three Military Governors of Shanghai, Kiangsu, and Chekiang held a meeting with the provincial delegates who remained in Shanghai. They decided that Nanking should be the seat of the provisional government and that Huang Hsing should be the Generalissimo and Li Yüan-hung the Vice-Generalissimo and Military Governor of Hupeh. This decision was immediately cabled to Hupeh and to the other provincial authorities; it was explained that the decision was imperative under the circumstances and that it would be made public and official after the delegates returned to Nanking from Hankow.[12] On the following day the representatives at Shanghai passed a resolution that the Generalissimo be put in charge of organizing the provisional government.[13]

Shanghai's decision reached Wuchang on December 5. Li Yüan-hung was displeased; with the military situation in Hupeh no longer critical because of the truce, he was ready to bid for power. In a circular telegram dated December 8 Li declared that the election of the Generalissimo should be disregarded because the Provincial Representative Council at Hankow had already decided to hold a meeting at Nanking for the purpose of electing a Provisional President, and that the election of a Generalissimo at Shanghai would cause confusion.[14] He was referring to the resolutions passed at the last meeting of the representatives of ten provinces held in Hankow on the previous day.

It may be recalled that during their five-day meeting in Hankow, the Provincial Representative Council adopted the Organic Law of the provisional government.[15] Before the meeting was adjourned, it was decided that all the delegates should gather at Nanking within a week to elect a Provisional President and that the election should be held when the representatives of more than ten provinces arrived at Nanking, which was to be the seat of the provisional government.[16]

By the middle of December delegates from fourteen provinces had arrived at Nanking. On December 14 they decided to hold the election two days hence. On the following day, however, they announced postponement of the election for a "special, important reason."[17]

The official documents do not reveal what this "special, important reason" was. According to one representative, it was the arrival of a Chekiang representative from Wuchang, who brought news to Nanking that Yüan Shih-k'ai, the premier of the Manchu government, was reported to be in favor of the republican form of government but could not say so openly. This alleged attitude of Yüan's was supposedly revealed by his peace negotiator, T'ang Shao-i, to Li Yüan-hung.[18] In any event the representatives decided on the 15th to postpone the election of a Provisional President. Instead, they formally recognized the Shanghai resolution of December 4, by which Huang Hsing had been elected Generalissimo and Li Yüan-hung Vice-Generalissimo. At the same time they passed an amendment to the Organic Law providing that prior to the election of a Provisional President, his power would be exercised by the Generalissimo.[19] Huang Hsing was chosen as the Acting Provisional President.[20]

However, according to the same source the commanders of the Kiangsu and Chekiang Joint Forces (who were responsible for the capture of Nanking) expressed unwillingness to accept Huang's authority because he had been defeated in Hanyang. These militarists had recently defected from the Manchu government, and they preferred to have as Generalissimo Li Yüan-hung, who would remain in Hupeh.[21]

On the following day, the 16th, some representatives suggested reversing the positions of Huang Hsing and Li Yüan-hung.[22] Meanwhile, however, the Provincial Representative Council received Huang Hsing's telegram from Shanghai, in which Huang declined to accept the position of Generalissimo and recommended Li Yüan-hung for the post.[23] Consequently, the representatives reversed their previous resolution and elected Li Yüan-hung as the Generalissimo and Huang Hsing the Vice-Generalissimo. They also passed another amendment to the Organic Law providing that "Prior to the election of the Provisional President, the power of the Provisional President will be exercised by the Generalissimo. In the case of the absence of the Generalissimo from the seat of the provisional government, the power of the Generalissimo will be exercised by the Vice-Generalissimo."[24]

The ranking members of the T'ung Meng Hui were indignant over the new decision. They blamed some of the representatives from the Northern provinces and even threatened to shoot them.[25] These incidents fully revealed the weakness of the revolutionary party. As Li Chien-nung comments:

We can see some of the weaknesses of the revolutionary army from these incidents. . . . One's contribution to the revolutionary cause should be considered as a whole; it should not be determined by one battle, whether won or lost. The capture of Nanking was, of course, a great contribution, but the defeat in Hanyang was not necessarily the fault of the commander. With a small Hunan army helped by newly recruited but untrained soldiers whose officers were strangers to them, [Huang Hsing] was able to resist the numerically superior and well-trained Northern Army for almost a month. Under the same circumstances, even the Kiangsu and Chekiang armies might not have won. Yet judging only from the result of one battle, the revolutionary leader who had been devoted to the cause for years was looked down upon as a defeated general. This fully revealed the arrogance and haughtiness of the militarists.

The second [weakness] was the opportunism of the politicians. Lacking a sound purpose and firm revolutionary principles, they changed their policy readily. Yüan Shih-k'ai was still the premier of the Manchu court, but once they heard that he also favored the republican form of government, they were willing to change the

Organic Law and recognize the [Shanghai] election [of Huang Hsing as the Generalissimo and Li Yüan-hung as Vice-Generalissimo] which they had previously considered illegal. But when they heard of the opposition of the Kiangsu and Chekiang militarists, they readily reversed the decision. Their actions were determined solely by expediency, and were lacking in revolutionary spirit.[26]

On December 20, four days after the election in Nanking, Li Yüan-hung cabled from Wuchang declining to accept the post.[27] On the following day, however, he declared that

the election of Generalissimo is a matter of extreme urgency for the organization of the provisional government. A man of great statesmanship, Mr. Huang K'o-ch'iang [Huang Hsing] is very well qualified for the position, but he is so modest that he has repeatedly recommended me for it. I am hardly qualified for such an important responsibility. . . . However, since the Vice-Generalissimo will exercise the power of the Generalissimo during the latter's absence, I shall reluctantly acquiesce to your request. In accepting the position of Generalissimo I hereby delegate my power to the Vice-Generalissimo, who will act on my behalf.[28]

Huang Hsing, however, declined even the position of Vice-Generalissimo; he wanted no position under Li Yüan-hung. The organization of a provisional government was unable to proceed because of this deadlock. The return of Sun Yat-sen solved the problem.

Sun Yat-sen was in Denver, Colorado, when he heard of the outbreak of the Wuchang Revolution. Instead of rushing back to his country, he sailed to Europe, for he thought that his proper "contribution to the revolutionary work was not in the battlefield but in diplomatic circles."[29] Since the attitude of the British government was the key to Chinese diplomacy at that time, he sailed from New York to England, and later to France. One of his most important plans was to negotiate a loan from the consortium, but he evidently had no success.[30]

In what capacity Sun Yat-sen would serve the republican government was by no means clear in the early days of the revolution. On his way home he cabled from Paris on November 12,

1911, that he was "happy to learn that the [Provincial Representative] Council was being organized in Shanghai and that Mr. Li [Yüan-hung] should of course be elected president. It would also be appropriate if Li would give up the post in favor of Yüan [Shih-k'ai] as reported."[31]

As previously mentioned, Kiangsu Military Governor Ch'eng Te-ch'üan's circular telegram to other provincial authorities dated November 14, 1911, had suggested inviting Sun Yat-sen to form a provisional government. This suggestion was offered by the Shanghai group only after the Wuchang group had insisted on having the Provincial Representative Council meet in Wuchang. The reaction to this proposal is not clear. The available clue is a telegram sent by Hunan Military Governor T'an Yen-k'ai to Li Yüan-hung a week later, in which T'an suggested appointing Sun as ambassador plenipotentiary for the purpose of seeking recognition from foreign powers.[32]

Sun Yat-sen's position was far from impregnable. As a Western critic has stated, "the Revolution had been started without his knowledge, directed without his presence or advice, and would have ended without his active participation, or any suggestion that he was the 'Father' of the movement, had he not arrived at a moment when it suited the real leaders to have a figure-head as a foil to Yüan Shih-k'ai."[33] To this it should be added that the provisional government would have been organized and the presidency filled without him had it not been for the deadlock between Huang Hsing and Li Yüan-hung for the position of Generalissimo. It should be stressed, however, that although Sun was not closely in touch with the developments in China, his leadership in the revolutionary movement was beyond question. It was logical that he should be chosen for the presidency when he was available.

Sun Yat-sen arrived at Hong Kong on December 21, 1911.[34] A story recorded by Hu Han-min bears witness to Sun's remarkable talents as a statesman.

It appears that when Sun arrived at Hong Kong, Hu Han-min, who was then the Military Governor of Kwangtung, came from Canton to meet him. Hu tried to persuade Sun to stay in Kwangtung instead of proceeding to Nanking. The gist of his argument was that Yüan Shih-k'ai, whose strength lay in his control of the Northern Army, was playing both sides against each other in order to enhance his own power. Unless Yüan's army were defeated, the revolution could not be a success. Now if Sun went to Nanking, the situation there was such that he would almost certainly be asked to head the government; but in this position he would have no army of his own. The reversals of decision over the election of a Generalissimo revealed the weakness of the revolutionary party and the fact that its chief of state was only a figurehead. Therefore Hu argued that it would be better for Sun to stay in Kwangtung, where he could build up revolutionary military forces, than to accept a nominal title without real power. Hu even ventured to suggest Canton as the seat of the provisional government if Sun stayed.

Sun Yat-sen contended, however, that for him to stay in Kwangtung would be a refusal to face hard political facts. What would the comrades say? he asked. It was true that Yüan Shih-k'ai was untrustworthy, but if he could be used to accomplish the overthrow of the Manchu dynasty it would be better than resorting to war, the outcome of which would be too uncertain. The first order of business, continued Sun, was to bring about the downfall of the alien dynasty; the problem of Yüan Shih-k'ai could be dealt with later. Besides, he added, the foreign powers had taken a neutral position only because the revolution had succeeded so rapidly; if the present stalemate were to continue, they might well decide to intervene.* The story of Gordon and Ward during the Taiping Rebellion must not be repeated.[35]

After a long discussion Hu Han-min was finally convinced. Following Sun's suggestion, he did not return to Canton but sailed with Sun for Shanghai, where they arrived on Christmas day.[36] On the following day the T'ung Meng Hui leaders held a conference to discuss the presidential election.[37] The account given by Hu Han-min probably best reflects the thinking of the Cantonese group in the party:

* This anxiety about foreign intervention was shared by many revolutionary leaders; it was one of the main reasons for their willingness to compromise with Yüan Shih-k'ai in order to bring the Manchu dynasty to a quick end.

Now that [Sun Yat-sen] had returned from abroad, the comrades decided to establish the provisional government with him as president. At that time Chang Ping-lin and Sung Chiao-jen had already been in Shanghai. Chang had often suggested that on account of his contribution Huang Hsing should be made president. . . .

However, because of the [opposition of] other party members, Huang in the end did not dare to take over the leadership. Sung Chiao-jen, who at first wanted to be the premier with Huang as the president, was also obliged to give in; but he still advocated the parliamentary system. Since Huang was responsible for restoring the provinces [from the Manchu government to the Chinese people] and since the representatives sent by the provincial military leaders were, with the exception of those from Chihli and Fengtien, members of the T'ung Meng Hui, the election [of the president] and the organization of the government would naturally be decided upon by the party.

Consequently, a conference of the T'ung Meng Hui hierarchy was held at Sun Yat-sen's residence to discuss the desirability of the presidential system as opposed to the parliamentary system. Sun said, "In the parliamentary system the chief of state does not have real power; it is the premier who is responsible to the parliament. At this time of emergency, we cannot adopt a political system which restricts the power of the man we trust. I myself will not go along with those who favor such an institution, which would be harmful to the revolutionary cause." Among those present at the meeting besides myself were Huang Hsing, Wang Ching-wei, Ch'en Ch'i-mei, Sung Chiao-jen, Chang Jen-chieh, Ma Chün-wu, Chü Cheng, and others. Chang answered first, saying, "Fine. . . . We'll all follow your idea." It was so agreed by the rest.[38]

Sung Chiao-jen's friend and biographer gives the following version of this important meeting:

On December 27 the leading members of the T'ung Meng Hui held a conference at Sun Yat-sen's residence. They decided that Sun was to be the president and Huang Hsing the premier. Huang, however, declined. Sun Yat-sen and Hu Han-min were opposed to having a premier.

Sung Chiao-jen, whose observations of both foreign and domestic politics had convinced him that the parliamentary system was desirable for the Republic, argued fervently for its adoption. Finally, Sun Yat-sen agreed. Since Huang Hsing had declined the premiership, Sun sent Chang Chi to ask Sung whether he would like to assume the post. Sung declined. Accompanied by Chü Cheng, T'ien T'ung, and Lü Chih-i, Sung Chiao-jen went to see Huang, urging him to accept the premiership. Finally Huang consented. Thus the decision that Sun Yat-sen was to be president and Huang Hsing premier was finally reached.

Then Sung Chiao-jen went to Nanking with other comrades to prepare for the election. Since the Organic Law of the Provisional Government had no provision for a premiership, Sung Chiao-jen submitted an amendment. But the representatives did not know of the decision reached at Shanghai. They opposed Sung's move, and the proposed amendment failed to pass.[39]

Hu Han-min's account seems inaccurate on two points. First, Sung Chiao-jen realized that in terms of age, ability, and prestige he was not the best candidate for Premier; it was not until a year later that he developed a serious aspiration for the position. Sung himself made this clear a year later in an interview with a newspaper reporter.[40] Second, it is not true that Huang Hsing had ever planned to "take over the leadership." After the deadlock over electing a Generalissimo he refused to accept any position until Sun Yat-sen's return, although the provincial representatives were still eager to organize the new government with him as Provisional President.[41] Furthermore, his wholehearted support of Sun Yat-sen eventually encouraged the representatives to elect Sun as president. As a more unbiased historian has recently commented, after what Huang had done for Sun Yat-sen "it was unfair indeed for Hu Han-min to state that 'Huang in the end did not dare to take over the leadership.' "[42]

It is also very doubtful that Huang Hsing ever consented to accept the position of Premier, as Sung Chiao-jen's biographer says he did. Whatever Huang thought of the parliamentary system, he clearly supported Sun Yat-sen's insistence on adopting a presidential system. On December 27 Huang himself went to Nanking to recommend the presidential system to the Provincial Representative Council. In fact, it was probably through Huang's influence on the Council that Sung Chiao-jen's proposed amendment to establish a premiership was defeated.[43]

On December 28 the provincial representatives nominated Sun Yat-sen, Huang Hsing, and Li Yüan-hung for President.[44] On the following day Sun Yat-sen was elected Provisional President by 16 of the 17 possible votes.[45] (Each province had one vote, although not all of the 17 provinces were under revolutionary control.) Huang Hsing received one vote.[46] There was not one vote for Li Yüan-hung. Chü Cheng interpreted this as a "clear indication of the thinking of the representatives (many of whom were not members of the T'ung Meng Hui), who respected the hierarchy of the revolutionary party and recognized its leadership as responsible for the success of the revolution."[47]

In the morning of January 1, 1912, Sun Yat-sen left Shanghai for Nanking, where he was inaugurated as Provisional President of the Republic of China that evening. The solar calendar was officially adopted in the place of the lunar calendar, and 1912 became the first year of the Republic. On January 3 the Provisional President appointed Huang Hsing Minister of War and made several other ministerial appointments. Sung Chiao-jen was of the opinion that former bureaucrats of the Ch'ing dynasty should not be allowed to take part in the new government, but the government later accepted a compromise formula: ministers who had been officials of the old regime should be given vice-ministers who had been revolutionists. Since no one from Hupeh was represented in the government, Huang Hsing suggested having Li Yüan-hung elected as Vice-President; Li was so elected.[48]

During the period of the Nanking Provisional Government, Huang Hsing seems to have exercised greater power in domestic affairs than Sun Yat-sen. As Hu Han-min recalled:

I was appointed by [Sun Yat-sen] as the Secretary-General of the President's Office. The ministers were appointed according to the suggestions of K'o-ch'iang [Huang Hsing]. [Of the nine ministers] only the Minister of War, the Foreign Minister, and the Minister of Education were members of the T'ung Meng Hui; the rest were high officials of the Ch'ing dynasty who had recently become sympathetic to the revolution.

However, all the vice-ministers were T'ung Meng Hui members. The name of Sung Chiao-jen was at first submitted for Minister of the Interior, but the Provincial Representative Council, which exercised the powers of the Provisional Parliament, . . . refused to give its consent because he advocated the parliamentary system and [allegedly] wanted to be the premier. Consequently, Ch'eng Te-ch'üan, the former Kiangsu governor who had gone over to the side of the revolution before the capture of Nanking, became the Minister of the Interior. Huang had recommended Chang Chien or Hsiung Hsi-ling to head the Ministry of Finance, but Sun was against the proposal. Sun said, "Finance should not be entrusted to outsiders. I know Ch'en Chin-t'ao will go along with us; besides, he is well known internationally because he helped organize the currency of, and negotiated foreign loans for, the Manchu government." As a result, Ch'en was appointed Minister of Finance. To Wang Ch'ung-hui, who first declined the post of Foreign Minister on the ground of insufficient prestige on his part, Sun said, "Don't worry. I shall handle foreign affairs myself. Besides, it is about time to get rid of the traditional conception about bureaucratic qualifications."

Chang [Chien, Minister of Industry] and T'ang [Shou-ch'ien, Minister of Communications] only briefly assumed duties and attended ministerial meetings; they soon moved to the foreign concession in Shanghai. Ch'eng [Te-ch'üan, the Minister of the Interior] had already been convalescing in the Shanghai Concessions. Being a representative for peace negotiations with the North, Wu [T'ing-fang, Minister of Justice] was unable to take care of the ministry affairs. [Finance Minister] Ch'en, who was busy with foreign loan negotiations, also lived in the Concessions most of the time. Consequently, the vice-ministers of these five ministries took charge of their respective ministries. The only ministers who were really active were Huang [Hsing], Wang [Ch'ung-hui], and Ts'ai [Yüan-p'ei, Minister of Education].

In those days the war was still going on. The power of the central government did not extend to the provinces, and the ministries actually existed only in name. But Huang Hsing was the Minister of War and concurrently Chief of the General Staff. Supreme military power was vested in him alone. He was in fact head of the cabinet, although he did not hold the title of premier.[49]

Chang Chi, who was also in a position to know the interplay of leadership within the government, recalled in his memoirs:

During the period of the provisional government, decisions were made by K'o-ch'iang [Huang Hsing], not by Sun Yat-sen. . . . Occasionally, when Sun attended a mass meeting there was no special seat reserved for him on the platform, and he would sit in one of the front rows. And the comrades still called him "Mister"; very seldom was he addressed as "President." However, all the power-worshiping comrades respectfully called Huang Hsing "K'o-lao."[50]

There were two major problems facing the leaders of the Nanking government. One was finance; the other was Yüan Shih-k'ai. The Provisional Government in Nanking was in dire need of money. When Sun Yat-sen landed at Shanghai, he was received by his comrades as a valuable financial asset. It was believed either that he actually had a large amount of money with him or that he could easily raise it to help the revolution. Indeed, the army commanders of the Kiangsu and Chekiang Joint Forces had opposed Huang Hsing for Generalissimo and had supported Sun Yat-sen because they hoped to take the lion's share of the money Sun would bring. Although Sun's arrival was most timely for the revolutionary cause, he brought with him no foreign loan nor any large sum of money.[51]

In preparing to organize the provisional government, Huang Hsing borrowed 300,000 *yen* from the Japanese firm of Mitsui. This was a private transaction, with Chang Chien serving as guarantor.[52] After the establishment of the Nanking Provisional Government, attempts were made to raise foreign loans on the security of the China Merchants' Steam Navigation Company and the Kiangsu Railway. Efforts were also made to borrow 5 million dollars from the Hanyehping Company (which consisted of the Hanyang Iron and Steel Works, the Pingsiang Coal Mines, and the Tayeh Iron Mines). In exchange for granting this loan, the company's capital was to be increased to 30 million dollars by funds from Japan, which would retain partial control. The company was to make the loan to the Provisional Government upon receiving the money from the Japanese. The negotiations were personally handled by Sun Yat-sen and Huang Hsing; Finance Minister Ch'en Chin-t'ao did not take part.[53] Chang Chien, the Minister of Industry, resigned in protest partly on the ground that "he had not been informed of the deal beforehand and could do nothing about it after the agreement was reached."[54] In a personal letter to Chang, Hu Han-min, the Secretary-General of the President's Office, explained:

Since January [1912], K'o-ch'iang [Huang Hsing] has been trying to support the armies with a pair of bare hands. . . . He can hardly sleep or eat. He is so overburdened with the task that he has become seriously ill. . . . He is not unaware of the undesirability of making this deal, but he is desperate. Since it is now an accomplished fact, we beg your forgiveness and understanding. . . . The Provisional Government is merely a revolutionary organization on a larger scale. . . . The criterion of judgment is whether the action is motivated by personal gain or for the sake of the cause. . . .[55]

The agreement was finally called off by the Nanking government because of objections from the Provisional Parliament and the Hupeh authorities.[56]

The other problem of the day was deciding how to deal with Yüan Shih-k'ai, who had become the most powerful figure in the Ch'ing government. Yüan had been active in domestic and foreign affairs for many years. He had been in charge of training the modern army in North China, and it had become his most important political asset. He had lost favor with the Court after the death of the Empress Dowager; in the edict of his dismissal issued on January 2, 1909, the Court had "showed clemency toward him" by ordering him "to vacate all his offices and return to his native province to convalesce from his present leg ailment."[57] But in its frantic search for someone to save the Empire after the outbreak of the Wuchang Revolution, the Court turned to him once again. This time he found an opportunity to become more than an important servant of the Imperial government; before long the very fate of the Ch'ing dynasty lay in his hands.

On October 14, 1911, four days after the outbreak of the Wuchang Revolution, Yüan Shih-k'ai was appointed Governor-General of Hunan and Hupeh. But he was not anxious to assume office. He set several conditions upon his acceptance of a government post, among them full power in military affairs and adequate funds for necessary expenditures. On October 27 he was appointed Imperial Commissioner with full power over land and sea forces.[58] Even then he did not leave his place of retirement in Honan province. It was obvious that the wider the spread of the revolution, the more the Court would need him and the more concessions he could win from Peking.

On October 29 the situation in the North took a drastic turn. On that day the officers of the Twentieth Division stationed at Luanchow (halfway between Mukden and Peking), headed by Chang Shao-ts'eng and Lan T'ien-wei, division and brigade commanders respectively, cabled the Peking government demanding a constitutional monarchy within a year. It was said that these officers and Wu Lu-chen, the commander of the Sixth Division, had plotted to seize Peking if their demands met with refusal.[59] This news struck the Court like a bolt of lightning and probably had much to do with Yüan's immediate departure for the front. On the same day Shansi seceded from the Empire. Peking was thus threatened on both flanks, and for a moment the Court considered fleeing.

On the 30th the Court accepted the demands of the army officers headed by Chang and Lan. The Imperial Regent, who had been primarily responsible for the dismissal of Yüan Shih-k'ai early in 1909, declared himself unfit to govern. On the following day Yüan arrived at the front in Hupeh and conferred with the Imperial War Minister, Ying Ch'ang, who had been helplessly directing the Northern army, the bulk of whose ranking officers were Yüan's men.

On November 1 Yüan was appointed Premier of the Peking government. A few days later Wu Lu-chen, who had just been appointed Governor of Shansi with orders to suppress the revolution in that province, was assassinated.[60] His death had little effect on the fate of the dynasty, but it had a direct bearing on the destiny of Yüan Shih-k'ai. For had Wu's alleged plot against the Court been successfully carried out, it would have cut off the powers on which Yüan was drawing to enhance his own position. The death of Wu Lu-chen was a great loss to the T'ung Meng Hui, which lacked real influence and military power in the Yellow River region.

With the danger of mutiny in the North removed, Yüan was able to direct his attention toward the South. From the very beginning he adopted a conciliatory attitude toward the rebels.[61] He made a series of peaceful overtures toward Wuchang, and the Court was acting on his advice when it ordered the government troops to halt their advance after the capture of Hankow.[62] On November 6 Yüan approached Li Yüan-hung for the third time within ten days. A few days later Yüan's emissaries came to Wuchang offering to engage in peace negotiations if the Hupeh leaders would recognize a constitutional monarchy. Huang Hsing, who was then defending Hanyang, found it necessary to issue a statement reaffirming his determination to fight for the republican form of government, for he was afraid that the peace offers might shake the determination of the people and the army.[63]

On December 7 Yüan Shih-k'ai appointed T'ang Shao-i as delegate of the Imperial government to negotiate with the South. The peace negotiations formally began on the 18th in Shanghai.[64] Two days later Ku Chung-ch'en, Chief of Staff of the Kiangsu and Chekiang Joint Forces, was authorized by Huang Hsing to sign a secret peace agreement with Liao Shao-yu, an unofficial representative of the North. The pact expressed agreement on five points: (1) that a Republic would be established; (2) that favorable terms of abdication would be granted to the royal family; (3) that whoever should first succeed in causing the downfall of the Manchu dynasty would become president; (4) that all war claims between the armies of the North and the South would be relinquished; and (5) that order would be restored and a provisional parliament organized.[65] These terms were substantially the same as those upon which the North and the South finally and openly agreed.

It was almost the unanimous opinion of the revolutionary leaders that should Yüan Shih-k'ai come to their side, he should be offered the presidency as a reward. Huang Hsing sent this assurance to Yüan through Wang Ching-wei, who had been released from prison; Wang gave the message to Yang Tu, who in turn passed it on to Yüan. Yüan did not accept the offer at once; he was quoted as having said that he hoped Huang would take up the presidency.[66] The offer to Yüan was reaffirmed by Sun Yat-sen after he had been elected President.[67]

The peace negotiations dragged on after the establishment of the Provisional Government in Nanking. Later Yüan personally conducted the negotiations by correspondence with revolutionary leaders in the South. The members of the Imperial family were naturally reluctant to give up the throne; but when they finally realized their hopeless situation, they agreed to step down under the most favorable conditions they could obtain.[68] The assassination of Liang Pi, the Manchu military leader who most strongly opposed abdication, and a declaration by Northern army generals and officers headed by Tuan Ch'i-jui advocating a republican form of government, accelerated the downfall of the Manchu dynasty. On February 12 the boy emperor, later known as Henry Pu Yi, abdicated. Thus the Chinese monarchical system of several millennia finally came to an end.

On February 13 Sun Yat-sen resigned and recommended that Yüan Shih-k'ai be made Provisional President. Subsequently Yüan was so elected by the Provisional Parliament in Nanking. However, Sun Yat-sen had made his recommendation contingent on three conditions. First, Nanking was to be the capital of the Republic. Second, Yüan was to come to Nanking to assume the presidency. Third, Yüan was to observe the Provisional Constitution then being drafted by the Provisional Parliament.[69] The second condition was obviously intended "to get the tiger out of the mountains."

The members of the Parliament, however, voted for Peking as the site of the capital. Chang Ping-lin and Sung Chiao-jen were among those who most strongly opposed making Nanking the capital; they believed that doing so would amount to abandoning Mongolia and Manchuria. Sun Yat-sen was upset and indignant. Largely through the influence of Huang Hsing, the Provisional Parliament reversed its decision and chose Nanking as the capital of the Republic.[70]

On February 18 Sung Chiao-jen, Wang Ching-wei, and other delegates of the Nanking government set out for Peking to "welcome" Yüan Shih-k'ai and "escort" him to the South. But he excused himself from leaving Peking on the ground that his presence was indispensable to the maintenance of peace in the North, a claim he bolstered by pointing to the soldiers' riots

135

which took place two days after the Nanking delegates arrived. The rioting began on February 29, and there was looting in part of Peking; on the night of March 2 the disturbance spread to Tientsin. There is probably no documentary evidence to prove that Yüan personally instigated the riots, but the time at which they occurred seems a sinister coincidence. Reluctantly, the leaders in Nanking agreed that Yüan might assume the presidency in Peking. On March 10 he was inaugurated. On April 1 Sun Yat-sen formally relinquished his post. After this, the Provisional Parliament once again voted for Peking as the capital and moved there. With unity between the South and North nominally achieved, the struggle between Yüan Shih-k'ai and the revolutionary leaders entered a new stage.

NINE

STRUGGLES AGAINST YÜAN SHIH-K'AI

IN THE MIDDLE of March 1912, Yüan Shih-k'ai appointed T'ang Shao-i as Premier with the task of forming a ministry. Shortly after T'ang arrived in Nanking on the 24th to negotiate with the leaders there, a dispute arose between the North and the South over filling the posts of Minister of War and Minister of Finance. The leaders in Nanking insisted that Huang Hsing be appointed Minister of War, but Yüan Shih-k'ai favored Tuan Ch'i-jui for that position. The difference was finally overcome by a compromise. The two posts were given to Yüan's candidates; but Huang was to be appointed Resident-General (Liu-shou)* at Nanking, with full power to command all the naval and military forces in the South.[1] The post of Military Governor of Chihli was to be given to Wang Chih-hsiang,[2] the former Lieutenant-Governor of Kwangsi in the Ch'ing government who had joined the revolutionists and served as an army commander under Huang Hsing in Nanking.[3]

By the end of March the cabinet members were approved by the Provisional Parliament. Four T'ung Meng Hui members joined the ten-man cabinet in a gesture of cooperation between South and North. They were Wang Ch'ung-hui, Ts'ai Yüan-p'ei, Sung Chiao-jen, and Ch'en Ch'i-mei, who were the respective Ministers of Justice, Education, Agriculture and Forestry, and Commerce and Industry.[4]

On March 31 Huang Hsing was officially appointed by Yüan Shih-k'ai as the Nanking Resident-General, a post which he held until June. The South had demanded the creation of the post

---

* *Liu-shou* (Resident-General) was an ancient title given to an official in charge of civil and military affairs during the emperor's absence from the capital.

not only because they wanted some administrative and military power during the transitional period but also because the revolutionists would need a central authority with supreme civil and military power in order to cope with the North in case of a split. Thus when the Nanking Provisional Government ceased to exist, the revolutionary forces remained intact.[5]

At the end of March more than fifty thousand soldiers were stationed in Nanking and its vicinity.[6] These troops had to be fed, but Huang had no means of maintaining them because the treasury in Peking withheld financial aid. Because of this difficulty, and also because he wanted to demonstrate the South's sincere acceptance of the central government,[7] Huang repeatedly asked to be relieved of his command and to have the post abolished.[8] This request was granted by Yüan Shih-k'ai, and Huang Hsing thereupon disbanded his troops.[9] While Huang's move weakened the revolutionary strength, his action received favorable comment from his current compatriots as well as from later historians. As Li Chien-nung stated: "Hereafter, no military man, no old-fashioned or new-style warlord, would be willing to disband his own troops [in order to show his support of a central government]."[10] From the standpoint of the power struggle, however, it was a mistake. Subsequent Chinese history has proved that no revolutionary party can achieve and maintain political power without the support of the army.

In the middle of June the nation was stirred by the resignation of Premier T'ang Shao-i. Although he was an old friend of Yüan Shih-k'ai's, T'ang believed that cooperation between the Provisional President and the T'ung Meng Hui was essential to the stability of the infant Republic. He had joined the T'ung Meng Hui when he was in Nanking in an effort to help organize the new government and had agreed to appoint Wang Chih-hsiang as the Military Governor of Chihli, and Po Wen-wei as the Military Governor of Shantung.[11] Yüan Shih-k'ai, however, had refused to support these commitments; on the pretext of opposition to Wang's appointment from Chihli army officers, Yüan sent Wang to help in the disbanding of the troops in Nanking. T'ang refused to countersign the order, but Yüan made it public without the Premier's signature. T'ang left Peking in protest.[12] The four T'ung Meng Hui cabinet members also resigned. For some time after this incident, it was widely rumored that Yüan was planning to become an emperor, and the Provisional President finally found it necessary to issue an official statement of denial.[13]

In July there was more political strife as a result of the Provisional Parliament's veto of the appointment of six ministers submitted for approval by the new Premier, Lu Cheng-hsiang.[14] There were constant conflicts between the executive and the Parliament, the latter being controlled by the T'ung Meng Hui. Yüan Shih-k'ai eventually found it desirable to talk with the revolutionary leaders and invited Huang Hsing, Sun Yat-sen, and Li Yüan-hung to Peking for a conference to iron out differences between the North and the South.

Li Yüan-hung, concurrently Vice-President and Military Governor of Hupeh, had become Chairman of the Republican Party (Kung Ho Tang) upon its founding early in May. The Republican Party was organized by several small groups which opposed the T'ung Meng Hui (and which included some of its former members). Li had not set foot outside Hupeh since the outbreak of the Wuchang Revolution, although as Provisional Vice-President he should have been with the provisional government. It was a cardinal rule in those days that the only safe way for a provincial leader to maintain power was to stay with his own army in his own territory. At that time Li had an additional reason for not going to Peking: the execution of Chang Cheng-wu and Fang Wei. These two high-ranking revolutionary army officers arrived at Peking from Hupeh in the middle of August. On the request of Li Yüan-hung, the Peking authorities arrested them for an alleged plot against the Hupeh Military Governor, and they were executed without trial a few hours after the arrest.[15] In joining the nationwide protest to Yüan Shih-k'ai, Huang Hsing stressed particularly the importance of the rule of law in a modern democracy.[16] Both the Peking government and Li Yüan-hung came under severe attack in the Provisional Parliament. The political atmosphere was such that Li deemed it unwise to leave Hupeh. However, as long as Huang Hsing and Sun Yat-sen accepted the invitation, Yüan's purpose of showing unity and harmony within the nation was accomplished.

The Peking government notified the foreign legations of the forthcoming arrival of the two revolutionary leaders, thus giving the fullest importance to their visit. It was also obvious that the government intended to extend the highest honors to these visitors.[17] The news of the summary execution of Chang Cheng-wu and Fang Wei reached Shanghai just as Sun Yat-sen and Huang Hsing were on the point of sailing for Tientsin on the 18th of August. Some of the comrades feared for the personal safety of their leaders and tried to induce them to abandon the journey. Sun Yat-sen, however, was determined to proceed on his way. Huang Hsing, who had been suffering from a sore throat for some time, left the steamer shortly before it sailed.[18] Wu Chih-hui and Ts'ai Yüan-p'ei were responsible for persuading him not to go.[19] They argued that he should remain so that both he and Sun would not be trapped at once in case of a plot against them. Sun went first, and Huang's trip was to depend upon Sun's report.[20] As a result the foreign press in Peking stated that Huang Hsing had been implicated in Chang's "conspiracy" and that this was why he canceled the trip. The Reuters correspondent in Hankow reported from the "most reliable sources" that Huang had secretly visited Hankow on the 12th, where he had stayed for two days at a hotel in the French Concession, meeting with Chang Cheng-wu and others.[21] The Reuters report was inaccurate, and the leading revolutionary newspaper in Shanghai, the *Min-li pao,* bitterly denounced the news as malicious gossip. Meanwhile, Sun Yat-sen cabled Huang from Tientsin stating that he had met a secretary of the President's office who made the same accusation of "conspiracy." Huang Hsing then wired Yüan Shih-k'ai demanding an investigation. The rumors finally stopped after Yüan privately denied that his office had such a secretary and publicly defended Huang's innocence.[22]

Sun Yat-sen arrived at Peking on August 24 accompanied by about ten persons. He arrived just in time to attend the formation meeting of the Kuomintang (Nationalist Party), which was to take the place of the T'ung Meng Hui. In thirteen meetings with Yüan Shih-k'ai during his twenty-six-day visit, Sun discussed such things as the single-tax theory, land reform, and the removal of the capital from Peking to the interior. But Sun's main interest lay in modernizing China by developing industry and railways. Considering Yüan "indispensable to the presidency in the next ten years,"[23] and having decided to refrain from entering politics, Sun proposed that Yüan begin training an army of two million men while he himself began work on building 200,000 miles of railroads.[24]

Since Sun was so enthusiastic about railway construction, on September 9 Yüan appointed him Director of Railroads with full powers "to consider and draft plans for a national system of railways," and to "submit and discuss the same with international financiers."[25] During their talks Yüan appeared to agree with Sun on practically everything, to Sun's great astonishment. In a conversation with Liang Shih-i, Yüan Shih-k'ai's secretary-general, Sun remarked:

When I talked with Hsiang-ch'eng [Yüan Shih-k'ai], I found that our ideas were more or less the same, and that he seemed to understand my political viewpoint quite well. But there's still one thing that puzzles me: China is an agricultural country. Without solving the basic problems of the peasants, no thorough reforms can be possible. In order to solve the agrarian problem, farmers must own their lands. When I mentioned this to him, I expected that he would object. But, on the contrary, he positively agreed with me and stated that that was undoubtedly so. And this is beyond my comprehension.[26]

Sun Yat-sen's favorable impression of Yüan Shih-k'ai is also indicated in a speech he delivered before the Shanghai Bureau of the Kuomintang on October 5 of the same year:

Among the Ch'ing officials, Yüan Shih-k'ai is really a man of ability. . . . Some people in the South still distrust him, but I definitely believe in his sincerity. . . .

I talked often with President Yüan when I was in Peking. . . . I believe that he is a man who can take up responsibility. His mind is also very clear. He understands world problems quite well. His ideas are also quite new, though the way he governs is rather old-fashioned. But things cannot be done entirely by new methods. . . . In order to govern the Republic, one must have the combination of new ideas, old experience, and old-fashioned method. And President Yüan is just the right man.[27]

Shortly after his arrival in Peking, Sun sent the following cable to Huang urging him to come to the North without delay:

Have talked with Yüan twice since my arrival in Peking. Regarding industries and related matters, his ideas are the same as mine. As to defense and foreign policy, our views are also quite similar. According to my observation, he is in a situation beyond suspicion and deserves our sympathy. The execution of [Chang] Cheng-wu was in fact carried out upon Li Yüan-hung's urgent request. . . . My trip here has greatly helped promote understanding in the North [about the South]. You should also come quickly so that the agitation in the South [against the North] may be stopped and unity of the nation may be satisfactorily reached. Please be sure you come here first before you go to Hunan.[28]

Accompanied by a large entourage, Huang Hsing sailed from Shanghai for Tientsin on September 6 and arrived at Peking by train on the 11th.[29] A French eyewitness gave the following account of Huang's arrival in Peking:

Sentinels were posted along the streets adjoining the Imperial palace, while Mongolian horsemen stood in the open space outside the station, and other soldiers lined the platform with their arms grounded, awaiting the train. . . .

There were also a number of young women and girls drawn up like a regiment, who belonged to modern schools, and who had come to do honour to the chief revolutionary fighter. They were dressed for the most part in light blue jackets and silk trousers of the same shade. . . .

On the arrival platform stood numerous groups of Chinamen, together with a few strangers [foreigners], all anxious to catch a glimpse of the Napoleon of the Chinese Revolution.

There was a puff of smoke in the distance, and at last the train drew up in the station. The bands played national airs. Every one rushed at the doors of the carriage to greet Hoang Hing [Huang Hsing], who stepped out of his compartment, and stood in the midst of a bodyguard composed of forty of his friends, who . . . wore European clothes, and were said to be armed with bombs.

Hoang Hing is a medium-sized, sturdy-looking man, with broad shoulders and powerful physique. He has a full face and a black beard. He wore a frock-coat and top-hat instead of a military uniform.

After shaking hands with his friends, he walked to the exit, accompanied by those privileged persons who had been admitted into the station. A coach, bought by the Imperial Government in anticipation of the visit of a German prince, was waiting outside the station. As the General passed between the lines of soldiers, the latter presented arms, while the suffragettes did not omit to salute the military hero. On reaching his carriage, he stood up and made a short speech to the crowds assembled in the open space outside the station.[30]

The meeting between Yüan Shih-k'ai and Huang Hsing was marked by the utmost cordiality.[31] Yüan treated Huang with the same courtesy he had extended to Sun Yat-sen, who left Peking on the 18th for a tour of China. The Peking officialdom was impressed by Sun Yat-sen's vision and by Huang Hsing's sincerity and practicality. Yüan openly stated that Huang was "not only a great, open-hearted man but also a sincere gentleman." They had long and intimate conferences almost every two days. Yüan was interested in Huang's views on the unification of the country as well as on foreign affairs. The chief problems in foreign relations at the time were the recognition of China by foreign powers and relations with Great Britain and Russia involving the refusal of Tibet and Mongolia to accept Chinese control.

Huang Hsing believed that the Tibetan and Mongolian problems should be solved by peaceful means and that China need not worry much about nonrecognition as long as the infant Republic was making some progress toward achieving its goals. In domestic affairs two things were uppermost in his mind. One was his hope of modernizing China by developing industry and mining, especially coal mining. The other was his desire to persuade Yüan Shih-k'ai to adhere to a parliamentary system, particularly the principle of letting the majority party in the Parliament organize the government. He believed that the Republic needed a strong central government and that in order to have a strong government it was necessary to have a strong political party standing firmly behind it. He hoped that Yüan would persuade his ministers to join the Kuomintang as a first step toward erecting an efficient parliamentary system, and he expressed willingness to use his influence to mediate between his party and the government.

Through Huang Hsing's influence, the government was organized with Chao Ping-chün as Premier. Since the veto of the six cabinet members by the Provisional Parliament in July, the Peking government had been without a Premier. According to a member of the Provisional Parliament, Yüan Shih-k'ai once asked Huang Hsing whether he would agree to the appointment of a Kuomintang member as Premier; the man Yüan had in mind, however, had no close relations with the party. Huang, who undoubtedly hoped to have a real cabinet government controlled by the Kuomintang after the forthcoming election, suggested that Yüan's colleague, Acting Premier Chao Ping-chün, head the cabinet; this would make it clear that the existing government was being directed by Yüan's man rather than by the Kuomintang members. The Provisional Parliament gave its approval on September 24.[32] The Premier and the majority of the cabinet members then joined the Kuomintang. Huang hoped that this would promote political stability and assimilate the conservative elements of the North into the Kuomintang.

On September 25 the Secretariat of the Provisional President's office made public the eight basic policies reached after the meetings between the President and the two Kuomintang leaders, Sun Yat-sen and Huang Hsing. The official statement reads as follows:

A season has passed since the unification of the Republic, and yet the work of the administration has been rather slow. In order to remedy this situation, basic policies had to be decided upon first. The President had thought a great deal about this and had long wanted to discuss the situation with the leaders of the other parties so as to find solutions. It happened that Messrs. Sun Yat-sen and Huang Hsing came to Peking in succession. In the most friendly atmosphere [the President] was able to confer with them daily. As a result, eight basic policies were decided upon; these were also agreed to by the members of the cabinet. Subsequently, a telegram was sent to Wuchang, asking Vice-President Li Yüan-hung's consent, which was immediately given. These eight policies can be looked upon as the basic agreement between the President and the leaders of the Kuomintang and of the Republican Party. These eight policies are:

1. To adopt a centralized government;
2. To reform undesirable social behavior;
3. To have temporary demilitarization, but to train army and naval men of ability;
4. To adopt an open door policy, to import foreign capital, to build railroads, to develop mines, and to establish iron and steel factories, all of which will benefit the people's livelihood;
5. To advocate government subsidies to private industries, starting with agriculture, forestry, industry, and commerce;
6. To concentrate power over military, foreign, financial, judicial, and communication affairs in the central government, giving certain powers to the provincial governments according to the local situation;
7. To place finance on a sound basis immediately;
8. To reconcile party differences, and to maintain order so as to seek recognition [by foreign powers]. . . .[33]

After Yüan Shih-k'ai's conferences with Sun Yat-sen and Huang Hsing, the Provisional Parliament ceased to attack the government. Political stability was temporarily achieved. A letter from the Peking correspondent of the British *Spectator* published on October 5, 1912, expressed optimism over the future of the Republic:

The position here has improved to an extraordinary extent; people are well satisfied with the Republic, and the opposition to the provisional President has subsided. He is certain to be elected President after the elections, and the pessimistic views of many publicists in the British Press seemed unwarranted. The writer has lived too long in China to claim special credit for his opinions, but it appears to him that in Yuan Shih-k'ai the nation possesses the strong man whom it needs at this juncture. He would even hazard the conjecture that Huang Hsing will be a worthy successor in the Presidency when the day comes for Yuan to leave public life.[34]

The Shanghai *National Review* of the same day published the following report:

[Huang's] visit undoubtedly resulted in a considerable strengthening of the government by continuing the policy of destroying party jealousies and party strife, which endangered the existence of the Republic prior to the arrival of Dr. Sun Wen [Yat-sen] and General Hwang Hsing. The latter has become surprisingly popular in Peking where, before his arrival, unfavorable reports had created much prejudice against him. It is believed that he will undertake the reorganization of the Hanyehping industries prior to taking up the task of exploiting the mineral wealth of China.

Before leaving Peking, Huang Hsing made courtesy calls on thirteen foreign envoys in the capital and invited them to a dinner party. His apparent interest in foreign relations is further suggested by current newspaper reports that he had advised Premier Chao Ping-chün to give special attention to diplomacy.[35] On October 3 the General Staff gave a farewell banquet for him. Of a guest who was a member of the Manchu royal family, Huang inquired about the former emperor. When told that the boy had cut off his queue and was studying diligently, Huang said, "Now that the five races of the nation are one family, a talented member of the royal family is also good for the Republic."[36] Two days later he left Peking for Tientsin, where the Japanese community gave him a welcoming party in the Japanese Club.[37] The speech he made on this occasion suggests his attitude toward Sino-Japanese relations. After expressing gratitude to the Japanese who had worked in the Chinese revolutionary movement, he said that the progressive Japanese government had been an inspiration to the Chinese and that he hoped the Japanese would now give brotherly advice and assistance to China in her efforts to make social and political progress. He added that he believed cooperation between the two countries could safeguard true peace in Asia.[38]

Huang left Tientsin by train on October 7 and arrived in Shanghai two days later. In a speech at the welcoming party given him by the Kuomintang in Nanking on the 10th, Huang emphasized the importance of supporting the government and advised the party members to refrain from making slanderous attacks on Yüan Shih-k'ai.[39] This was the same advice he had given before in Peking: personal interests should be sacrificed in order to consolidate the Republic, and criticism of the government should be constructive.[40]

On October 27 Huang Hsing arrived in Wuhan (from Shanghai) on a government cruiser sent by Li Yüan-hung, who prepared an elaborate reception for him.[41] This was the first stop on his journey to Hunan.

After two days in Wuhan, he proceeded to Changsha. This was the first time he had openly visited his home since the abortive revolt eight years before.[42] His Hunanese wife had joined him in Nanking early in 1912, but in August she had returned to Changsha, where their second daughter, Te-hua, was born in February of the following year.[43] During his stay in Changsha, Huang spent most of his time investigating mines, making speeches, and attending banquets. He modestly declined to have a city gate and a street named after him as proposed by the provincial officials.[44]

On November 28 he was appointed by Yüan Shih-k'ai as director-general of the Hankow-Canton and Szechwan Railways.[45] Consequently, he left for Hankow on December 17 to assume this position. About this time the Mongolian situation took a serious turn, and he cabled to the Kuomintang headquarters in Peking advocating a firm position; he believed that if war between China and Russia were to break out over Mongolia, the Tsarist government might collapse under a revolutionary attack from within.[46] Late in January 1913 Huang resigned from the railway post under the pretext of "ill-health," the real reason being that the Ministry of Communications had restricted his power. He went back to Shanghai near the end of January.[47] The national election was then under way, and Huang Hsing began to remind his comrades of the importance of writing a good constitution.[48]

Article 28 of the Provisional Constitution provided that the Provisional Parliament should be dissolved upon the establishment of the formal parliament, the National Assembly. In the middle of December 1912, the national election began. Sung

147

Chiao-jen, who was an ardent advocate of a parliamentary system, was wholeheartedly engaged in the campaign for the Kuomintang. By this time he had emerged as the most important leader of the party next to Huang Hsing and Sun Yat-sen. Hu Han-min explained his rise in these words: "Sung had studied parliamentary theory in Japan, and he became important within the party because [he had the ear] of Huang Hsing and because he won the support of prominent constitutionalists outside the party . . . who were happy to cooperate with him."[49]

Sung Chiao-jen had been primarily responsible for reorganizing the T'ung Meng Hui into the Kuomintang. When the T'ung Meng Hui became a recognized political party in March 1912 (with Sun Yat-sen as chairman, and Huang Hsing and Li Yüan-hung as vice-chairmen), it adopted the following program, which was aimed at "consolidating the Republic and carrying out the Principle of People's Livelihood": (1) unification of the country; (2) the development of local government; (3) the development of unity among the five races; (4) the application of national socialistic policies; (5) the spread of compulsory education; (6) equality of the sexes; (7) compulsory military service; (8) readjustment and reorganization of fiscal and taxation systems; (9) efforts toward gaining equality with other nations; and (10) development of agricultural and colonizing enterprises and of the natural resources of the country.[50] The most formidable opponent of the T'ung Meng Hui in the Provisional Parliament after the legislature moved to Peking was the Republican Party (Kung Ho Tang), which was formed in May 1912; although Li Yüan-hung was its titular head, the Republican Party soon became little more than Yüan Shih-k'ai's own political tool. In order to make the T'ung Meng Hui the majority party in the National Assembly after the coming election, Sung Chiao-jen advocated its amalgamation with four other parties. A number of political parties and associations had sprung up during the first year of the Republic; many of them were merely loose associations of personalities without large followings. By the middle of August an agreement was reached by which four other parties would join the T'ung Meng Hui to form the Kuomintang. The political philosophy behind this action was

148

the belief that in a republic it was desirable to have only two big and powerful parties opposing each other, not innumerable small splinter groups.[51]

In a telegram jointly issued from Shanghai on August 13, 1912, Sun Yat-sen and Huang Hsing informed all branches of the T'ung Meng Hui that negotiations for incorporating four political parties within the T'ung Meng Hui had been successfully concluded in Peking. The purpose of the Kuomintang, as the new party was to be called, was to "strengthen the Republic and achieve democracy." Its five basic policies were as follows: (1) to enhance political unity; (2) to promote the development of local government; (3) to encourage racial assimilation; (4) to improve the people's livelihood; and (5) to maintain international peace.[52] This party program was drafted by Sung Chiao-jen, and he probably contributed more political ideas to it than did any other party leader.[53]

The formation meeting of the Kuomintang was held in Peking on August 25. Sun Yat-sen, Huang Hsing, Sung Chiao-jen, Wang Ch'ung-hui, Wang Chih-hsiang, and four others were elected as directors of the party. Among the thirty councilors elected were Chang Chi and Hu Ying; Hu Han-min was an alternate councilor, along with nine others.[54] Sun Yat-sen remained the titular head of the party. As the acting chairman of the Kuomintang, Sung Chiao-jen was primarily in charge of party affairs in the Peking headquarters. A point which has generally been overlooked should be stressed here. For almost a year after he relinquished the presidency, Sun Yat-sen was inactive not only in national politics but also in party affairs. During this period the cleavage between the two most important groups that had formed the T'ung Meng Hui seven years before (the Hsing Chung Hui and the Hua Hsing Hui) became more and more apparent, not by design of their leaders but by the natural course of events. Huang Hsing and his followers emerged as the strongest group in the party.[55] The division apparently did not reflect ideological differences but only personal preferences for different leaders within the party.

The weakening of Sun Yat-sen's position in his party after the revolution is not difficult to explain. Before 1905 Huang

Hsing had been working independently of Sun, and the majority of Huang's followers and associates were the Japanese-educated students who later came to lead the T'ung Meng Hui. The leaders of the Restoration Society were also close to Huang. An examination of the Revolutionary leaders of 1911 would suggest that many of them were closer to Huang's group than to Sun's. Then, too, Huang had personally directed most of the military revolts; by 1912 he was no longer a young underground leader but a national figure. In the months following the outbreak of the Wuchang Revolution, while Sun Yat-sen was abroad, Huang had handled many important civil and military affairs and had passed all the tests of leadership in practical politics. By background, temperament, and social connections, he could probably get along more easily with the elite of Chinese society than could Sun Yat-sen, who had few connections in China. Furthermore, as the military leader of the revolution, Huang naturally enjoyed real power; he could count on the support of large portions of the army. Finally, Sun Yat-sen was regarded by many of his contemporaries as an impractical theorist and visionary and the young Republic had little appetite for theory.[56]

There is no evidence that Huang Hsing had ever planned to capture leadership of the movement from Sun Yat-sen. He was not an ambitious man thirsting for power, but a capable leader who could be prevailed upon to serve when duty called. As Hu Han-min stated:

After the Canton Revolution of March 29 and the battles of Hanyang, Huang Hsing enjoyed tremendous prestige both within and outside the party. But he was by nature a man of kindness, honesty, and modesty. However, he lacked vision, and he had not thoroughly studied political theory. When suddenly thrown into the company of the constitutionalists, he felt inferior. His own comrades appeared to him more violent than ever, which was good in the time of revolution but not for the period of national reconstruction. Whether his views were progressive or backward he himself did not know. On the one hand, he tolerated Chang Chien and T'ang Shou-ch'ien in order to win the support of the gentry; at the same time Yang Tu . . . and others who were suspected of being opposed to the revolution also were shielded by him. And his political views became more and more Right-wing.[57]

It is not very useful to describe Kuomintang politics in the first years of the Republic with such labels as "Left-wing" or "Right-wing." It was true that in the first years of the Republic Huang Hsing called for moderation and conciliation in national affairs in order to put the state on a sound political basis.[58] But this was the same position taken by Sun Yat-sen.[59] Nor is there any evidence to show that the policies of Sun Yat-sen or Hu Han-min differed in any way from Huang's policy as far as "toleration of the gentry class" was concerned. From the correspondence exchanged during the period of the Nanking provisional government between Chang Chien on the one hand and Sun Yat-sen and Hu Han-min on the other, it appears that Sun and Hu were just as eager as any other revolutionary leader to have Chang's services.[60]

The Kuomintang scored a great victory in the national election, which began in the middle of December 1912 and ended in February of the following year.[61] In the first two months of 1913 it was widely reported in Peking political circles that Huang Hsing was to run for the presidency against Yüan Shih-k'ai.[62] If the rumor reflected Yüan's concern, it was unwarranted. "With regard to the presidency," a Kuomintang member of the National Assembly recalled in an article written in the winter of 1913, "no decision was made [by the Kuomintang] to support Yüan Shih-k'ai. Nor, on the other hand, was there any plan that he should be challenged. It was generally held that if Yüan would abide by the law it was all right to elect him to the presidency."[63] Sun Yat-sen, who had traveled to Japan in the middle of February, also made this clear. He was quoted as saying publicly in Japan: "I have insisted on not running for the presidency. The Kuomintang will try to persuade Mr. Huang K'o-ch'iang [Huang Hsing] to be the presidential candidate, but I am sure that he will not accept the nomination. The presidency cannot but fall on Mr. Yüan Shih-k'ai."[64]

Since the belief seemed firmly established, even among the revolutionary leaders, that Yüan Shih-k'ai was indispensable, the Kuomintang did not plan to challenge him for the presidency. Under the leadership of Huang Hsing and Sung Chiao-jen, it aimed instead at capturing control of the cabinet. By the end of February it appeared certain that the Kuomintang would be the majority party in the National Assembly and would take over the government by organizing a Kuomintang cabinet. The press began to predict inevitable conflict between the future president and the premier, with Huang Hsing's name frequently mentioned as the possible premier.[65] Actually Huang was to remain in the South while Sung Chiao-jen was to conduct party affairs in the North.

Through February and March of 1913, numerous Kuomintang members who had been elected to the National Assembly stopped at Shanghai to seek the advice of Huang Hsing and Sung Chiao-jen before proceeding to Peking. The policies of the Kuomintang, which reflected some of the ideas of Huang and Sung at this time, may be summarized as follows: First, the president should be elected after the adoption of the constitution; this was opposed to the view held by Yüan Shih-k'ai that the election of the president should be held prior to the adoption of the constitution. Second, the parliamentary system should be adopted; that is, the cabinet should be organized by the majority party in the National Assembly. Third, provincial governors should be elected by provincial assemblies.[66]

The National Assembly was scheduled to convene in April, and Sung Chiao-jen thus set out for Peking on March 20. Among those who saw him off at the Shanghai railway station that evening were Huang Hsing and Ch'en Ch'i-mei. At 10:40 P.M., as they walked from the waiting room toward the entrance gate to a special express train, Sung was shot by an assassin and critically wounded. An operation failed to save him, and he died in a hospital on the morning of March 22. In a fortnight he would have been thirty-one years old.

Sung Chiao-jen had not suspected that his political enemies would use such extreme methods. Indeed, he died believing that he was shot by mistake, that his assassin was actually aiming at someone else. He had requested Huang Hsing to send a cable to Yüan Shih-k'ai for him, reporting the incident and expressing the hope that the Provisional President would "protect human rights" and that the National Assembly would adopt "an everlasting constitution."[67]

Peking officialdom viewed the assassination as caused by the internal struggle for leadership within the Kuomintang. This explanation seemed incredible to those who were well-informed on party affairs.[68] Yüan Shih-k'ai was "reliably reported to be shocked" by the news of Sung's death.[69] He immediately ordered the Kiangsu Military Governor, Ch'eng Te-ch'üan, to "investigate the case thoroughly."[70]

The culprits were quickly captured by the police and brought to a preliminary hearing before the Mixed Court of Shanghai. Ying Kuei-hsing, a secret society leader and the direct instigator of the crime, was arrested at midnight on March 23 in the International Settlement; Wu Shih-ying, the assassin, was captured on the following day in the French Concession. A search of Ying's home yielded numerous coded telegrams and letters concerning the murder plot exchanged among Ying, Premier Chao Ping-chün, and Hung Shu-tsu, a confidential secretary to the cabinet.[71]

After the preliminary hearings, which established a *prima facie* case of murder, the Mixed Court transferred the prisoners and the evidence to the Kiangsu provincial authorities in the middle of April. The day after the findings of the Mixed Court were made public by Military Governor Ch'eng on April 25, Huang Hsing and Sun Yat-sen jointly issued a circular telegram demanding that the real murderer behind the scenes be brought to justice.[72]

In May Premier Chao Ping-chün was subpoenaed to appear before the local court at Shanghai, but he avoided the summons by claiming illness.[73] The Peking authorities then ordered Huang Hsing to appear before the local court at Peking on the ground that they had discovered assassination plots against prominent Peking government officials, which an assassin had confessed were organized by Huang Hsing.[74] On June 11 Huang Hsing appeared before the Mixed Court of Shanghai and stated that he would appear whenever the court received evidence against him from Peking.[75] No further requests were made of Huang, but by this time the Premier had succeeded in evading the issue by creating confusion.

Yüan Shih-k'ai sent Liu K'uei-i, an old friend of Huang

Hsing and Sung Chiao-jen, to attend Sung's funeral. Liu was then Minister of Industry and Commerce. He brought a secret message from Yüan to Huang: if Huang would say no more about the assassination of Sung, Yüan would use his influence to assist Huang and his party. Huang refused to consider such a proposition. Shortly afterward, Liu returned to Peking and resigned from his post.[76]

On April 26 the Reorganization Loan contract of £250,-000,000 was signed by the Peking government and the five-power banking consortium. The conditions for securing the loan included not only the government's pledging of particular taxes, especially on salt, but also the administration of these taxes, especially the salt gabelle, by foreign agents.[77] In the eyes of the South, the real purpose of concluding the loan at that time and on such terms was not to promote reconstruction; it appeared more like an overt action against the South. The National Assembly was then in session, but the government had not submitted the loan contract for approval as required by law. The Assembly immediately declared it null and void, and telegrams of protest flew to Peking from all corners of the nation. Huang Hsing was most outspoken. He bluntly accused Yüan Shih-k'ai of wanting the loan only to fight the Kuomintang; in support of this charge he quoted the newly discovered correspondence between Hung Shu-tsu (the confidential secretary of the cabinet) and Ying Kuei-hsing, in which Hung expressed the hope of obtaining some money from the loan then under negotiation in order to pay Ying for arranging Sung Chiao-jen's death.[78] The signing of the Reorganization Loan thus speeded the deterioration of relations between Yüan Shih-k'ai and the Kuomintang leaders.

Huang Hsing and the other leaders of the Kuomintang, however, still hesitated to make an unequivocal break with the Peking government; they fully realized their own military weakness.[79] Huang insisted on settling the two outstanding issues by legal means. Replying to Li Yüan-hung's telegram of May 9, he stated: "I have maintained that the Sung [Chiao-jen] case should be settled only by due process of law and that the Reorganization Loan should be approved by the National Assembly.

My position on these issues has been consistent . . . as is clearly and fully revealed by my earlier statements."[80]

In contrast to the conciliatory attitude of Huang Hsing, Yüan Shih-k'ai was resolute. Following the denunciation of the National Assembly by the Northern provincial military governors, Yüan gave orders, on May 15, to deprive Huang of the title "General of the Army," which had been conferred upon him on September 9 of the previous year, and which Huang had repeatedly declined to accept.[81] Shortly after this seven Northern military governors denounced Huang Hsing, and Yüan's generals pledged their loyalty to the government. Huang Hsing shouldered the brunt of Yüan Shih-k'ai's "psychological warfare" against the Kuomintang. He was accused of being the leader of a conspiracy to overthrow the government by force. Sun Yat-sen's name was rarely mentioned in the government's accusations.[82]

In June the Kuomintang declared that it did not object to the Peking government's obtaining the Reorganization Loan and that it opposed only the procedure by which the contract had been made. It declared itself willing to approve the contract if the government would submit it to the National Assembly, even at this late date.[83] But even such a large concession as this failed to please Yüan Shih-k'ai, who seemed determined to crush the Kuomintang by force. As early as April 7 he had made war plans and had secretly ordered a partial mobilization.[84] With financial resources secured, he became increasingly belligerent. In an article published on May 27, 1913, a well-informed Chinese journalist predicted that war was imminent, quoting what Yüan had said to his close aides a few days earlier: "Tell the Kuomintang members that I have made up my mind. Sun [Yat-sen] and Huang [Hsing] only want to make trouble. I can't . . . tolerate it. . . . If they have the ability to organize another government, I am sure I can destroy it."[85]

On June 9 Yüan ordered the dismissal of Li Lieh-chün, the Military Governor of Kiangsi. Five days later Kwangtung Military Governor Hu Han-min was dismissed, and Anhwei Military Governor Po Wen-wei was dismissed by the end of the month. Of these three Kuomintang military governors Li Lieh-chün was, in the eyes of Yüan Shih-k'ai, the most aggressive and arrogant.[86] Li was also the only one who had any real military strength; upon the dissolution of the office of Nanking Resident-General, Huang Hsing had sent a well-equipped brigade to Kiangsi and it later became the main source of anti-Yüan strength in Kiangsi province.[87] Shortly after his dismissal, Li came to Shanghai to consult with Huang Hsing and Sun Yat-sen. He told the two leaders that he could still regain control of Kiangsi from Yüan Shih-k'ai if other provinces would support him. Sun enthusiastically encouraged him. A policy of war was then agreed upon, and Li returned to Kiangsi early in July.[88]

Although Huang Hsing had advocated peaceful opposition, he had made certain military preparations against a possible war. Shortly after the assassination of Sung Chiao-jen, he had sent an emissary to Hupeh with a letter to Chiang I-wu and the other army officers in that province. According to Kuo Chi-sheng, who read the letter, Huang warned the comrades to be vigilant and advised them to consult his emissary about any further action. An Army Officers' Corps was subsequently organized for the purpose of "improving Hupeh administration and carrying on the revolutionary tasks." The Officers' Corps was not especially created to overthrow Li Yüan-hung, but some of its members soon began working toward that end. In May the organization was smashed by Li, who ordered the arrest of several high-ranking officers. Throughout June and early July, Huang Hsing's men made several attempts to seize the Hupeh government, but all of these failed.[89]

Kuomintang underground activities and army coups were more prevalent in Hupeh than in any other province. This was probably because Huang believed that for political and strategic reasons, control of that province was essential to any effective military action against Yüan Shih-kai in the Yangtze regions.

On July 12 Li Lieh-chün declared war on Yüan Shih-k'ai, and the "second revolution" began.[90] On what must have been the evening of July 14, Wu Chih-hui recalls that a number of people at Huang's house in the Shanghai International Settlement were waiting for an emissary from Nanking. When the emissary arrived, he reported that the commander of the Eighth Division in Nanking was weakening in his resolve to support

Huang. The First and Eighth Divisions were the main military forces in Nanking upon which Huang had counted for support against Yüan Shih-k'ai. As soon as Huang heard the report, he picked up a manifesto prepared by Chang Shih-chao and rushed to Nanking with a dozen aides.[91]

On the following day, with the support of the army, Huang Hsing forced Military Governor Ch'eng Te-ch'üan to declare Kiangsu province "independent" from the central government. Within a day or two Ch'eng left Nanking for Shanghai, and Huang took over the administration and reorganized it for war. Since his resignation as Nanking Resident-General a year before, Huang had had no official position of any kind. It was therefore necessary for him to force Ch'eng to appoint him to a military command. In the manifesto issued in the name of the Commander-in-Chief of the Punitive Expedition in Kiangsu Province against Yüan Shih-k'ai, Huang summed up his attitude toward the war as follows:

Ever since the assassination of Sung Chiao-jen, which was followed by the illegal contract of a foreign loan, the treachery of Yüan Shih-k'ai has been wholly unmasked. It was only natural that our citizens should feel at once shocked and anguished. In sorrow and indignation, I occasionally telegraphed my protests in mild terms to the central government. Motivated by their patriotic love of the Republic, the military governors of four provinces—Hunan, Kiangsi, Anhwei, and Kwangtung—had also frankly expressed their views. But during all this time Yüan harboured evil thoughts and made preparations for war. Upon the exposure of his crimes, we would have been justified in taking up arms against him. But we realized that the nation had just been stabilized and that foreign aggression was imminent. Therefore we refrained from resorting to force in order to avoid civil war, hoping that he might gradually come to his senses. Consequently, I ignored the insulting telegrams he sent me. The four governors, who were dismissed in succession without reason, also decided to accept their dismissals and return to private life. We thought Yüan would be satisfied then. But this wicked man of wolfish nature was unmoved. Instead of directing his attention to the frontiers where Mongolia is in danger, he suddenly sent troops to the peaceful interior and coastal provinces. We can only conclude that he is determined to exterminate all the southern armies and to liquidate all his opponents. Until he does this he will not

157

stop. . . . Who can sit by and tolerate such inhuman conduct and ruthless demolition of republicanism? . . . I regret very much having hesitated for so long, but it is not too late to fight him. . . . My sole object is to overthrow him. As soon as he is ousted I shall disband my army and retire to private life, making way for more worthy men to conduct the affairs of the state. Heaven will condemn me if I have any ulterior motives for personal gain.[92]

The last three sentences quoted above were Huang's answer to the hostile criticism that it was his ambition to become President that lay behind the current troubles.[93] Huang also issued a manifesto to the foreign press stating that the war against Yüan was begun "to overthrow a despotic ruler who has betrayed the trust of the people," and requesting "all financial groups to cease making further advances of money" to the Peking government.[94] This manifesto had little effect on the foreign financial groups that supported Yüan Shih-k'ai. Few members of the foreign press in China or abroad realized the significance of the events that led to the revolt. As the London *Times* of July 19, 1913, commented in its editorial:

It is the rebellion of jealous and rapacious politicians. . . . Huang-Hsing has been spoken of, in rather exaggerated fashion, as China's "Man of Destiny" and as a possible successor of Yuan [Shih-k'ai], from whom he has suffered many slights of late. . . .

The revolt should decide whether China is to be subjected to strong centralized control or whether the provinces are to be a law unto themselves; . . . The rebel leaders are certainly no patriots striking a manful blow against tyranny. . . . President Yuan may have been rough of late in handling of the provincial Governments . . . he may have treated the South with too much disdain, but to onlookers he still appears, for the present, the only man who can prevent the Chinese Republic from falling to pieces.

The editorial of the *New York Times* of August 6, 1913, is another example of the view the foreign press took toward the revolt:

The present so-called rebellion is not so much an uprising of the people against the Government at Peking as an effort by disaffected politicians and place hunters to force themselves into power. . . . The end of the civil war, which cannot be much longer deferred, will leave Yuan Shih-kai more strongly established than ever as ruler of China; an event in which the rest of the world cannot fail to find cause for congratulation.

The victory which the *New York Times* considered "desirable for the peace of the world" was easily won by Yüan Shih-k'ai.[95] Between July 12 and August 4, seven provinces (Kiangsi, Kiangsu, Anhwei, Kwangtung, Fukien, Hunan, and Szechwan) declared "independence" from Peking. By September 12, exactly two months after the revolt had started, the war was over. The Southern armies, lacking sufficient ammunition and practically penniless, fought hard for a while but never became a serious menace to the central government. In some provinces the declarations of revolt were merely gestures, and were not followed by military action; only Kiangsi and Nanking saw real fighting. Indeed, Chinese historians have come to call the "second revolution" "The Battles of Nanking and Kiangsi."

From the very beginning Huang Hsing did not seem to have much confidence in winning the war. When he saw that defeat was inevitable, he issued this statement on July 26:

On account of our lack of funds, food and ammunition, our army may meet defeat, although with wide support and determination, we might ruin the country and make it untenable for even Yuan Shih-kai.

Yet I think that it is a useless and ruinous struggle, and should we carry it to the bitter end it will so despoil and devastate our fair land that, even if we win, our beloved country will be in bankruptcy, and in danger of the unspeakable disaster of foreign partition . . . The truth [about the revolt] has been kept back by inspired editorials and papers, and our cause has been grossly misrepresented to foreigners in their own country.[96]

With this in mind and having decided to let fate take its course, Huang left Nanking on July 28.[97] The next day Ch'eng Te-ch'üan returned to Nanking and declared his allegiance to Yüan Shih-k'ai. The Nanking campaign would have ended then but for a coup d'état ten days later by Ho Hai-ming, a member of the Kuomintang, who declared independence again and offered strenuous resistance to the Northern troops. Nanking was not finally captured by Yüan's army until September 2.

In commenting on the "second revolution" and the politics of the early years of the Republic, Chinese historians have generally been influenced by a hindsight argument found in two documents. One of these documents is a long letter from Ch'en Ch'i-mei to Huang Hsing, dated February 4, 1915. As far as the revolt of 1913 was concerned, the gist of Ch'en's argument was that if Sun Yat-sen's policy had prevailed over Huang's, the South would have declared war against Yüan shortly after the evidence of Sung Chiao-jen's assassination was revealed, or after the conclusion of the Reorganization Loan. On both occasions public opinion throughout the nation turned strongly against the Peking government. The South would therefore have started the war at a better time and the outcome might have been different. By insisting on dealing with Yüan by legal means, argued Ch'en, Huang gave Yüan both the opportunity to consolidate his power and the time to prepare for war. As time passed anti-Yüan sentiment in the nation ebbed, to the great disadvantage of the South.[98]

The other document is a letter Sun Yat-sen wrote to Huang Hsing in March of 1915, which reads in part:

In 1913 I advocated most strongly declaring war against Yüan Shih-k'ai. The reason for its failure was not because Yüan had stronger military power, but because of the disunity among our comrades. I still remember the conference held at your house five days after the death of Sung Chiao-jen. . . . At that time you said that the Republic had been established and that law was not useless. You suggested that we adopt a calm attitude and advocated a legal solution of the murder case. . . . You believed that the military strength of the South was not great enough to make war against the North and that once war started it might bring disaster to the nation. I did not agree with you, but you did not listen to me.

Later Li Lieh-chün and Po Wen-wei were dismissed . . . and the South was threatened. . . . In an angry moment I . . . wanted to conduct the revolt myself in Nanking. But you suddenly decided to take the command on the ground that military affairs were not my strong point and that one mistake might bring disastrous consequences. I did not want to create internal strife at a time when we were facing the common enemy, so I gave up my plan in favor of yours. You went to Nanking . . . but you abandoned the city because of a shortage of funds to support the army. . . . As a result the strong anti-Yüan sentiment of the people faded away. In the final analysis, who was to blame, you or me? The answer is obvious.[99]

Judging by its ignominious collapse, it is very doubtful whether the war would have gone much differently if it had started in April 1913 instead of three months later. The military strength of the South and the popular sentiment against Yüan were not reliable, as Huang had maintained. A noted Chinese journalist observed from Peking in a dispatch of August 7, 1913, that the people in the capital received the war news calmly and showed little surprise when the Northern army scored one victory after another, "because, though one might question the wisdom of Yüan Shih-k'ai's political judgment, in the matter of military affairs no one doubted his ability." This, the journalist said, was in great contrast to the situation in Peking immediately after the outbreak of the Wuchang Revolution, when the people had shown little confidence in the government and the capital had been in panic.[100]

It should be pointed out that in 1913 the Chinese people longed for peace, law, and order above everything else. In the eyes of conservative citizens, the revolutionary faction in the Kuomintang was still a violent and disturbing force in the nation. If Huang Hsing had launched a punitive war against Yüan in March or April, historians probably would have said that he should have exploited every peaceful and legal means before resorting to war. A policy of restraining Yüan Shih-k'ai by legal means was doomed to failure, for Yüan took the law into his own hands when it suited his purpose. Huang Hsing at least demonstrated to the nation that he had done everything possible to avoid bloodshed. If his intentions were not clear to the nation at that time, they later became clear to historians. His peace policy failed, but it is doubtful that a war policy would have succeeded.[101]

TEN

LAST YEARS

HUANG HSING reportedly arrived at Yokohama on August 18, 1913, together with Chang Chi and Sun Yat-sen.[1] At first it seemed possible that the Japanese government would deny asylum to the refugees in order to avoid diplomatic troubles with Yüan Shih-k'ai's regime in Peking. Through the efforts of Inukai Tsuyoshi and other Japanese friends, however, permission for them to land had been secured in advance.[2] Once again Tokyo became the headquarters of the Chinese revolutionary exiles; from the Japanese capital they watched helplessly as Yüan Shih-k'ai tightened his autocratic rule.

While the Kuomintang leaders had been waging war against Yüan Shih-k'ai, the National Assembly had continued to hold its sessions in Peking, although Chang Chi, President of the Senate, and a number of Kuomintang members who formed the old guard of the T'ung Meng Hui had fled to the South. The party headquarters in Peking was soon under the control of the non–T'ung Meng Hui factions of the party. On July 30, 1913, two days after Huang Hsing's flight from Nanking, Yüan Shih-k'ai ordered the local police to call upon the executives of the Kuomintang to find out whether the party was involved in the "second revolution" or whether it was only the work of "ringleaders such as Huang Hsing, Li Lieh-chün, Ch'en Ch'iung-ming, Ch'en Ch'i-mei, and Po Wen-wei." If the party was not involved in the rebellion, the Presidential Mandate continued, "it should publicly declare its attitude within three days and expel from the party the rebels named above."[3]

At first the Peking members of the party indicated that they were unable to comply with the government's demands, but realizing that Yüan would not tolerate vacillation, they eventually notified the government that the party as such had no connection with the revolt and that the party committee had removed the names of the five leaders mentioned in the Mandate from the membership rolls of the party.[4] The party authorities announced in the newspapers that although the expulsion of Huang Hsing and the others could normally be effected only by the party convention, they had to be expelled according to the government order because it was impossible to summon the convention on such short notice.[5]

Sun Yat-sen was not among those expelled, perhaps because the Peking government thought he was not involved or because they found it politically expedient to pretend belief in his innocence in order to divide the Kuomintang leadership. Huang Hsing, on the other hand, was generally considered to be the leader of the war faction in the Kuomintang. This is interesting in view of Sun's later claim that he insisted on war with Yüan from the beginning.[6]

No one seemed interested in questioning the legality of the party action, not even those who were expelled. The expulsion was probably considered expedient by the Kuomintang members in the National Assembly, who were still trying to keep their positions either out of personal interest or in the illusory hope of carrying on their work under Yüan's regime. No other incident more clearly reveals the weakness of the party.

The causes of disunity in the Kuomintang were manifold. On the one hand, Yüan Shih-k'ai successfully divided it through bribery and political maneuvering. On the other hand, after the assassination of Sung Chiao-jen, neither Huang Hsing nor Sun Yat-sen went to the North to direct party affairs. Consequently, there was no leadership at headquarters; no one there was capable of uniting the party members, to say nothing of winning the support of the other political parties. The views of the members in Peking often differed from those of their leaders in the South.[7]

Yüan Shih-k'ai still tolerated the legal position of the Kuomintang because its votes were necessary to his election as President of the Republic. The election was held on October 6, 1913, beginning at eight o'clock in the morning. After Yüan had not received the required number of votes on the first two ballots, a mob calling itself a "citizen corps" surrounded the assembly building and refused to let the assemblymen leave until Yüan was elected. The election closed at ten o'clock that night, after Yüan had been elected on the third ballot.[8] Four days later, on the second anniversary of the Wuchang Revolution, Yüan was inaugurated as the first President of the Republic of China.

Five days after the inauguration, the Peking government issued an order for the arrest of several "chief rebels" headed by Huang Hsing, including "Chang Chi and Sun Yat-sen, who were connected with the rebellion."[9] On November 4, less than a month after the election of the President, the Peking government revoked the credentials of the 438 Kuomintang members of the National Assembly; even those who had severed their relations with the party before the "second revolution" were not exempt. The Senate and the House of Representatives were unable to convene on the following day because neither had enough members remaining to form a quorum.[10] Thus Yüan succeeded in dissolving the parliament, and the Kuomintang lost the last vestige of its power in the country.

The Kuomintang now faced more than extinction from without; a serious crisis within its leadership was also developing. In Japan, the relationship between Huang Hsing and Sun Yat-sen was under strain, and it deteriorated with the constant quarrels of their respective followers. The two leaders did not see each other for months at a time. Their mutual Japanese friends, Miyazaki and Kayano, tended to see more of Huang than they did of Sun. The daily reports of the secret agents of the Japanese Foreign Office made it clear that Sun was no longer in undisputed control of the revolutionary movement.[11] An open disagreement finally came when Sun Yat-sen attempted to reorganize the party in order to establish his undisputed leadership.

A reorganization of the Kuomintang had been on Sun's mind ever since he had escaped to Japan in the fall of 1913. By the end of January 1914, he had a definite conception of the new organization he proposed to create.[12] The purpose of the new party, to be called the Chinese Revolutionary Party (Chung-hua

Ko-ming Tang), would be "to eliminate the bureaucrats and the sham revolutionists."[13] According to the party's charter, party members were to be classified in three groups for the duration of the "revolutionary period."[14] Those who had joined the party before the outbreak of the revolution against Yüan were to be Initial Members; in the new state, they would be called "privileged citizens" and would enjoy special power. Those who had joined the party after the outbreak of the revolution but before the establishment of the revolutionary government were to be Assistant Members; they would be called "meritorious citizens" and would have the right to vote and to be elected to public office. Those who had joined the party after the establishment of the revolutionary government were to be Common Members; they would be called "progressive citizens" and would have the right to vote but not to be elected. Nonparty members were to have no political rights during the "revolutionary period." This classification of citizenship was to be abolished after the promulgation of a constitution; the "constitutional period," however, was not to begin until the successful conclusion of a "period of military administration" and a subsequent "period of political tutelage." Certain tasks appropriate to each period were outlined, but no time limits were set for accomplishing them.

The charter also specified that candidates for membership in the party would be required to take an oath of personal loyalty to Sun Yat-sen ("to follow and to obey Mr. Sun") and to sign a pledge to that effect with a fingerprint as a seal. Even those who had previously joined the T'ung Meng Hui or the Kuomintang would be required to take this oath in order to become members of the new party. This was the condition that Huang Hsing and many other Kuomintang members found most unacceptable, and it was this clause in the charter that provoked the final split in the revolutionary camp.[15]

In a letter to Teng Tse-ju, dated April 18, 1914, Sun Yat-sen offered the following explanation for his stand:

The reason I demand obedience from the members of the new party is that during the Wuchang Revolution of 1911 as well as in the "second revolution," our party members did not take unified action but acted independently. . . . It has been correctly pointed out by some people that lack of party discipline was the cause of our failure. I may mention here that during the period of the Nanking Provisional Government, although I had the honor of being the President, I was in reality a puppet. Nothing was decided by me. When Yüan Shih-k'ai claimed to receive the presidency from the Ch'ing regime, I strongly argued against it because, as a matter of principle, his power should be thought of as conferred on him by [the people of] the Republic. No other interpretation is permissible. I would go to war rather than accept his claim. But I was blamed by my comrades [for obstructing peace negotiations]. . . . At that time I also insisted that Nanking should be the site of the national capital and that Yüan should leave for the South to assume the presidency. My policy was again opposed by the comrades. When the evidence in the case of Sung Chiao-jen was revealed, I advocated war against Yüan; but K'o-ch'iang [Huang Hsing] did not agree. Because of the postponement, we were defeated as soon as the war broke out. Therefore, unless the comrades are united and obey me personally, the revolutionary cause is doomed to failure.[16]

It has long been assumed in China that Sun's arguments are borne out by the facts of history. However, there are reasons to suspect that the facts were not identical with Sun's retrospective interpretation of them. Until the question of war or peace arose in the spring of 1913, there is no evidence of disagreement between Huang Hsing and Sun Yat-sen on the policies mentioned above by Sun; nor does it seem that the two leaders had any basic difference of opinion on other issues. The surrender of power to Yüan Shih-k'ai and the repeated concessions made to him by the revolutionary leaders before and shortly after the abdication of the Manchu emperor were not really made by the party members against Sun's wishes. Rather, the decisions were made reluctantly by the revolutionary leaders as Yüan refused to comply with their terms; compromise undoubtedly seemed necessary in view of the superior military strength of the North. An analysis of the documents and events of the time will not support the conclusion that Sun shared no responsibility for the compromise with Yüan.

In this connection we might also examine the familiar claim that Sun's political ideals were often disregarded by the party members after the overthrow of the Manchu dynasty. It should be pointed out that Sun Yat-sen's "Three People's Principles" were not systematically expounded until the 1920's. Even so, fervent advocacy of a parliamentary system by Huang Hsing and Sung Chiao-jen was undoubtedly in line with the "Principle of People's Rights." As to the "Principle of People's Livelihood," it was not neglected in the postrevolution T'ung Meng Hui or in the Kuomintang programs. It was not an issue within the party in the early days of the Republic. The Nanking Provisional Government existed for only three months, and it is doubtful whether the revolutionary leaders ever had a real opportunity to begin implementing the "Principle of People's Livelihood." Furthermore, there is no evidence that Sun Yat-sen himself ever complained that disregard of this principle by the party members was a cause for their failure.

There is no question that the Kuomintang needed to be reorganized and strengthened. It is undoubtedly true that the party had been infiltrated by many opportunists since the outbreak of the Wuchang Revolution, and it is reasonable to believe that the members who had no firm dedication to the party cause should have been eliminated. The party disunity during the "second revolution" was an even stronger justification for organizing a highly disciplined party. But Sun's proposal for establishing discipline was extreme. He took the position that the failure of the Kuomintang was due to the failure of his comrades to follow his personal leadership, and that the only way to correct the past mistakes was for them "to follow and to obey" him alone. This was unacceptable to many of his comrades.

It was understandably difficult for the revolutionists, who had just overthrown a monarchy for the purpose of establishing a modern democracy, to take an oath pledging loyalty to one person. Huang Hsing was strongly against it. He argued that such a demand violated the spirit of the Republican Revolution: one worked for the cause, he said, not for an individual, and besides, the demand of a fingerprint was an insult to the party members.[17] Sun Yat-sen made a dramatic visit to Huang's residence to argue for the proposal, but Huang remained unconvinced.[18]

Huang Hsing's refusal to join the new party was of course the most serious blow to its unity. Efforts were made by Sun's followers to find a compromise formula. It was suggested that former members of the T'ung Meng Hui should not be required to take the oath and that the pledge "to follow and to obey Mr. Sun" should be replaced by the wording "to follow and to obey the chairman of the party" without mentioning Sun's name. Thus allegiance would be owed only to the presiding chairman of the party. Whether Huang would have accepted such a formula is not clear; the question never arose because Sun refused to consider any change in his original plan.[19] It is known, however, that in one of the two letters to Huang Hsing in which he argued the necessity of obedience to a personal leader, Sun suggested that if he should be unsuccessful after two years of leadership, he would be willing to turn over the chairmanship of the party to Huang.[20]

The charter of the Chinese Revolutionary Party provided for a vice-chairmanship. Huang Hsing was the logical choice, but when his attitude became clear, Sun Yat-sen declared that any comrade who had been a provincial military governor would be qualified to fill that post. The only Kuomintang governors who were willing to join the new organization were Hu Han-min and Ch'en Ch'i-mei, and neither considered himself an appropriate choice for vice-chairman. Li Lieh-chün, Ch'en Ch'iung-ming, Po Wen-wei, and the rest were never close to Sun and refused to follow him.[21] They refused to join the party unless the oath and fingerprint requirements were changed and Huang Hsing would also join it.[22] It is one of the best examples of Huang's influence in the revolutionary movement that the vice-chairmanship remained open throughout the life of the Chinese Revolutionary Party.[23]

With a few exceptions, none of the well-known revolutionary leaders joined the new party, which elected Sun Yat-sen as its chairman in June 1914. It is significant that even by Sun's own claim, only "eight provinces were represented" at the meeting. This stands in great contrast to the formation of both the T'ung Meng Hui and the Kuomintang as far as geographical distribution of party membership is concerned. By July 8, when the Chinese Revolutionary Party was formally founded, Huang Hsing was en route from Japan to the United States.[24]

On July 9 Huang arrived at Honolulu, where the overseas Chinese gave him a welcoming party before he sailed again the same day. It was the "most enthusiastic meeting of the overseas Chinese in the history of Honolulu," according to a contemporary report.[25]

It is significant that, of all nations, Huang wanted most to visit the United States. This was the country where his comrade Sun Yat-sen had spent many years soliciting funds. This was the first and only time Huang himself made direct contact with the West; he eventually gave up his intention of proceeding from America to Europe. Accompanied by four aides, he arrived at San Francisco on July 15. His eldest daughter, Chen-hua, who had been studying with her older brother I-ou and her sister-in-law in New York for the last two years, came to meet him; he was joined later by his wife Hsü Tsung-han and their one-year-old son I-mei.[26] His Hunanese wife and their daughter Te-hua remained in Tokyo where they had taken refuge after the failure of the "second revolution."

In an interview with a reporter for the *San Francisco Examiner,* Huang accused Yüan Shih-k'ai of imperial aspirations. When asked about the price on his head, Huang could not suppress this short burst of enthusiasm: "I do not think they will ever have to pay it. Young China is awake. We are educating ourselves and the masses are awakening. We are going through a crisis. The monarchy has been overthrown and things will work out eventually."[27]

Yüan Shih-k'ai had asked that Huang be prevented from entering the United States, but the American government refused his request.[28] After Huang's arrival the Chinese Minister in Washington formally requested the State Department to arrest him and his associates on the ground that they were "setting on foot a military expedition" from this country and were collecting money for it throughout the United States.[29] The matter was referred to the Department of Justice, which decided to take no action. Meanwhile, Huang denied that his motives for visiting America were other than peaceful. He stated: "China is ripe for a republican government. . . . We have hoped, and still hope, to solve China's problems through peaceful procedures."[30]

In San Francisco, where he took a suite in the Fairmont Hotel, the overseas Chinese gave numerous welcoming parties for him. In a letter to Kayano Nagatomo dated July 27, 1914, he described his first ten days in the United States:

I trust that you have already received my postcard sent from Honolulu when I arrived there on the 9th of this month, and also my telegram informing you of my safe arrival in San Francisco on the 15th. Members of the Chinese parties besides the Kuomintang also came to welcome me when I arrived at the port, and in the following days I was enthusiastically entertained by various organizations. It is gratifying that the overseas Chinese are so enthusiastic regardless of my success or failure. I have also met the acting Japanese consul-general and the staff of the consulate in San Francisco once. . . . They were very friendly. . . .

I stayed in San Francisco for nine days, exhausted by making speeches and attending banquets. On the 23rd I moved to Pacific Grove, about one hundred odd miles from San Francisco, and four hours by train. . . . This is a summer resort close to the sea. The weather is beautiful here. The flowers are blooming and the grass is green all year long and the trees and the woods are flourishing and shady.

Have temporarily rented a small house. I do some reading and do my own cooking. In the morning I can pick up clams and abalones along the beach. They are delicious. There are two Japanese grocery stores here, which can supply the food we need.

I am planning to employ an expert on American government to lecture me on that subject and also on self-government on the local level. After I know something about these subjects, I shall travel to the east coast of the country.

The American government and people have been quite friendly toward us. Before we landed at San Francisco, the administration in Washington had ordered the immigration officers to greet us. Yesterday I received several letters and telegrams from Chambers of Commerce and private individuals on the east coast, expressing their welcome and sympathy. Although Yüan Shih-k'ai through his envoy to this country attempted to make difficulties for us, the

American government has ignored his requests. There is justice in this world after all.

I am determined to reveal the wickedness of Yüan's dictatorship, and I will make it clear to the nations of the world that as long as he is in power China will never have peace. He must be ousted before there can be peace in Asia. . . .[31]

From the accounts of his activities published in the *Young China* (*Shao-nien Chung-kuo ch'en-pao*) of San Francisco, Huang Hsing apparently visited the city and its vicinity from time to time. On August 15 he was invited to deliver an address on "China under the Republican Form of Government" before the members of the city's Commonwealth Club. He made a bitter attack on Yüan Shih-k'ai and predicted that unless Yüan changed his policy or someone replaced him, another revolution would start in the southern provinces; he declared that the majority of Chinese are strongly in favor of closer relations "with the outside world and especially with America."[32] On September 19 Huang and his entourage left for Los Angeles, the first stop on their journey to the east coast. During their three-day sojourn in the city he paid a courtesy call on Mrs. Homer Lea and placed a wreath of flowers on the tomb of her husband.[33]

On September 29 Huang reached Chicago, where he stayed at the Congress Hotel.[34] It was in "one of those suites of the great hotel that looks out over Lake Michigan" that Paul Linebarger went to see him. A former American judge in the Philippines and a sympathizer with the Chinese revolution, Linebarger expressed the hope that someday he might write a story of Huang's life "in some hermit place of China." He asked Huang to write him something he could use as the foundation for a biography. "Some little time after this," Linebarger recalled, "I received a bulky package from Hwang. I think my fingers must have trembled as I opened it. Therein lay (as I thought) what was to serve as the foundation of the life story of one of the bravest of generals. I opened the package carefully, like the [*sic*] pilgrim opening a sacred book." What Linebarger found was a long, typewritten document in which Huang made no mention of himself; it was an appeal to the American public to support Chinese

171

democracy in its struggle against the usurpations of Yüan Shih-k'ai.[35]

On October 2 Huang Hsing arrived in New York. He lived first at the Astor and then at the Hotel Bonta, Broadway at Ninety-fourth Street.[36] He was enthusiastically welcomed by the local Kuomintang and the Chinese community generally, as in the other cities he had previously visited.[37] To a reporter for the *New York Times,* he explained his mission in the United States and expressed his views on a number of subjects, including the European war which had broken out two months before:

It has been said that I have come here to collect funds for a third revolution. . . . I have not mentioned the subject of raising money, and my object is not that. It is to study the way government is administered in this great Republic after which Chinese patriots hope their own government will be fashioned, and to do what I can to make Americans and Chinese more friendly. . . . The ideals of China and the United States are now absolutely the same, and the sympathy of the American people with China in its aims would have tremendous effect at home. . . .

Yuan Shih-kai . . . has been thrusting two propositions before the world. . . . In the first place he has been insisting that the Chinese are not prepared for the republican form of government that they have adopted. For another reason, Yuan has been saying and causing his agents to say that he was the only man in China strong enough to rule it. . . .

You may be assured that time is near when Yuan Shih-kai must step down from his pinnacle of power, and give way to a form of government the people desire and which they propose to establish. Europe is now in arms against imperialism and despotism: The effect upon China must be tremendous. . . .

Out of this war the United States must inevitably arrive as the universal arbitrator, not only in the affairs of this Continent and of Europe, but of the Orient as well. . . .

In looking over the European situation, although it is evident that Germany has thoroughly prepared herself for the present struggle, and has been preparing for it for years, I can see no possibility of her ultimate triumph. The Allies, fighting on the broader ground of liberty, and resistance to unwarranted aggression, certainly have all the moral advantage in their favor. I believe in the triumph of right over might, and that the Allies must win. . . .

As for the neutrality of China, I do not know how far he [Yüan] will succeed in preserving that. The Chinese people, as usual, will want to be neutral. . . . Unfortunately, the people of China, who wish to preserve strict neutrality, have no voice in the matter.[38]

In a private letter, Huang called the China policy of the Japanese government, by which troops were sent to occupy the German-leased territory in Shantung, "shortsighted" and "harmful to the future of the Yellow race."[39]

In New York, Huang was occasionally attacked in the press by Americans who favored Yüan's regime. The *New York Times* of November 24, 1914, published a statement given out for Huang by Professor Charles A. Beard of Columbia University. It was a reply to a charge by Professor Jeremiah W. Jenks, Director of the Far Eastern Bureau at New York University.

It is with regret and disappointment that I read of the unwarranted attack by my friend, Dr. J. W. Jenks, upon myself. Only two weeks ago he gave out a report to the effect that Dr. Sun [Yat-sen] and I were to be invited by Yuan Shih-kai to come back and assist in the regeneration of China. I denied it, and now Dr. Jenks replies to my denial by saying that I am a traitor, discredited and disowned by friend and foe. To an intelligent public it must be very humiliating to be treated with the doctor's glaring contradictions.

As to Dr. [Frank J.] Goodnow's allegations I will only remark that I have not had the honor of meeting that distinguished gentleman. But as he is still in the employment of Yuan Shih-kai and publicly stated last Thursday night that during his stay in China the liberal statesmen of China avoided him and he was thrown entirely into the hands of the northern reactionary party, it is hardly to be supposed that he has introduced into his study of Chinese politics a completely unbiased and unpartisan view.

It is lamentable that Dr. Jenks has declared that I am trying to raise money in the United States. I distinctly assured him, as he admits, that I am not. I earnestly request him to submit proofs that I am trying to get Chinese to subscribe a dollar a month apiece toward the support of a new revolution.

I do not find that Dr. Jenks or Dr. Goodnow denies that Yuan has established a despotic military power in China. . . .

As to the crucial question of the loan which Yuan is trying to raise in America, Prof. Jenks denies that Yuan's commissioners are seeking a loan, but he admits Yuan's dire need for money and says that any one who finds it will be amply rewarded. The distinguished doctor's admission will be sufficient for the wise American public. . . .

By keeping out of this loan the American people will not only maintain the respect of China but may thereby compel Yuan Shih-kai to abandon his despotic policy and adopt one more consistent with true democracy.

Taking advantage of the European war which had broken out in the summer of 1914, the Japanese government submitted its Twenty-one Demands to the Peking government in the middle of January 1915. Had they been accepted, these would have made China a virtual protectorate of Japan. Negotiations between the Chinese and the Japanese governments began early in February. By this time a rumor was being widely circulated in China, chiefly by Yüan's Peking government, that the revolutionary leaders were attempting to make use of foreign powers to overthrow their own government in Peking. In a long circular telegram dated February 25, 1915, Huang Hsing denied the charges and made known his political views on current events; this was the first important public statement he had made in two years. Although it was issued jointly by Huang and four other former military governors (Ch'en Ch'iung-ming, Niu Yung-chien, Po Wen-wei, and Li Lieh-chün), there is little doubt that it was primarily Huang's work. It was probably its moderate tone, its well-written phrases, and the sincerity of the writers that prompted a young Chinese student by the name of Hu Shih in the United States to copy it in full in his diary. Since Huang's public statements are rare and seldom seen, it may be worth while to quote it at some length. In the following translation, the word "we" has been substituted for the Chinese phrase "[I, Huang] Hsing and the rest [of the undersigned]."

My fellow countrymen:

It has been two years since we left you. . . . Since then the [Peking] authorities have done everything conceivable to smear us. Whenever there is trouble in the nation, it is always Huang Hsing who is to blame, and sometimes the rest of us are also accused of being involved. Recently the whole nation has been shocked and puzzled by the serious diplomatic pressure being exerted upon our country. Once again the rumor is widespread, both in and out of China, that we are trying to use a foreign power to overthrow our government. . . . We are obliged to make our position clear not only for the purpose of refuting the wicked men who deliberately invented this lie but also to prevent any foreign power from making use of it to threaten our weak government in order to obtain concessions from it. . . .

It may be recalled that China was in great danger [from foreign aggression] under the corrupt rulers of the Ch'ing dynasty. Our people arose and the Revolution of 1911 broke out. Although the purpose of the revolution was declared to be the overthrow of the Manchus, the real aim was in fact to save the country. If the nation could not be regenerated, what purpose could the revolution serve? After the unification of the North and South, political powers were concentrated in the central government. Within the framework of law, our party did criticize and restrain the government. In those days the Chinese people lived under a republican form of government for the first time in their history. It was inevitable that some of our party members should behave with unnecessary aggressiveness. We fully realize our shortcomings.

As to the war of 1913 . . . had there been any other way to reform the country, we would have taken it even at the cost of our own lives. At the time when we started to revolt, the outcome of the war was already a foregone conclusion. When we failed to crush the enemy with one blow, we immediately abandoned our efforts because we sincerely did not want our country dragged into a devastating war by our army, which could not possibly defeat the enemy. Therefore, we have a clear conscience even though we have been criticized by our own comrades for cowardice. If we did not want to fight to the bitter end even when we still possessed some real military strength, why should we be talking of another war now, when we have no foothold on our motherland and not one soldier in our command. . . .

As to the accusation that we are attempting to use foreign forces, this is the most preposterous of all. . . . We all know that the internal affairs of one's nation should only be solved by the people themselves; to rely on another country inevitably puts one's own nation in danger. This is only common sense, and yet we find it necessary to state it. . . .

It must be understood that a revolution cannot be forced by a small group of people; it must truly represent the popular will of the country. The Revolution of 1911 is a good example of this. . . .

At the present time we do not wish to outline vague programs or make empty declarations. We are willing to wait and see, as our people wish to wait and see, whether our nation can be regenerated by any means short of revolution. War is devastation. . . . Who would not agree [to wait] if it can be avoided? The condition of the state is such that any unwise move may bring catastrophe to the nation. We fully appreciate the thinking of our countrymen who fear revolution.

But the cause of a revolution cannot be found in the act of revolt itself; whether a revolution breaks out or not depends upon whether the government is good or bad. In this sense the Revolution of 1911 was not a success for the revolutionary party but only a defeat for the Manchu government. Our countrymen should know how much worse is the present Peking regime than the Manchu government. When we took part in politics, the central authorities [in Peking] always excused themselves under the pretext that the government did not have a free hand. The falsehood of that argument is not worth debating. But if that was so, what explanation can they give for the condition of our country today? Since we are now exiled from the country, the government should be in a much better position; and yet the condition of the country has been deteriorating to such an extent that the Republic exists only in name, and the corruption of power surpasses that of real autocracy. . . . In a word, the authorities of the present regime have only selfish aims, and under their corrupt rule everything is possible short of changing men into women or women into men. "Disunity in the nation" is a poor excuse for this.

While foreign aggression can sometimes be provoked by the international situation, fundamentally it is made possible by the corrupt administration of the victim nation. One-man rule does not appear in modern times not because it is impossible but because it is not good. . . . In our country today we see only one person. The interests of the nation and of the people do not count. It is not surprising that a foreign power can write off China easily as long as it can handle that man to its advantage. . . . What should be done about this will depend solely upon the wishes of our people.

Being exiled abroad, there is not much that we can do about it. Concerning the important national affairs that involve us, the best we can do under the circumstances is to make sure that no harm will be done to our country because of what we may do. . . . Of course, we will not shrink from our duties as citizens.[40]

Fearing that the Peking government, which faced both internal and external difficulties, could not resist Japanese pressure, many Kuomintang members and some of Sun Yat-sen's followers in the Chinese Revolutionary Party advocated a temporary cessation of all revolutionary activities against Yüan so that he could concentrate on resisting Japanese aggression. This was the position taken by the Association for European Studies.[41] This organization had been founded in Japan by prominent Kuomintang members who had not joined Sun Yat-sen's Revolutionary Party; most of them were followers of Huang.[42]

By late November, Huang had taken up residence in Media, Pennsylvania.[43] He wrote to Feng Tzu-yu, asking him to tell Sun Yat-sen "not to get rid of a tiger to let in a wolf." But Sun Yat-sen maintained that the necessary condition for protecting China from foreign aggression was the overthrow of Yüan's government.[44] In May, Yüan accepted most of the Japanese demands, and in spite of his repeated denials, a movement toward monarchy was definitely under way. These events seemed to argue the necessity of a "united front" against Yüan, and the revolutionists began to seek for agreement within their own camp. During the summer the two factions, the Association for European Studies and the Chinese Revolutionary Party, conducted negotiations in Japan, but they made no significant progress toward unity.[45]

The Chinese Revolutionary Party remained somewhat isolated from other political groups in China, but Sun Yat-sen still exercised his predominant influence among the overseas Chinese, especially in the United States. In Southeast Asia, however, he engaged in a bitter rivalry with Ch'en Ch'iung-ming and Li Lieh-chün for the support of the overseas Chinese; each side was trying to raise funds abroad. Sun's letters to his comrades in Malaya during this time are full of angry and bitter words denouncing his rivals. At this point it should be emphasized that although Huang Hsing did not join Sun's new party, he himself never planned to organize a party to oppose Sun; nor was he willing to do anything that might hamper Sun's efforts. The contemporary rumor that the Association for European Studies was intended to offer rivalry to the Chinese Revolutionary Party was unfounded.[46]

Thus, while the overseas Chinese in Southeast Asia were divided into two camps after Ch'en, Li, and Po had traveled there, a similar division did not occur in the United States, despite Huang's long visit there. The Kuomintang Bureau of the United States reorganized itself according to instructions from Sun Yat-sen in Tokyo, although the name of the party remained unchanged because of its legal status (in the United States the Kuomintang was registered under the name of the Chinese Nationalist League). The party members in the United States respected Huang as their leader despite the fact that he did not join the new organization. When the Kuomintang Convention of the United States was held in San Francisco in August 1915, Huang was elected honorary chairman.[47]

Huang lost no time in denouncing Yüan Shih-k'ai when he finally "consented" to become emperor. On December 14, 1915, two days after Yüan announced that he intended to restore a monarchical system and to be crowned as emperor on January 1, Huang sent a cable to the American envoy in Peking declaring his determination to fight for the Republic.[48]

To his friends who were preparing to take up arms against Yüan, Huang wrote from New York on December 18, 1915:

Now I am glad . . . that all patriots of our country will be able to work together for a common cause . . . although I am unable to return to China at the present time. . . . Regarding fund-raising in the United States, I will do whatever I can. The Chinese in this country have already started a fund-raising campaign, and I will tell them to remit money to you as soon as they collect it.

I have already cabled to the Diplomatic Corps in Peking, expressing our people's determination to oppose a monarchical system. I have also cabled to English-language newspapers in Peking and Shanghai expressing the same view. I am drafting a letter to a foreign government, its parliament, and its industrialists for the purpose of seeking their good will and support for us. As to the military leaders in China, I will write to those who may listen to me. I will try to win their good will and their support for you. . . .

There is one more thing I should like to say. The trouble with our people is their own disunity; too many of them are trying to organize their own followers to serve their own personal interests. As a result, numerous factions and cliques exist. This is a great obstacle to the progress of our nation at a time of revolution and national reconstruction. I think that one of the reasons which accounts for the prosperity of the United States is that during her war for independence from Great Britain her people and leaders were willing to sacrifice personal gains in the interest of the nation. You will of course appreciate the importance of preventing factional feuds before they start. . . .[49]

Eight days later the *Philadelphia Press* (December 26, 1915) published a long letter written by Huang appealing to the American people to support the Republican cause of the Chinese people.[50] About the same time the people of Yunnan revolted.

Yunnan was the first province to revolt against Yüan Shih-k'ai. On December 25 the provincial authorities declared independence and the military campaigns began. The credit for the revolt, which finally led Yüan to abandon his ambition of becoming a monarch, has generally been given to Ts'ai O, a Japanese-educated Hunanese army general. An examination of the accounts written by top-level participants reveals that two other military leaders, Li Lieh-chün and T'ang Chi-yao, were equally responsible for effecting the coup.[51] T'ang was the Military Governor of Yunnan; from his letter to Huang Hsing reporting the declaration of independence,[52] it is clear that Ts'ai and Huang had communicated with each other before Ts'ai's arrival in Yunnan in the middle of December after a dramatic flight from Peking.[53]

Huang Hsing remained in the United States and engaged in propaganda and fund-raising. In a letter dated January 4, 1916, he revealed:

I received a letter from Mr. Ts'ai yesterday. He informed me that other provinces in Southeast China have decided to support the action taken by Yunnan. I think the overthrow of the dictator will not take long.

Perhaps I, too, should have gone back to China to take up arms, but the European War is still going on and the only nation in the West that can help us resist Japanese aggression is the United States. Therefore I remain here in the hope that I may accomplish

179

something in this direction and obtain some financial support from the American government. Ts'ai is an able commander, and I am sure he will do his job very well . . . Of late I have been in great financial difficulty, because prior to the outbreak of the Yunnan revolution, I had remitted all the money I had, as well as all I had borrowed from others. . . .[54]

Having failed to win the support of foreign governments, Yüan now faced internal opposition; on March 22, after several postponements, he formally abandoned his scheme to ascend the throne. But he still hoped to maintain his presidency, and the war went on. On May 8 a military council was established in western Kwangtung with T'ang Chi-yao as chairman and Ts'en Ch'un-hsüan as vice-chairman. This council was intended to create a unified military regime in the South to oppose the Peking government; it was dissolved on June 14 of the same year, eight days after the death of Yüan Shih-k'ai.

On the whole, it was Ts'ai O, Li Lieh-chün, T'ang Chi-yao, and other leaders of the military council who played the key roles in overthrowing Yüan's monarchical scheme. Yüan's death conveniently finished their work. Politically, they were close to the Progressive Party and the Association for European Studies. Isolated from the other groups opposing Yüan, Sun Yat-sen's Chinese Revolutionary Party played a secondary role; its chief contribution was a few military actions taken in Shanghai by Ch'en Ch'i-mei and in Shantung by Chü Cheng. In March Sun was still obsessed with the idea of the loyalty oath to his leadership.[55] But within two months the other anti-Yüan groups in the nation had become so powerful that he was willing to order his troops to abandon his favorite blue-sky flag for the five-star flag used by other anti-Yüan forces in order to show a "united front" against Yüan Shih-k'ai.[56]

By April Huang Hsing had moved back to New York City. His residence at 404 West 115th Street became a favorite haunt for *New York Times* reporters, for while there, Huang received a constant flow of cablegrams from military leaders in China reporting the progress of the movement against Yüan Shih-k'ai.[57] In order to gain closer contact with political events in

China, Huang set sail for Japan from San Francisco on April 22.[58] To the Japanese reporters who interviewed him in Honolulu, he stressed that the war against Yüan would be continued until Yüan stepped down from office, and he denied any rift with Sun Yat-sen.[59] In order to avoid possible assassination, he left the ship shortly before its arrival at Yokohama, boarded a steamship prepared in advance by Miyazaki Torazō, and disembarked secretly at Yokosuka. When the representatives of Sun Yat-sen and Ts'en Ch'un-hsüan went to greet him on the ship at Yokohama, they found only Hsü Tsung-han and her boy I-mei in his cabin.[60]

Huang Hsing arrived in Japan on May 9, just a few days after Sun Yat-sen had left for Shanghai (April 27).[61] Sun had repeatedly asked Huang to return to Japan but without avail. Hearing now that he was on his way back, Sun cabled to Honolulu on April 24, asking the comrades there to relay a message to Huang; Sun wanted him to sail directly to Shanghai without stopping in Japan.[62] But Huang seemed to think that the political situation in China was not yet ripe for his return and he considered Sun's return somewhat premature. He also declined Chü Cheng's request that he come to Shantung, where Chü was commanding an army in the name of the Chinese Revolutionary Party; military men of other parties were also organizing anti-Yüan forces there and Chü was having difficulty controlling the situation.[63] However, Huang considered Sun Yat-sen's recent anti-Yüan statement issued in Shanghai "unselfish and admirable."[64] Furthermore, at Sun's request, he promised to negotiate with the Japanese General Staff on Sun's behalf for a shipment of arms which Sun had previously made an effort to obtain.[65]

On June 7, the day after Yüan Shih-k'ai's death, Vice-President Li Yüan-hung, who had come to Peking at Yüan's request in 1913 after the "second revolution," succeeded to the presidency under the provision of the Constitution of 1914, which had been promulgated after Yüan had dissolved the National Assembly. Huang Hsing vigorously denied the validity of Yüan's "private law." He declared in Japan that Li should succeed to the presidency according to the Provisional Constitution of 1912 and the Presidential Election Law of 1913, which were Organic Laws of the Republic illegally abrogated by Yüan Shih-k'ai.[66]

The dispute over the succession remained a matter of national importance until the end of the month, when Peking finally admitted the legality of the argument. In a telegram dated June 20, 1916, Huang answered questions from Li Yüan-hung on national affairs; he maintained that the restoration of the Provisional Constitution, the reconvention of the National Assembly, and the organization of a responsible cabinet were steps which the central government should take without delay.[67] These were the same actions named by Sun Yat-sen and other leaders of the South as the conditions under which the South would cease to make war against the North. Sun had previously asked Huang whether he would agree to the restoration of the Provisional Constitution and the reconvention of the National Assembly as conditions for a settlement between the South and the North.[68] It may be noted here that in endorsing this policy Huang had suggested that Sun "take charge" of affairs, thereby implying that he recognized Sun's leadership. At the same time he expressed the hope that their "unselfishness and impartiality" would be recognized by the nation.[69]

It appears that Huang returned to Shanghai from Japan on June 22.[70] There he remained, at 393 rue Ferguson in the French Concession, until his death four months later.[71] During these last days he and Sun saw each other frequently. They may have realized that their former rift had been caused by differences of temperament and method, but not of purpose; at any rate, their disagreements had not destroyed the mutual respect and trust they had developed during the years of comradeship. Now that Sun had ceased to insist on the oath of personal obedience and the fingerprinting procedure, it was possible to restore unity among the leaders. In fact, Sun was then contemplating a reorganization of the Chinese Revolutionary Party in order to make possible the return of those who had previously refused to join it.[72] When the National Assembly reconvened, the former Kuomintang members returned to their seats, but the Chinese Revolutionary Party remained in existence, abroad as well as in China. Clearly, something had to be done.

Sun's first step was to halt the activities of the Chinese Revolutionary Party. On July 25 the party headquarters (now in Shanghai) issued a statement calling for the cessation of "all party activities and affairs" pending a future reorganization.[73] Next, Sun ordered all party branches to resume the name of the Kuomintang. His third measure was to send Hu Han-min to Peking to consult with the Kuomintang members in the capital.

Unity among the Kuomintang members in Peking was urgently needed; although they comprised the majority party in the National Assembly they were without leadership. Huang Hsing used his influence to have Chang Chi re-elected to the National Assembly by Hunan province in the hope that he could bring about the unity desired.[74] Huang also thought very highly of Hu Han-min, and he advised his friends in Peking to heed the counsel of the former Minister of Political Affairs of the Chinese Revolutionary Party. "[Hu] Han-min went along with the Chinese Revolutionary Party," Huang wrote, "but he did not really agree with its policies. Many people have the impression that he is a critical, sharp-tongued, narrow-minded person. Personally, he may be so, but in matters of official business he is a hard worker, very sincere and very reasonable."[75]

Huang Hsing declined to follow the suggestion of some of his followers that he go to Peking. He still believed that he could do more for the party by staying away from the capital. More particularly, he did not want to be directly involved in Peking politics because it might affect his long-standing plans for developing China's industries.[76] During this time Huang seems to have been interested chiefly in education, city planning, and the development of commerce and industry.[77] These interests were probably developed during his two years in the United States. He took a pessimistic view of the Peking government, and correctly predicted that the National Assembly would be dissolved again when it no longer served the purpose of the northern militarists.[78]

On October 10, the fifth anniversary of the Wuchang Revolution, Huang Hsing fell ill. He seems to have had a stomach hemorrhage during the period of the Nanking Provisional Government, and he suffered from the ailment for more than a month when he was in the United States. This time, however, his illness was much more serious. His Hunanese wife and all the members of the family who had remained in Tokyo were urgently called back to Shanghai. On October 31, 1916, he died at the age of forty-two.[79] On the following day Sun Yat-sen sent the following announcement to all the party branches and members:

It is well known to our comrades that since the founding of the T'ung Meng Hui, Mr. Huang K'o-ch'iang [Huang Hsing] and I have been working hand in hand for the revolutionary cause. On the last National Celebration Day, the 10th of October, he suddenly developed a hemorrhage in the stomach. After vomiting a great deal of blood, he fainted for an hour. A German doctor by the name of Kelli [phonetic transliteration] was immediately brought in, and he said that the ailment would not be fatal. Later [Huang] had chest pains. By the end of the month there were signs of enlargement of the liver. At five o'clock in the afternoon of the 30th, he was vomiting blood continuously and his condition was critical. He was given an injection and the vomiting ceased. At two o'clock on the morning of the 31st, he suddenly began to vomit blood again. Another injection was given, but he died soon after.

K'o-ch'iang was by nature a man of sincerity and honesty, in the prime of life. Although we did not fight against Yüan Shih-k'ai shoulder to shoulder this time, I had hoped that we might cooperate and work together again some day. Alas! I am deeply grieved by his sudden death, which is a profound loss to the nation and a deep personal loss to me.[80]

The National Assembly subsequently passed a resolution to honor Huang Hsing with an official national burial. He was buried in the Yo-lo Mountain, Changsha, Hunan.

ELEVEN

CONCLUSION

HUANG HSING'S contribution to the revolutionary movement is difficult to assess in terms of his political thought; materials that shed light on his political ideas are scant, and Huang himself left no political writings. The most important sources of his political views are probably his speeches published in the Shanghai *Min-li pao* during the first year of the Republic, when his attention was drawn to the immediate problems of the day.

Like most revolutionists of his time, Huang admired Western institutions; he was doubtless also impressed by the Japanese example of modernization. Politically, at least, he gave little more than traditional deference to the masses, and in this he was no different from most of his revolutionary comrades.

Huang had some ideas about social reform, but they are not easy to categorize. He repeatedly stressed the importance of implementing the "Principle of People's Livelihood," a term he used interchangeably with "national socialism"; however, he also professed a high regard for the traditional culture of China. He believed that the new Republic should undertake social reforms simultaneously with political reforms, and he even advocated a revolutionary flag that symbolized socialism. But how socialistic his ideals really were is not clear. The Revolution of 1911 was primarily a political, not a social, revolution.

In accounting for the failure of the revolutionary leaders to maintain political power and implement a coherent program of reform, much could be said about the shortcomings of the Kuomintang, which harbored many opportunistic politicians from the very beginning. Still, its formation was a great political success in 1912. It enabled the revolutionists to capture a majority of the seats in the National Assembly, and thus gave them an opportunity of wresting political power from Yüan Shih-k'ai by peaceful means. Political control of China was actually within reach of the revolutionists until Yüan Shih-k'ai took the law in his own hands. With the Kuomintang functioning as something like a Western political party, a democratic system might have slowly taken root in China if Yüan Shih-k'ai, in the interests of national reconstruction, had been willing to maintain his presidency in a parliamentary government.

It may be argued, and perhaps more convincingly, that China in 1912 was not prepared to make a democratic system work. Huang was familiar with this argument, and he rejected it with characteristic idealism. In a letter to the editor of the *Philadelphia Press,* published in that newspaper on December 26, 1915, he said:

Considering the statement, "the Chinese people are not prepared for self-government," it may be conceded, and is only reasonable to expect, that the principles of modern democracy are not so well defined in the average Chinese mind as they are in the minds of Americans. But how many years has it taken the United States to arrive at its present degree of perfection? The Americans have been learning for over a century, and the great advancement in the art of government that the next hundred years will bring to America will, without doubt, surpass its progress of the past. How absurd if future generations should say that the Americans of the present day were unsuited for a republic. It would be equally absurd for your present generation to assert that your forefathers were unfitted to organize a great democracy. . . . The best and only school for democracy is democracy.

In any event, a revolutionary reform of government based on Western ideas was never realized; party politics of the Western sort were not given a chance to work. Judging by the subsequent events, it may not be an exaggeration to say that with the assassination of Sung Chiao-jen, the first real opportunity for establishing a Western-style democracy in China was lost.

It has been said of Sun Yat-sen and Huang Hsing that the "success of the Revolution of 1911 was due to their wholehearted cooperation; the failure of the Republic was to a great extent due to Huang's later disagreement with Sun."[1] This, of course, is an oversimplification. Without the historical forces at work it is doubtful that the Manchu dynasty could have been overthrown. As for the failure of the Republic, meaning the failure of the "second revolution" against Yüan Shih-k'ai, it cannot be attributed solely, or even largely, to Huang's disagreement with Sun's policy after the assassination of Sung Chiao-jen. The causes of the failure lay rather in the course of the revolution itself.

The Manchu regime collapsed too quickly; this was not because it was conquered by the revolutionary party (which had no army of its own), but partly because of Yüan Shih-k'ai's maneuvers and partly because the constitutionalists in the provincial assemblies quickly went over to the side of the revolution. The T'ung Meng Hui never had a chance to establish any real military strength in the North, and even in the South its control over some provincial governments was only nominal.

Chinese historians, too conscious of the fact that Yüan Shih-k'ai made use of the revolution to enhance his own power, have often failed to see that the expedient was mutual: the revolutionary leaders were just as anxious to make use of Yüan as he was to use them. And under the circumstances, their decision may be considered a fairly successful maneuver; the alternative would have been a prolonged civil war, the outcome of which could not have been predicted. The revolutionists succeeded in forcing a change in the form of government; after that, their fortunes began to decline rapidly.

Realizing that the revolutionists were militarily weak even in the South, and wishing to put the state on a sound political foundation, Huang advocated curbing Yüan Shih-k'ai's power by legal and peaceful means. When he realized that he had underestimated Yüan's ambition and ruthlessness, Huang saw no alternative but open resistance. In fighting against Yüan in 1913 the revolutionary leaders were without the powerful argument that had previously appealed to the people; they were no longer fighting an alien regime. The contemporary belief, both in China and abroad, that Yüan was an indispensable "strong man" considerably weakened popular support for the revolutionary cause. The financial aid and support Yüan received from foreign powers also worked against the republicans. In this situation, the disunity within the Kuomintang during the "second revolution" proved disastrous. A party under iron discipline and served by a loyal and well-trained army might have been able to fight Yüan Shih-k'ai effectively; but the methods required to maintain such effectiveness were incompatible with the republican spirit of the time and with the fundamental goals of the revolutionists.

The alternative to resisting Yüan Shih-k'ai was proposed by Sun Yat-sen. After relinquishing the provisional presidency, Sun exhorted his followers "to accept the role of a party not in power in order to promote educational and industrial enterprises that will lay a permanent foundation for the nation . . . [and] to let Yüan assume full political powers in the country."[2] To be sure, the pursuit of this policy might have avoided the conflicts that led to the assassination of Sung Chiao-jen and the ensuing "second revolution." But it was too much to ask that the revolutionists relinquish power and abstain completely from politics after the success of the Revolution. Besides, it is hard to imagine how the revolutionary party could have pushed through fundamental social reforms without having political power. It is not surprising that Sun's policy was rejected by his comrades as "fanciful and idealistic."

Most Chinese historians, influenced after the 1920's by the political theories and practices of either the Kuomintang or the Communist Party, have tended to criticize the outright imitation of Western political systems that was advocated by Sung Chiao-jen and many other Kuomintang members during the first years of the Republic. But what other political system could republicans advocate in 1912? Until 1917 the model for a new government anywhere in the world, even in Russia, was liberal democracy after the British, French, or American pattern. Huang Hsing, like every other revolutionary leader, had his shortcomings; but his faith in Western political philosophy and institutions at that time cannot fairly be counted as one of them.

NOTES

NOTES

In the following notes, bracketed numbers refer to sources listed in the Bibliography, pp. 225–46; roman numerals in citations may indicate either *chüan* or true volumes.

CHAPTER ONE

1. Huang Hsing's stepmother died in 1929 and was honored by an official funeral.

2. The information relating to the family background of Huang Hsing was furnished by his eldest daughter, Huang Chen-hua, who has been a member of the Legislative Yuan in the Chinese Nationalist Government since 1948. It is contained in a letter to the author from Taipei, dated April 28, 1955.

3. [121], p. 1.

4. *Ibid.*

5. Huang Hsing's eldest son, I-ou, was born in 1893. A daughter, Chen-hua, was born in 1896. She is married to Ch'en Wei-lun.

6. [28], X, 1–3.

7. *Ibid.*

8. [33], pp. 7–13.

9. *Ibid.* and [78], pp. 71, 73, 86, 87, 106, 125, 157, 161, 184.

10. [30], XXIX, 33–34.

11. [33], p. 10.

12. Letter from Huang Chen-hua to the author, dated April 28, 1955.

13. [121], p. 1. It is commonly believed in China that calligraphy expresses the personality of the writer. In former times the ability to write well was the passport to a successful official career.

14. *Ibid.*

15. For an English biographical sketch of T'an Ssu-t'ung, see [89], II. 702–5.

16. For an account of this revolt, see [67], I, 70–89. Some Chinese sources state that Huang Hsing took part in the revolt.

17. *Ibid.*

18. *Ibid.,* p. 127.

19. [56], II, 114–15.

20. Letter from Huang Chen-hua to the author, dated April 28, 1955. The

Shanhua district was incorporated into Changsha after the establishment of the Chinese Republic. Huang I-chung was educated in Japan.

21. This chronology is corroborated by a directory of Hunan students in Japan published in [253], No. 10 (July 15, 1903). The record shows that Huang Hsing had returned to China at the time the magazine was published. It should be mentioned that practically all other Chinese sources have erroneously given the date of Huang's arrival in Japan as the winter of 1901.

22. [121], p. 1.

23. [70], I, 142, 146–47.

24. [110], pp. 188–89.

25. [70], I, 128–37, 143–45, and [67], I, 51. Publication of the monthly *Kuo-min pao* ceased after four issues.

26. [50], I, 486.
27. [70], I, 84–89, 151–54.

28. *Ibid.*, I, 192.
29. [155], p. 11.

30. [121], p. 1.
31. [80], III, 8.

32. [121], p. 1.

33. [253], No. 2 (November 15, 1902).

34. *Ibid.*

35. [221], No. 4, pp. 130–38.

36. *Ibid.* and [70], I, 155–59; V, 34–39.

37. For the regulations of the Association for Universal Military Education passed on May 11, 1903, see [221], No. 5, pp. 147–51.

38. [70], I, 162–65.

39. *Ibid.*, I, 165–66; the date is given in [105], I, 120.

CHAPTER TWO

1. An article written in 1954 by Chang Shih-chao on the *Su-pao* case is published in [62], I, 387–90. For an English biographical sketch of Tsou Jung and an account of the case, see [89], II, 769.

2. [253], No. 2 (November 15, 1902).

3. *Ibid.*, No. 5 (February 15, 1903).

4. The Chinese Educational Society was founded in 1902; according to one source, its purpose was to publish new school textbooks. Many modern schools had been established after the change of the educational system, and translations from Japanese textbooks, although commonly used until that time, were found inadequate for Chinese students. [70], I, 173–74. According to one of the earliest members of the Society, its founding members harbored revolutionary ideas. [50], p. 485.

5. *Ibid.*, pp. 489–90.

6. [37], I, 368.

7. [24], p. 233.

8. The text of the *Ko-ming chün* can be found in many publications, one of which is [164], II, 419–35. The writings of Tsou Jung were the first docu-

ments of the revolutionary movement to outline the fundamental principles upon which the future republic would be founded; they appeared two years before Sun Yat-sen put his formative ideas of democracy into writing. Tsou's book has been called "a synthesis of the modern political ideas of the West known to China since the Opium War." [167], pp. 50–51.

9. Letter of Wu Chih-hui to Feng Tzu-yu, June 8, 1943, on the *Su-pao* case; see [70], III, 174–82.

10. *Ibid.*

11. Chang Ping-lin was sentenced by the Mixed Court to three years' imprisonment. Tsou Jung was sentenced to two years; he died of illness on April 3, 1905, a few weeks before his term was to expire. Chang Ping-lin was released from prison on June 29, 1906. For the 189 telegrams exchanged among Ch'ing government officials on the case, see [62], I, 408–80.

12. [50], p. 494.

13. The note of introduction is reprinted in facsimile in [162], I. The note was not dated, but Ts'ao mistakenly dated it as spring of 1902 instead of June 1903.

14. [162], I, chap. 1; see also [123], p. 116.

15. [85], Part II, p. 91.

16. [121], p. 2.

17. *Ibid.*

18. [85], Part II, p. 91.

19. [25], pp. 137–38. Chang also recalled with dismay that he almost accidentally killed Huang one evening while cleaning his gun; see [24], p. 234.

20. [85], Part II, p. 91; see also [124], pp. 5, 7–8.

21. [121], p. 3. In [176], p. 100, the founding date of the Hua Hsing Hui is given as February 15, 1904 (Chinese New Year's Eve). The source for this date is unknown. I know of no other sources that give a specific date for the founding of the organization, and no original documents relating to the founding, organization, and programs of the Hua Hsing Hui can be found.

22. [121], p. 3.

23. Among the initial Hua Hsing Hui members listed by Liu K'uei-i were Chang Chi, Chang Shih-chao, Ch'en T'ien-hua, Hu Ying, Sung Chiao-jen, and Wu Lu-chen. *Ibid.*

24. *Ibid.*, p. 4.

25. *Ibid.*; but Liu and others mistakenly state that the attempted revolt was planned to take place on the occasion of the sixtieth birthday of the Empress Dowager.

26. *Ibid.*

27. *Ibid.*

28. [40], p. 55. On pp. 56–57, Chang lists forty-eight persons including himself as members of the Science Study Group.

29. [132], I, 553–54.	30. [40], pp. 62–64.
31. [103], IV, 4.	32. [40], pp. 55.
33. [164], IV, 1536.	34. [109], p. 238,

35. This conclusion is reached after comparing the subsequent events with the following records of participants: [148], entries for the 28th day of the 9th lunar month (November 5, 1904); [124], p. 7; [162], I, 1–3; [121], p. 5; and a letter from Huang Hsing's eldest daughter to the author, dated April 28, 1955. For the text of the official bulletin calling for the arrest of Huang Hsing and his accomplices, see [164], III, 676–77. Marius B. Jansen, in [92], p. 116, erroneously dates Huang's Changsha revolt in 1903.

36. [121], p. 5. 37. [85], p. 9.

38. [162], I, 1–3. 39. [40], p. 56.

40. [148], entry for the 11th day of the 10th lunar month (November 17, 1904); see also [121], p. 5.

41. [162], I, 7–8.

42. [148], entry for the 11th day of the 10th lunar month (November 17, 1904).

43. [121], p. 6.

44. [121], pp. 6–7. For the testimony of Huang Hsing and his friends and for the official exchange of correspondence regarding the case, see [164], III, 679–83.

45. [121], pp. 7–8. It is difficult to ascertain when this second adventure took place. Liu stated that he and Huang Hsing returned to China in March 1905, heard of Ma Fu-i's arrest in April while traveling in Hunan, and returned to Japan in June. In his diary, however, Sung Chiao-jen mentions seeing Huang and Liu (in Japan) quite frequently between January 26 and June 26 of 1905; he also states that on May 1 Liu personally informed him of Ma Fu-i's execution. It should be noted that although Huang and Liu first escaped to Japan before Sung arrived in Tokyo (Dec. 13, 1904), they are not mentioned in Sung's diary until January 26, 1905; from this, we might speculate that Liu's memory failed him and that he and Huang were in China some time between early December 1904 and January 26, 1905.

CHAPTER THREE

1. In a brief autobiographical sketch written for Herbert A. Giles in London in 1896, Sun Yat-sen stated that he was born on November 22, 1866. After a thorough investigation by the Kuomintang authorities many years later, that date was proved erroneous. [164], IV, 1194. But see also [105], I, 6.

2. [105], I, 45–50. Cf. [92], p. 61, and [141], p. 32; both Jansen and Sharman date Sun Yat-sen's trip to Tientsin as having occurred in 1893 instead of 1894.

3. For the text of this letter to Li Hung-chang, see [146], V, 1–12.

4. [164], I, 26.

5. [105], I, 55, n.13, and [103], III, 1.

6. [103], III, 16–18. Sun took $100 with him when he returned to Hong Kong; $1,040 (equivalent to HK$2,000 at that time) was subsequently sent to

him. His elder brother's "shares" were $200. If Sun Mei had contributed more than this amount, as is generally supposed, it is difficult to understand why it was not recorded, since all the contributions appear to be business investments.

7. Feng Tzu-yu and practically all the Kuomintang publications in the past have given February 21, 1895, as the founding date of the Hong Kong Hsing Chung Hui; for example, [70], V, 10. But in [105], I, 56, the date is given as February 18, 1895.

8. For a biographical sketch of Yang Ch'ü-yün, see [206]; [70], I, 6–8; [196], p. 55. Yang's father, a native of Fukien province, was born in Penang, returned to China when he was about sixteen, and then settled in Hong Kong.

9. [205], p. 8.

10. For an analysis of the Fu-jen Wen-she, see [171].

11. Tse Tsan Tai was born in Sydney, Australia, on May 16, 1872, six years after his parents (natives of Kwangtung province) had immigrated there. He received his elementary education at the Grafton High School. At seven he was baptized (in old age, he called himself a "Christian" and "also a staunch supporter of Confucius and his teachings"). At fifteen he returned to Hong Kong, where he completed his education at Queen's College (high school); he then entered the Hong Kong government service, where he remained for ten years, chiefly performing clerical duties connected with public works. See [205], pp. 6–7, and [198], p. 1.

12. Cheng Shih-liang was a graduate of a German missionary school in Canton. Having studied briefly at the Canton Hospital School, where he came to know Sun Yat-sen, Cheng returned to his native village in eastern Kwangtung and opened a Chinese medical store. Ch'en Shao-pai attended briefly the College of Medicine for Chinese in Hong Kong; he was probably Sun Yat-sen's closest friend during the Hsing Chung Hui period. For biographical sketches of both men, see [70], I, 5, 37–38; [197].

13. For the texts of both sets of regulations of the Hsing Chung Hui, see [103], III, 2–6. [141], p. 36, erroneously describes the regulations of the Hong Kong Hsing Chung Hui as if they were the regulations of the Honolulu branch; some Chinese publications also fail to distinguish between the two.

14. [119], pp. 48–49. Liu claimed that Sun Yat-sen personally revealed this story to him one day in the former's newspaper office in San Francisco. No specific date was given, but it was probably in 1910.

15. For example, [69], p. 16, and [195], p. 33.

16. [205], p. 10, and [196], pp. 9–10. Many Western sources have given September 9, 1895, as the date of Sun Yat-sen's first revolutionary attempt. For example, [141], p. 39; [45], p. 32; and [136], p. 15.

17. [164], IV, 1229.

18. [205], p. 9. On August 29 the revolutionists and their sympathizers met at a hotel, where the policy of the revolutionary government was outlined. Among the sympathizers were Ho Kai (Ho Chi), a barrister and a member of the Hong Kong Legislative Council; Thomas H. Reid of the *China Mail*; and Chesney Duncan of the *Hongkong Telegraph*. Reid agreed to work to create

sympathy and support in England. Later, he and one T. Cowen drafted a proclamation to the foreign powers for the revolutionists.

19. According to [196], pp. 10–11, Sun Yat-sen was at first elected, but was somehow forced to resign in favor of Yang Ch'ü-yün. However the defeat came about, it was a "great blow" to Sun and "always rankled in his breast." [205], p. 9. Up to this time the chairmanship of the Hsing Chung Hui was apparently open. Two dubious sources, however, give different versions. In [206], pp. 8–9, it is stated that on September 30, 1895, Huang Yung-shang resigned from the chairmanship in favor of Yang Ch'ü-yün. This is also stated in [203], p. 4, but with the variant date of February 21, 1895.

20. Memorial of Kwangtung Governor T'an to the Throne, reporting the attempted Canton revolt of October 26, 1895; reprinted in [67], I, 27–29. Both the scale and scope of the attempted revolt have been exaggerated in subsequent accounts. Several thousand rebels are said to have been mobilized, and the number has increased with each telling. For example, see [195], p. 35 (otherwise a careful study). For Sun Yat-sen's own account, written about a year after the event, see [204], pp. 20–27; it is significant that at that time he did not claim to be the leader of the revolution.

21. Sun Yat-sen did, however, occasionally pass by Shanghai and Hong Kong on shipboard; and on two occasions (January 1902 and January 1903) he stayed in Hong Kong for a few days; see [70], IV, 71; [205], p. 21; and [105], I, 108, 113. Many fantastic and fanciful accounts of Sun's adventures in the interior of China after 1895 have been written in the West. For example, an entire chapter in Bishop Henry B. Restarick's book, *Sun Yat-sen: Liberator of China* (New Haven: Yale University Press, 1931) is devoted to "The Unlucky Plan of Revolt in 1904," in which Sun was found at secret headquarters in Canton personally directing the plot with a certain Chang Chau. Restarick presumably obtained the information from Chang himself, whom he describes as "a public notary of the Territory of Hawaii." In [141], p. 102, Sharman gives (rather skeptically, perhaps) a full page to Restarick's "vivid narrative" of this revolt, and "corrects" the date to 1906.

22. Sun Yat-sen was detained in the Chinese legation in London on October 11, 1896. Thanks to his former teacher, James Cantlie, and to the British government, he was released twelve days later. His *Kidnapped in London* was written a short time after his release. For a source book on the episode, see [200].

23. For an autobiographical sketch of Miyazaki Torazō and the story of his acquaintance with Sun Yat-sen, see [202], pp. 117–83; also [92], pp. 54–58, 64–68. Miyazaki's book was first published in 1902. Marius Jansen, in [92], has ably given a full account of the role of the Japanese in Sun Yat-sen's career up to 1915.

24. [196], pp. 36, 41. Ch'en did not disclose the source of Sun's funds.

25. [202], p. 183; [196], pp. 39–41; and [105], I, 87–88. [205], pp. 17ff., mistakenly identifies the new organization as the T'ung Meng Hui, which did not come into existence until 1905. In his autobiography, Sun Yat-sen called the event a "merger of secret societies in the Yangtze Valley, Kwangtung,

Kwangsi, and Fukien provinces into the Hsing Chung Hui." [146], I, 36. This has been criticized by a Communist historian as "farfetched." See [93], p. 542.

26. About two weeks after the abortive revolt of 1895, Yang Ch'ü-yün fled from Hong Kong to Saigon with a price on his head. He then proceeded to Singapore, Madras, Colombo, and South Africa. He returned to Yokohama on March 21, 1898. See [205], pp. 10, 12, 13. According to [196], p. 35, Yang's arrival did not seem to be a very pleasant surprise to Sun Yat-sen. Nevertheless, Sun and Yang might have reached some kind of understanding on the leadership when they met.

27. [205], pp 16–17.

28. For the details of this attempt, see [199], pp. 315–16.

29. Letter of Sun Yat-sen to Hirayama Shū, dated July 24 [1900]. [146], V, 20.

30. [196], pp. 46–47.

31. *Ibid.*; [70], V, 16–22; and [202], pp. 260–67. The memorial of the Kwangtung Governor Te Shou to the Throne reporting on the Waichow revolt is reprinted in [194], pp. 10–12.

32. [196], pp. 52–54; [205], p. 20; and [70], V, 13–14. For the background of Yang's assassination, see [199], pp. 316–17.

33. [70], I, 39; *cf.* [92], p. 96.

34. The relations between Sun Yat-sen and K'ang Yu-wei, on the one hand, and between Sun and Liang Ch'i-ch'ao, on the other, have been discussed briefly in [199], pp. 314–15, and [92], pp. 78–80.

35. [70], I, 111–12. Feng also reprinted Pi Yung-nien's letter to Hirayama Shū explaining his reasons for entering the Buddhist priesthood.

36. [105], I, 104–47.

37. [70], I, 192–94, and [67], I, 146–47. Of the fourteen students who studied in this military school, twelve were Sun's fellow provincials; the other two were from Fukien province. In less than six months the school was closed down owing to the continuation of internal dissension among the students. For an article on the subject written by a former student of the school, see [103], II, 107–11.

38. [42].

39. [173], V, Book ix, 46–49.

40. [70], I, 218–19. Feng stated that Liu Ch'eng-yü also enrolled at Stanford University for the purpose of compiling the immigration regulations of the United States. The *Stanford Register* for the years 1903 through 1910, however, does not contain his name; of course, it is possible that he registered under a different name.

41. This account is based on an article written by Ho Chih-ts'ai, who played host to Sun Yat-sen in Brussels during Sun's trip to Europe in the spring of 1905. The article was written in 1925 at the request of Feng Tzu-yu and is reprinted in [70], II, 135–41.

42. [56], pp. 115–17.

43. *Ibid.*

44. *Ibid.,* p. 117.

CHAPTER FOUR

1. [67], I, 54, estimates that before 1900 the Chinese students in Japan numbered fewer than 100, but that the number increased to 1,500 in 1901. [70], IV, 104. The following figures, given in [71], p. 142, appeared in the *Japan Weekly Mail*: 570 in February 1902, 1,200 to 1,400 in 1904, 3,000 in July 1905, and 13,000 in September 1906. The figures given in [252], Vol. I, No. 2 (April 10, 1904), p. 45, are: 579 in February 1902, 1,058 in October 1902, and 1,400 in 1904. Of the 1,400, 249 studied at the Kōbun Institute, and the great majority of them were Hunanese.

2. [80], p. 13.

3. [70], II, 148; [103], II, 7; [178], p. 32.

4. [252], Vol. I, No. 12 (January 30, 1905), p. 455. In commenting on the report that the Changsha revolutionary attempt involved students returned from Japan, the editor of the magazine lightly dismissed the case, quoting an old Chinese saying which satirized the inaction of the traditional Chinese literati: "A Hsiu-ts'ai [holder of the first literary degree] who attempts to revolt will accomplish nothing in three years." *Ibid.,* Vol. II, No. 1 (February 28, 1905), p. 6.

5. [92], pp. 116–17.

6. [148], entries for January 27, February 2, April 20, and May 7, 1905.

7. [130], pp. 115–16. [92], p. 251, n.36, gives Kayano Nagatomo's version of what he takes to be the first meeting of Sun Yat-sen and Huang Hsing; but the Japanese text of Kayano's book describes the "first meeting after a long separation."

8. [148], entry for July 28, 1905.

9. [162], I, 15.

10. Unless otherwise noted, the account of the founding of the T'ung Meng Hui given in this chapter is based on the following personal accounts of the participants: [70], II, 146–51; [162], I, 15–16; [148], July 28–August 20, 1905; and [159], II, 2–5.

11. For the text of this speech, see [164], I, 44–46, and [146], III, 1–6. For an account of the meeting written by "Kuo-t'ing" (Ch'en T'ien-hua), see [239], No. 1 (2nd printing; December 8, 1905), pp. 68–76.

12. [103], II, 1, and [105], I, 151. The personal accounts of the participants on the founding of the T'ung Meng Hui are substantially the same, but dates and places vary slightly. The diary of Sung Chiao-jen, [148], is most reliable. For an able study of the subject, see [156], pp. 106–7. This was originally a memorandum submitted to the Kuomintang in 1936 by Teng, who was also present at those meetings. [109], pp. 239–41, uses direct quotes from Sung's diary without noting that the dates recorded in the diary after Sung's arrival in Japan are in Western style. This accounts for the erroneous dates on the founding of the T'ung Meng Hui given in the Teng and Ingalls translation of Li's book, [110], p. 203.

13. For the complete text of the T'ung Meng Hui's regulations as amended in the spring of 1906, see [103], II, 98–100.

14. For a study of the origin and meaning of the policy of "equalization of land rights," see [137].

15. The term "Shu-wu" nowadays signifies an unimportant position with miscellaneous duties. Teng and Ingalls, in [110], p. 203, render it "treasurer." 16. For the lists of the names of the T'ung Meng Hui officers in the three departments, see [159], pp. 3–4, and [70], II, 150–51. Both T'ien and Feng were officers of the Reviewing Department.

17. [103], II, 18–77. The record also indicates the following membership in 1906, by provinces: 127 from Szechwan; Anhwei, 59; Kiangsu, 36; Chekiang, 20; Yunnan, 21; Fukien, 10; Kiangsi, 8; Shantung, 53; Chihli, 35; Shansi, 55; Shensi, 4; Kweichow, 8; and Honan, 9.

18. [70], IV, 25–65. This is a revision of an earlier list, [70], III, 31–122, in which Feng listed many others who belonged to other organizations. Even in this revised list Feng included some persons who were probably no more than sympathizers with the revolution.

19. [146], II, 88.

20. Hu Han-min was born in Canton in 1879. His father, who was a government official or clerk, died when Hu was twelve years old. When his mother died, two years later, the family was so poor that the funeral had to be postponed for two months for lack of money. Three of his four brothers and one of his two sisters died of malnutrition. Hu made a meager income as private tutor. In 1902 he passed the provincial examination with the *Chü-jen* degree. In 1903 he sailed to Japan and enrolled at the Kōbun Institute, where Huang Hsing was then studying. He returned to China after three months. [80], III, 1–13.

Wang Ching-wei was born in Kwangtung in 1883 and took his first degree, the *Hsiu-ts'ai*, in 1902. In 1904 he was sent by the provincial government to study in Japan, along with a group of students which included Hu Han-min. He and Hu studied at the School of Public Law and Government in Tokyo. Wang was graduated in 1906. [153], pp. 14–19. According to T'ang, Wang came to Japan in 1903, but Hu Han-min dated his departure with Wang from China as 1904. [80], III, 10.

21. [152], p. 55.

22. [154], p. 10. According to Chang Chi, the organization of the Restoration Society was begun by Chang Ping-lin in June 1903, shortly before his arrest; see [24], p. 40.

23. [154], p. 21.

24. [152], p. 49.

25. For the text of the manifesto and regulations of the Lung Hua Hui drafted by T'ao Ch'eng-chang early in 1904, see [62], I, 534–44.

26. [70], II, 152–53; IV, 156–57.

27. *Ibid.*, IV, 156–81.

28. [148], August 20, 27, 28, 1905; September 20, 21, 1905.

29. [80], III, 16.

30. *Ibid.*

199

31. The text of this editorial can also be found in [164], II, 438–39, and [146], VI, 236–38.

32. [127], pp. 78–89, first published in the Nanking [224], Vol. VII, No. 7 (June 1932). "Man-hua" was a pseudonym of T'ang Tseng-pi, assistant editor of the *Min-pao* in 1908. *Cf.* [92], p. 119, which gives February 1906 as the publication date of the first issue. [70], II, 154, and [105], I, 156, give November 17, 1905, as the date of first publication. According to [162], I, 17, the first issues of the journal were printed in five thousand copies: two thousand for the Chinese students in Japan, and three thousand for circulation in China.

33. [127], pp. 79, 91. The text of Hu Han-min's article can also be found in [164], II, 446–55. According to [24], p. 235, cooperation between the Chinese and the Japanese people was really not a policy advocated by the T'ung Meng Hui, but an expedient policy under the circumstances. But Chang wrote his memoir during the Sino-Japanese war, and perhaps was influenced by the political atmosphere of the time.

34. [127], pp. 79–80.

35. There are still quite a few articles published in the *Min-pao* under pseudonyms whose authors cannot be identified; see [127], pp. 87–90.

36. For example, [152], p. 49: the T'ung Meng Hui "would have been an unworkable organization but for the overpowering personality of Sun Yat-sen." See also [128], p. 103.

37. [80], p. 21; also [70], I, 28.

38. [148], February 28, 1907.

39. [80], pp. 21–22.

40. In 1928 this three-colored flag was finally adopted as the national flag of the Republic of China by the newly established Nationalist Government at Nanking. Before that time, several flags were used. In the Wuchang revolution of 1911 the Hupeh revolutionaries used the eighteen-starred flag. The revolutionists in Shanghai used a five-starred flag. The Kwangtung revolutionary government used the three-colored flag favored by Sun, but Ch'en Ch'iung-ming used the "well-field" flag in the eastern part of the province. In the early days of the Republic the five-starred flag became the national flag, the eighteen-starred flag the army flag, and the three-colored flag the navy flag; this use of three flags was approved against the wishes of Sun Yat-sen.

41. [70], I, 26–37.

42. The amount of money given to Sun Yat-sen by the Japanese government varies according to different sources. [121], p. 16, gives the figure at 5,000 *yen*; but [92], p. 123, gives the figure at 70,000 *yen*.

43. [189], p. 212. 44. [70], V, 125.

45. [80], p. 27. 46. [121], p. 16.

47. *Ibid.* 48. *Ibid.* and [67], I, 201–2.

49. [36], p. 524. Chang Huang-ch'i came to know T'ao Ch'eng-chang in 1907.

50. *Ibid.* The fifteenth issue of the *Min-pao* (July 5, 1907) published an announcement of Chang Chi proposing the formation of the Socialism Study Group. Chang was also interested in anarchism and translated certain works

on the subject. The twentieth issue of the *Min-pao* (April 25, 1908) published an introduction by Chang Ping-lin to the works of Chang Chi.

51. [70], V, 72.
52. [67], III, 149.
53. [127], pp. 83–84.
54. The circular statement was reprinted in part by the Paris *Le Siècle Nouveau* (*Hsin shih-chi*), January 22, 1910.
55. [100], p. 532.
56. Quoted by the Paris *Le Siècle Nouveau,* November 13, 1909.
57. [36], p. 525.
58. This is based on the reminiscences of Yang Chao-jung, who saw Huang Hsing in Semarang; see [225], No. 19 (No. 2 of 1958), p. 40.
59. Letter from Hu Han-min to the T'ung Meng Hui members in Southeast Asia in answer to charges against Sun Yat-sen; reprinted in part in [164], I, 120, n.5.
60. Seven letters from Sun Yat-sen to Wu Chih-hui, August 1909 to January 3, 1910, in [146], V, 82–90. In these letters Sun answered the charges against him and requested Wu to make a vigorous counterattack on his behalf; Wu was then publishing *Le Siècle Nouveau* in Paris, and he was known to be antagonistic to Chang Ping-lin.

CHAPTER FIVE

1. Huang Hsing believed that the secret societies, although unreliable in the long run, were useful in the initial stages of an uprising; see [135].
2. [105], I, 155.
3. [70], IV, 156.
4. [121], p. 9.
5. [184], p. 45.
6. *Ibid.* The same source indicates that Huang Hsing arrived in Singapore from Penang on July 12, 1906. (This assumes that Chang followed the lunar calendar in his diary.) It appears that Huang Hsing traveled through Malaya in the summer of that year.
7. [40], pp. 81–82. Chang lists 128 persons as members of the Society for the Daily Increase of Knowledge; *ibid.,* pp. 89–92.
8. [67], II, 98, and [103], IV, 6.
9. [148], September 17 and 25, 1906.
10. [80], III, 18.
11. [168], p. 223. The various Chinese accounts on this incident are vague about the day of the protest. This article was originally written in Tokyo by a Chinese student on February 18, 1906. Also see [71], pp. 153–54.
12. For the text of the letter, see [162], I, 32–35, and [239], No. 2 (3rd printing, May 8, 1906), pp. 1–10. An explanatory note to the letter was published by "Ch'iang-chai," and Ts'ao mistakenly attributed the authorship to Huang Hsing instead of to Sung Chiao-jen. For a verification of the pen names that appeared in the *Min-pao,* see [127], pp. 86–90.
13. [80], p. 19.

14. For an account of the meeting, see [239], No. 10 (2nd printing, December 23, 1906), pp. 81–114.

15. *Ibid.,* pp. 83–96.

16. *Ibid.,* pp. 102–3.

17. Announcement in [239], No. 10.

18. [105], I, 167. Pingsiang was an important mining district. Liling and Liuyang were strongholds of Hunan secret society members who wanted to avenge the death of their leader, Ma Fu-i, who had been executed for the abortive Changsha revolt with Huang Hsing the year before. It happened that there were famines that year, and the workers and peasants in these areas suffered greatly.

19. [67], I, 245–56. For the official correspondence and memorial relating to the uprisings, see [62], II, 480–522.

20. [148], January 5 and February 15, 1907. At about this time Huang Hsing's eldest son, I-ou, joined his father in Japan. Huang asked Sung Chiao-jen to teach his fourteen-year-old son classical Chinese. *Ibid.,* February 20, 1907.

21. [105], I, 169.

22. For some of the English correspondence exchanged among the American Legation, the American Church Mission at Wuchang, and the Chinese Foreign Office, see [162], Vol. I, chap. 1.

23. [40], p. 83. Chang was among those arrested with Hu Ying.

24. [97].

25. For the testimonies of Sun Yü-yün and the others, see [67], I, 273–89.

26. Hunan Governor Ts'en Ch'un-hsüan's Memorial to the Throne, dated January 30, 1907, reprinted in [67], I, 261–62.

27. [103], IV, 6. For the official offer of the reward posted by Governor-General Chang Chih-tung, see [67], I, 259–61.

28. For the testimony of Hsü Hsi-lin and his accomplices and for the official documents relating the case from the Ch'ing archives, see [70], V, 82–89; [154], Part III, pp. 6–7; and [62], III, 80–98, 112–76. It is interesting to note that Tsou Lu, in reprinting Hsü's testimony in [164], III, 728–29, changes the original testimony which showed some disrespect for Sun Yat-sen: "I do not agree with Sun Yat-sen and he is not qualified to give me an order to assassinate" is changed to "I do not agree with Sun Yat-sen and he did not ask me to assassinate."

29. [121], pp. 9, 14. For an English biographical sketch of Ch'iu Chin, see [89], I, 169–71. For Ch'iu Chin's testimony dated July 13, 1907, as well as the testimony of her comrades and the official correspondence and memorials concerning the case, see [103], Vol. I, Part II, pp. 1–44.

30. [105], I, 175.

31. The conflicting sources are the autobiography of Hu Han-min, [80], and Feng Tzu-yu, [67], I, 179, and [70], III, 236. Hu Han-min says that Huang left Japan two days before Sun did, or March 2, 1907. Feng says that Huang and Sun arrived in Hong Kong about March 15, 1907, and that whereas

Sun went on to Annam, Huang remained in Hong Kong for a few days and then returned to Japan. It is possible that Feng simply misdated a description of Huang's trip to Hong Kong in early January of 1907; in Hu's autobiography, the character for "months" could easily have been misprinted as "days," so that Hu also may have meant to refer to Huang's January trip.

32. [105], I, 177–81; *cf.* [141], p. 102, which dates the "third attempt" in 1906 and states that its objective was the "Viceroy's yamen" [office] in Canton.

33. See [70], IV, 189; V, 125.

34. For the imperial edict of October 3, 1907, condemning the Kwangtung governor on the loss of Fangcheng, see [70], V, 122–23.

35. [70], V, 120–21, and Sun Yat-sen's letter to Teng Tse-ju, dated October 8, 1907, reporting the battles. In this letter Sun stated that the revolutionary forces had 20,000 men. The exaggeration was probably due to a desire to make a good impression while fund-raising. [192], pp. 5–7.

36. [146], II, 91; the translation, with minor changes by the present author, is from [76], pp. 68–69.

37. The dates given here are based on [91], pp. 35–71. Kyōkichi's account, originally published in the Osaka *Asahi* in May and June of 1908, seems more reliable than the later accounts by Feng, in [70], V, 136–37, and by Hu Han-min, in [80], p. 23, and [70], V, 215–19. For a Chinese translation of reports on the Chengnankuan campaign issued by the French press in Tonkin, see [70], V, 139–40.

38. [105], I, 194. See also [70], V, 140–43, and [189].

39. Sun Yat-sen's preface (dated June 1908) to [91].

40. Letter of Sun Yat-sen to Teng Tse-ju, dated March 7, 1908, [192], pp. 8–9.

41. [151], p. 37. T'an Jen-feng, a schoolteacher in Hunan, took part in Huang Hsing's attempted Changsha revolt in 1904 and joined the T'ung Meng Hui in Tokyo in 1906.

42. [189], p. 223.

43. [151], p. 37.

44. [70], V, 144–48. The Hong Kong *Chung-kuo jih-pao* had a correspondent in Huang Hsing's forces. Feng was then concurrently in charge of that newspaper.

45. [146], II, 91; the translation is from [76], p. 69, with minor changes by the present author.

46. Letter of Hu Han-min to Sun Yat-sen, dated April 24, 1908, reprinted in [70], V, 149–56.

47. [70], V, 146.

48. [121], p. 19.

49. Letter of Hu Han-min to Sun Yat-sen, dated April 24, 1908, in [70], V, 153. The letter was based on an oral report by Huang Hsing's lieutenant in the army, who had retreated to Hanoi before Huang did.

50. Sun Yat-sen called this campaign, like all the previous ones, "my" seventh attempt. Leonard Hsü has it translated as "our" attempt, but this does

not correspond to the original text. For Kuo Jen-chang's report to the Governor-General of Kwangtung and Kwangsi concerning the campaign, see [70], V, 47–48.

51. [70], V, 47; also Hu Han-min's letter to Sun Yat-sen, dated April 24, 1908, reprinted in [70], V, 149–56.

52. Hu Han-min's letter to Sun Yat-sen, dated May 8, 1908, and Sun Yat-sen's letter of May 20, 1908, to Teng Tse-ju; see [192], pp. 12–18.

53. [70], V, 161.

54. [80], pp. 24–25; [189], pp. 224–27.

55. [146], II, 91.

56. In the preface to [67] Feng Tzu-yu points out that Sun Yat-sen's autobiography, in describing the Hokow campaign, makes it appear that Huang Hsing never set foot in Hokow. For official documents from the Ch'ing archives relating to the revolt, see [62], III, 269–320.

57. [141], p. 110.

58. The twenty letters written by Sun Yat-sen to Teng Tse-ju and other overseas Chinese comrades in Malaya between the fall of 1907 and the end of 1908 were primarily concerned with fund-raising. See [192], pp. 5–26.

59. Two letters from Sun Yat-sen to Teng Tse-ju, dated November 10, 1908, and December 19, 1908, respectively, in [192], pp. 24–26.

60. *Ibid.*, p. 22, and [105], I, 206.

61. Wang Ching-wei's letter to Teng Tse-ju, dated January 10, 1910, in *ibid.*, pp. 32–34.

62. Sun Yat-sen's letters to Teng Tse-ju, dated November 10, 1908, and December 19, 1908, respectively, in [192], pp. 24–26.

63. Sun Yat-sen's letter to Teng Tse-ju, dated April 6, 1909, in *ibid.*, pp. 27–28.

64. [105], I, 214.

65. [151], p. 39.

66. [127], pp. 83–84.

67. *Ibid.*

68. [146], V, 70.

69. [151], p. 40.

70. *Ibid.*

71. [121], pp. 20–21.

72. The testimony of Hsiung Ch'eng-chi, reprinted in [67], III, 142–46. For an annotation of the testimony by Ch'ien Ch'ao-hsiang, see [62], III, 240–43.

73. [121], pp. 20–21.

74. [164], I, 77–78; III, 784.

75. Letter from Wang Ching-wei to Sun Yat-sen, dated January 11, 1910, in [67], III, 150–53; Wang to Hu Han-min, dated May 8, 1909, in [170], I, 247–51; and Wang's letter to his comrades in Southeast Asia, dated December 27, 1909, *ibid.*, pp. 255–58. In some sources the last letter is dated December 22, 1909.

76. [67], III, 149–50.

77. [70], IV, 158–59; but Hu Han-min gives the number of converted soldiers as 3,000. [103], III, 32–33.

78. About the loan of 500 *yen,* see Huang Hsing's letter to Kayano Naga-

tomo, dated [January] 25, [1910], in [9], Part I, pp. 20–25. *Cf.* the editor's note, *ibid.*, Part II, p. 9, which takes the date as being from the old-style calendar and converts it to March 6, 1910. The date of Huang's arrival in Hong Kong is given in his letter to Miyazaki Torazō of February 4, 1910, in *ibid.*, Part I, pp. 28–30.

79. [70], IV, 159.

80. *Ibid.*, IV, 173–75.

81. Letter from Huang Hsing to Miyazaki Torazō, April 28, 1910, in [9], Part II, p. 11; also [80], pp. 31–33, and [164], Vol. III, chap. 20. The best non-revolutionary source on the Canton army riot is [108].

CHAPTER SIX

1. The Canton Revolution of 1911 occurred on the 29th day of the 3rd lunar month in the old-style calendar, and March 29 became the national memorial day instead of its Western calendar equivalent, April 27.

2. [80], p. 34.

3. [9], Part I, pp. 1–18.

4. Hu Han-min's note of January 20, 1928, in [9], Part II, p. 6. The letter was preserved by a piece of luck. According to the note by Chü Cheng, it was accidentally found many years later in a wastepaper basket among other discarded documents in the Kuomintang headquarters at 44 rue Vallon, Shanghai, where voluminous and uncatalogued party archives were kept from 1916 to 1928. [250], No. 4, pp. 3–4. Yang Shu-k'an, a leading party member, stated in 1932: "Huang Hsing's great planning can be seen from this letter. To those who may think that Sun Yat-sen's contribution to the revolution was merely his earliest advocacy and that he did less [for the movement] than Huang, this letter can show that the two leaders really worked together and shared the credit for founding the Republic together." *Ibid.* Huang's letter was dated the "5th day of the 4th month," so the equivalent in Western style would be May 13, 1910; but the editor [9], Part II, p. 5, renders it as May 22, 1910.

5. Letter from Sun Yat-sen to his comrades in New York, dated June 22, 1910. [146], V, 106–7. In a letter written about the same time to his comrades in Hawaii, Sun stated that he had arrived in Japan on the morning of June 10, 1910. *Ibid.*, p. 103.

6. [95], pp. 381–83. [92], p. 251 n.36, presents this as the first meeting between Huang Hsing and Sun Yat-sen.

7. For Lü Chih-i's own account, see [164], IV, 1421–26.

8. Letter of Sun Yat-sen to Teng Tse-ju, dated July 14, 1910, in [192], pp. 74–75. Sun Yat-sen's mother died in the same month.

9. After the reorganization new members were not required to pay dues, and the regular minimum fifty-cent monthly membership fees became optional. Letters from Sun Yat-sen to Teng Tse-ju, dated August 11 and 24, 1910, in [192], pp. 75–76.

10. Letter of Sun Yat-sen to Teng Tse-ju, dated October 28, 1910, in [192], p. 78.

11. [192], p. 37.

12. Hu Han-min's letter (n.d.) to Teng Tse-ju, in [192], p. 42.

13. Sun Yat-sen's letter to Teng Tse-ju, dated December 10, 1910, in [192], p. 50.

14. [105], I, 235.

15. Huang Hsing's letter to Teng Tse-ju, dated January 9, 1911; also Hu Han-min's letters to Teng Tse-ju, dated February 9 and 23, 1911, respectively, in [192], pp. 52-54.

16. [192], pp. 42-43.

17. Two letters of Huang Hsing to Teng Tse-ju, dated January 9 and 12, 1911, respectively, in [192], pp. 54-55.

18. [9], Part I, pp. 35-37.

19. Unless otherwise mentioned, the account of the Canton Revolution of March 29, 1911, is based on the following sources: letter (n.d.) of Huang Hsing to the comrades abroad reporting on the Canton Revolution, in [9], Part II, pp. 19-22; Huang Hsing and Hu Han-min, "Joint Report on the Canton Revolution of 1911," in [9], Part I, pp. 57-75; Huang Hsing's speech delivered on March 29, 1912, in Nanking at the first anniversary of the Canton Revolution, reprinted in [232], No. 5, pp. 7-8, and [165].

The Joint Report was not dated, but probably was written in the latter part of May or sometime in June 1911. There are no records of contributions from Siam and French Indo-China. The estimated figure given here is based on the balance of the total expenses from the total contributions of other places and also the two letters of Hu Han-min to Teng Tse-ju, dated February 9 and 23, respectively, in [192], pp. 52-53. For detailed figures of each town or city both in Malaya and in the Dutch East Indies, see [164], III, Part I, pp. 805-7, and [165], pp. 13-15.

20. Letter of Huang Hsing to Teng Tse-ju, dated January 24, 1911, in [192], pp. 55-56.

21. [103], II, 23.

22. [9], Part I, pp. 45-47.

23. [9], Part I, p. 65, and the testimony of Sung Yü-lin after arrest, quoted in [165], p. 63. Sung was Chao Sheng's personal representative in Canton. His testimony was also reported in [238], May 7, 1911.

24. For a biographical sketch of Hsü Tsung-han, see [70], III, 334-37. Hsü Tsung-han has generally been mistaken by Western historians as Huang Hsing's only wife. Actually Huang's Hunanese wife was still alive in Changsha, and she remained devoted to him and his children although he was seldom in Hunan. After 1911 Hsü Tsung-han was with Huang most of the time, wherever he went; Huang's love for her seems to have been much in the nature of comradeship. Apparently the question of divorce was never raised in the Huang family by any of the parties concerned. This was not unnatural, how-

ever, since the system of monogamous marriage was not legally established in China until after the passage of the Marriage Law in 1930.

25. [80], pp. 39–40.

26. Some of these letters can be found in [165], pp. 136–38, 142–45.

27. Of the 85 rebels, who came from six provinces, there were nine Japanese-educated students, one Chinese-educated student, four teachers, one journalist, thirteen army men, fourteen peasants, three workers, thirty-one overseas Chinese from Southeast Asia (one of them a journalist, one a teacher, thirteen workers, and sixteen tradesmen), and nine of unknown occupation. In terms of known age, forty-eight of them were between twenty-one and thirty years old; the average age was twenty-nine. [122]. My finding is based on the eighty-five names listed in the last part of Lo's book, but it varies slightly from Lo's.

28. Quoted by Lo Chia-lun, *ibid.,* introduction.

CHAPTER SEVEN

1. For example, when Chang Yü-k'un, a leading member of the Literary Society and a participant in the Wuchang Revolution, submitted his "A Factual Account of the Wuchang Revolution Initiated by the Literary Society," written in 1935, to the Committee for the Compilation of Materials on the Party History of the Central Committee of the Kuomintang, his work was refused on the ground that the author claimed too much credit for the Literary Society. Some suggested changing the title of the book to the "Fourteenth Revolutionary Attempt of Sun Yat-sen." See Li Liu-ju's Introduction to the 1952 edition of Chang's book, [43].

2. [43], pp. 4–8. 3. *Ibid.,* pp. 12–17.

4. *Ibid.,* pp. 18–21. 5. [40], p. 166.

6. *Ibid.;* but [43], p. 11, dated Chiang I-wu's trip to Shanghai in the spring of 1909.

7. [43], pp. 11, 17, 21. 8. [84], I, 13–15; also [40], p. 179.

9. [157], p. 11. 10. [90], I, 2.

11. [179], pp. 37–38. For the declarations of the Common Advancement Society, see [225], No. 13, pp. 94–98; also [157], pp. 13–15. However, Teng's version of the "ten purposes" of the Society is questionable, although he was once chairman of the Society. According to him (p. 16), the Common Advancement Society also aimed at the return of foreign settlements and the abolition of extra-territoriality and unequal treaties. These were popular slogans in China after the 1920's, but they were practically unheard of in the Republican Revolutionary period. Since Teng admitted making slight changes in the declarations at the time when he wrote this article in the summer of 1955, it is not unlikely he distorted them somewhat.

12. [41].

13. [157], p. 11.

14. [160], p. 55.

15. [83], p. 7.

16. [40], pp. 189–90.

17. [151], p. 44.

18. [59], pp. 2–3.

19. [151], p. 44.

20. [84], I, 18.

21. [40], p. 63.

22. [43], p. 27.

23. [59], pp. 1–2.

24. [151], p. 42. In June 1910 T'an quarreled with Sun Yat-sen about party affairs when the latter arrived in Japan.

25. [166], p. 93.

26. [151], pp. 42–43.

27. Declaration proposing the formation of the Central China Bureau of the Kuomintang, reprinted in [40], pp. 209–10.

28. [9], Part I, pp. 88–95.

29. *Ibid.*

30. [59], pp. 19–29.

31. [166], pp. 97–98.

32. [59], pp. 35–36.

33. [90], I, 71.

34. [43], p. 24; but Yang Yü-ju, in [179], pp. 40–41, denied having made such a suggestion.

35. [43], pp. 25–26.

36. *Ibid.*, pp. 28–29; [40], p. 238, and [83], p. 16. According to [179], pp. 48, 50, it was decided at the meeting of September 14 to leave the commander-ship open for Huang Hsing, and it was in the meeting of September 24 that the compromise formula was offered by Sun Wu.

37. According to [84], p. 23, the revolt was postponed to the 9th of the same month. But [43], pp. 30–31, states that the revolt was set for October 11, 1911. It was most likely that no firm date was set. There was much discussion about starting the revolt on the Chinese Mid-Autumn Festival Day (October 6 in that year), but no resolution is recorded.

38. [59], p. 38. Before Chü's arrival in Shanghai, the leaders of the two revolutionary groups in Hupeh had cabled T'an Jen-feng, requesting his presence in Hupeh. T'an was then ill. On September 20 Sung Chiao-jen agreed to go for him, but postponed his departure when informed of Chü's coming. When the date for revolt was tentatively set, the leaders in Hupeh repeatedly cabled Chü to bring T'an and Sung to Wuchang. Sung agreed at first to go on October 7, but when the time arrived he declined to make the trip under some excuse. According to Chü (who did not know it then), Hu Ying had secretly informed Sung that the situation in Hupeh was not yet ripe for success. The truth of this allegation cannot be verified. In anger, T'an went to Nanking on October 8 and then set out with Chü for Hankow two days later. On their way they heard that the Wuchang Revolution had broken out. *Ibid.*, pp. 39–40; and [151], pp. 50–51; also [90], II, 18.

39. A biographical sketch of Huang Yü-ying written by Lü Chih-i, reprinted in [164], IV, 1421–26. Lü was one of the signatories of the Declaration Proposing the Formation of the Central China Bureau of the T'ung Meng Hui.

40. From May to June 16 (1911), the Shanghai *Min-li pao* published more than twelve news dispatches concerning Huang Hsing, whose whereabouts after the Canton revolt was much discussed. Some reported that he had been

killed in the revolt; others stated that he had escaped to Hong Kong and then to Annam.

41. [9], Part I, pp. 77–79.

42. The assassination of an important Manchu general, Feng Shan, at the end of October, 1911, in Canton was the result of Huang's careful planning. According to Hu Han-min, this was the most successful assassination in the history of the revolutionary movement because the assignment was carried out without loss to the revolutionary party. He credited it to Huang's initiative and planning, although by the time the assassination took place the Wuchang Revolution had broken out and Huang had left Hong Kong for Wuchang. [80], p. 41.

43. [151], p. 50. Lo Fu-hsing, the revolutionary leader of Taiwan, recalled that after the failure of the Canton Revolution, he went to Batavia, Java, in June to see Huang Hsing; Huang returned to Hong Kong on September 12, 1911; see [72], p. 47. If this information is correct, Huang must have taken refuge in Batavia for a while.

44. [9], Part I, pp. 84–87.

45. [70], I, 336.

46. [146], II, 95–96. This translation is substantially based on [76], pp. 77–78. The most obvious error in Hsü's translation is the rendering of "Hong Kong" as "Hankow."

47. [90], I, 29.

48. [183], V, 44–45. Kung Hsia-ch'u was among those revolutionists arrested in Wuchang on the evening of October 9, 1911. His article was originally published in 1912 with an introduction by Sung Chiao-jen, dated October 3, 1912, and an introduction by Chiang I-wu dated June 1912.

49. Ibid. and [43], p. 31. There is some disagreement on the date of the bomb explosion and the subsequent discovery of the revolutionary headquarters in Hankow. Some maintain that it was October 8, but the majority date it on the 9th. For a discussion of this point, see [112], p. 81.

50. For the text of the order, see [183], pp. 46–48; and [43], pp. 32–34.

51. [84], I, 25–30 (with a reprint of Governor-General Jui Cheng's report to the throne); and [43], pp. 36–40.

52. [146], II, 95.

53. [40], pp. 258–59.

54. [112], pp. 84–85.

55. Letter of Li Yüan-hung to Admiral Sa Chen-ping, dated October 20, 1911, reprinted in [40], pp. 324–26; [174], p. 825; and [74], pp. 92–93. Li Yüan-hung had the reputation of being on good terms with the soldiers. According to Wan Hung-chieh, he had been mentioned as a possible military governor as early as April 1911, in a meeting of the leaders of the Literary Society. [90], I, 121–23. Even if Li's selection was more than an accident, its connection with the Literary Society's meeting was probably remote, judging from the events of October 10–11. It might also be noted that the Literary Society and the Common Advancement Society were not yet unified in April 1911.

56. [63], p. 33, states: "Had there been no Li Yuan Hung, whose name

to-day is known in civilization everywhere, there would probably have been no Revolution."

57. Hu Ying was released from prison immediately after the revolutionists had captured Wuchang. He soon became the military governor of Shantung. Subsequently his position as head of foreign affairs was taken by C. T. Wang. This was the culmination of Hu Ying's revolutionary career. He later became one of the "six gentlemen" who supported Yüan Shih-k'ai's monarchical movement in 1915.

58. [40], p. 268.

59. [90], I, 16.

60. [75], Vol. I, Part I, p. 5.

61. Hsü Tsung-han's recollections, as told in an interview with a reporter of the Communist Chungking *Hsin-hua jih-pao* (New China Daily News), October 10, 1942, p. 5.

62. [40], pp. 312–13. [152], p. 77, gives October 20, 1911, as the date of Huang Hsing's arrival at Wuchang; [109], p. 317, dates the arrival on November 3; [126], p. 135, dates it November 5. The last two are obvious mistakes, because Huang Hsing arrived at Hupeh before the recapture of Hankow by the Manchu government troops, which took place on November 2, 1911.

63. [40], pp. 332–33.

64. [81], p. 64.

65. Unless otherwise stated, the account of the Hankow and Hanyang battles described in this chapter is based on [40], pp. 314–89, and [112], pp. 148–84.

66. Less than two weeks after he had captured Changsha, Chiao Ta-feng became a victim of a coup instigated by the conservative leaders and local gentry of the province. He died in his mid-twenties.

67. [162], II, 210–13. Ts'ao was not present at the meeting, but his book is reputedly based on the private papers of Wu Chao-lin; see [40], p. 312.

68. [112], pp. 147–48. But Li Shu-ch'eng, Chief of Staff to Huang Hsing in Hanyang, maintains that Huang's power and authority were not confined to Wuhan but extended over all the revolutionary troops of the South. [90], I, 193, n.2.

69. [59], pp. 69–70.

70. [16], XLIII, 14–15.

71. [40], p. 364.

72. [95], p. 156. Several Japanese volunteers lost their lives in the Hanyang battles.

73. [164], III, Part II, 920.

74. [112], p. 184; also [40], pp. 376–77.

75. [40], p. 379.

76. [112], pp. 147–48; [70], I, 349; and [109], p. 321.

77. [59], pp. 71–72. For detailed accounts of the revolts in each province, see [103], IV, and [62], VII.

78. [70], I, 348–49.

CHAPTER EIGHT

1. [113], p. 64; [80], pp. 52–53; [179], pp. 181–82; and [83], p. 48.
2. [112], pp. 184–85.
3. *Ibid.* Li Shu-ch'eng, Chief of Staff to Huang Hsing in Hanyang, is quoted as having said that T'ang Shou-ch'ien and other leaders in Shanghai requested Huang to come there. [90], I, 139, n.2. It should also be mentioned that the Hupeh army leaders made no effort to detain Huang, and that friction had developed between Hunan and Hupeh troops; see [59], pp. 77–78. Chang Ping-lin's biographical sketch of T'an Jen-feng, reprinted in [40], p. 213, errs in stating that Huang Hsing went to Kwangtung after the fall of Hanyang.
4. [238], December 2, 1911. According to the report of a Manchu agent, Huang Hsing arrived at Shanghai at 1:00 P.M., December 1, 1911. [62], V, 398. Chü Cheng recalled that one day he visited Sung Chiao-jen, who told him that Huang Hsing was coming to Shanghai from Hupeh. And they went to see Ch'en Ch'i-mei, Military Governor of Shanghai, who enthusiastically promised full support to Huang's leadership if, and when, Huang came. [59], p. 79.
5. [103], I, 1, 3.   6. *Ibid.*, pp. 2–3.
7. *Ibid.*, pp. 3–4.   8. *Ibid.*, p.4.
9. [40], p. 390.
10. [103], I, 4; but the date of the telegram is based on [164], III, Part II, 1009.
11. [164], III, Part II, 1010.
12. [116], I, 21–22. The text of this circular telegram to the representatives of the revolutionary provincial military governments, dated December 4, 1911, can also be found in [103], I, 6, but it is there dated December 1, 1911.
13. [164], III, Part II, 1012.
14. [116], I, 22.
15. For the text of the twenty-one articles of the Organic Law, see [164], III, Part II, 1010–12. According to this law, the provincial military governments had an important voice in the central government: the provisional president was to be elected by the representatives of the provincial governments, and the members of the provisional parliament were also appointed by the Governors of the provinces.
16. [103], I, 7.   17. *Ibid.*, p. 8.
18. [98], p. 48.   19. *Ibid.*
20. [238], December 17, 1911.   21. [98], p. 48.
22. *Ibid.*   23. *Ibid.*
24. Telegram from the Provincial Representative Council to Li Yüan-hung, dated December 16, 1911, in [103], I, 8–9. The text of the telegram can also be found in [116], II, 2. The telegram was probably dated December 18, 1911.
25. [98], p. 49. Ku Chung-hsiu was a representative from Chihli province. His account of the events relating to the election of the Generalissimo has generally been accepted by Chinese historians. It should be borne in mind, how-

ever, that politically Ku belonged to the constitutionalist group who went to the side of the revolution after the outbreak of the Wuchang Revolution. He seemed to believe that the reversal of the election was justified. *Ibid.*

26. [109], p. 321. These paragraphs do not appear in the English translation by Teng and Ingalls.

27. [116], III, 1.

28. *Ibid.,* p. 6; also [103], I, 9.

29. [146], II, 96; translation found in [76], pp. 78–79.

30. [76], pp. 81–82.

31. [103], I, 1.

32. The telegram reached Wuchang on November 24, 1911. See [116], I, 12.

33. [136], p. 42.   34. [105], I, 286.

35. [80], p. 54.   36. [105], I, 287.

37. [59], pp. 85–86.   38. [80], pp. 55–56.

39. [75], p. 7. Chü Cheng, in [59], pp. 85–86, states that the conference was held in the evening of December 26, 1911. It is probable that the discussion lasted through that evening and the following day.

40. [238], March 12, 1913.   41. [151], p. 59.

42. [142], p. 89.   43. [59], p. 86.

44. [101], Part III, p. 145.

45. Telegrams from the Provincial Representative Council to Sun Yat-sen, dated December 29, 1911, in [103], V, 10.

46. According to [113], p. 49, the representative from Chekiang did not vote for Sun Yat-sen; but according to [166], p. 117, the Hunanese representative, T'an Jen-feng, voted for Huang Hsing. The second version was more probable because T'an had strongly opposed electing Sun to the presidency. [151], p. 59.

47. [59], p. 87.

48. *Ibid.,* p. 88.

49. [80], pp. 57–58.

50. [24], p. 238. In Chinese officialdom, it was a customary expression of respect to greet a person by his first courtesy name followed by the word *lao,* meaning "old one."

51. [52], VII, 55–56.   52. [35], p. 171.

53. [98], pp. 65–67.   54. [27], IV, 5–6.

55. [35], p. 176.

56. For the exchange of telegrams on this matter between the Nanking government and Hupeh Military Governor Li Yüan-hung, see [116], VI, 23–24; VII, 2. Abrogation of the agreement providing for joint control of the Hanyehping Company was agreed upon by Sun Yat-sen and Huang Hsing by the middle of February 1912.

57. [16], IV, 12.

58. *Ibid.,* XL, 15.

59. [40], pp. 33–34. Wu Lu-chen and Lan T'ien-wei were leaders of the

Japanese-educated officers who had gradually gained power in the Northern Army without belonging to Yüan's clique. Wu had belonged to Huang Hsing's Hua Hsing Hui and had taken part in the initial stage of Huang's attempted Changsha revolt of 1904. *Ibid.*, p. 29; [121], p. 3; and [40], p. 37. Lan T'ienwei, it may be recalled, was the captain of the Chinese student army corps organized in Tokyo in 1903. During their student days in Japan Lan and Huang belonged to a small secret revolutionary group whose members were of Hupeh and Hunan origin. [112], p. 146.

60. In the words of the Imperial edict, Wu Lu-chen was accused of "instigating the army at Luanchow in the East, plotting with the rebels at Taiyuan [the capital of Shansi] in the West, detaining arms which were sent to the front, and attempting to block communications between South and North. . . . Consequently in less than ten days Peking was endangered and the Court was threatened." [16], XL, 62–63.

61. *Ibid.*, XLIII, 10.

62. *Ibid.*, XL, 46.

63. [112], p. 214. This is based on a Japanese consulate report of November 10, 1911 (3:00 P.M.).

64. For the records and documents of the peace negotiations, see [99].

65. [53], pp. 103, 106. Ch'ien was on the staff of Ku Chung-ch'en. For an account of this inside story, see [117].

66. This was revealed by T'ang Shao-i in the second meeting of the peace negotiations held on December 20, 1912. [99], p. 12.

67. Telegram of Sun Yat-sen to Yüan Shih-k'ai, dated December 29, 1911. [146], IV, 144.

68. For a personal account of the conference of the Imperial family to discuss war or abdication, see [62], VIII, 110–15.

69. [103], I, 51.

70. [80], p. 59.

CHAPTER NINE

1. [54], 1913, p. 496. 2. *Ibid.*, p. 497.

3. [142], p. 148. 4. [59], pp. 118–24.

5. [59], p. 154. For the authority of the Resident-General and the regulations of his office, see [238], April 16, 1912; English translations are available in [54], p. 498.

6. [238], April 16 and June 12, 1912.

7. Huang Hsing's messages to the army and to the nation upon his resignation, dated June 14, 1912. For the texts of the messages, see [238], June 17, 1912, and June 18, 1912; also [59], pp. 156–58.

8. For the text of Huang Hsing's telegram to Yüan Shih-k'ai (dated May 13, 1912) requesting the abolition of his post, see [238], May 15, 1912; also [59], pp. 154–56.

9. [103], VI, 126. It is interesting to note that in June and July of 1912

Huang Hsing sent a number of men to Taiwan for the purpose of recruiting local revolutionists; [72], p. 44.

10. [109], p. 380.

11. Letter of the T'ung Meng Hui headquarters in Peking to its Shanghai branch, in [238], July 1, 1912.

12. [113], pp. 87–88.

13. For the text of Yüan's statement published by the Shanghai *Shih-pao* (Times) on June 27, 1912, see [133], pp. 43–45.

14. [98], p. 105.

15. Telegram of Li Yüan-hung to Yüan Shih-k'ai, dated August 11, 1912, and the telegram of the Ministry of War of the Peking government to Li Yüan-hung, informing the latter that his request had been acted upon. The telegram reached Wuchang on August 16. [116], XIII, 8–9.

16. For the exchange of telegrams on the case between Huang Hsing and Yüan Shih-k'ai, see [181], VI.

17. [240], August 17, 1912, p. 133.

18. [238], August 19, 1912.

19. Wu Chih-hui's article in [238], August 28, 1912.

20. Wu Chih-hui's note on Huang Hsing's letter to Hsü Tsung-han, in [9], Part II, p. 53.

21. [240], August 31, 1912, p. 172.

22. [238], August 27, 28, and 31, 1912.

23. Telegram of Sun Yat-sen to Yüan Shih-k'ai, July 1913, in [103], VI, 2: "When I was in Peking last year . . . I told you that you were indispensable to the presidency in the next ten years."

24. [113], pp. 91–92. In a letter to Sung Chiao-jen, dated August 1912, shortly before going to Peking, Sun Yat-sen had expressed his plan of "building 200,000 miles of railroads in ten years." [146], V, 155.

25. Quotations from the Presidential Mandate in [54], 1913, p. 525.

26. [66], I, 123.

27. [238], October 7, 1912, p. 2.

28. [146], IV, 223; also [238], September 6, 1912.

29. [238], September 6 and September 12, 1912.

30. [64], pp. 258–59.

31. Unless otherwise mentioned, the source on Huang Hsing's visit in Peking is [238], September 12 to October 9, 1912. A brief account is also available in [125], pp. 160–65. The current press dispatches of Huang Yüan-sheng, dated October 5, 1912, and October 12, 1912, respectively, can be found in [88], II, 151–54 and 158–60.

32. [98], p. 107.

33. [103], VI, 127; [133], pp. 47–48; also [238], October 1, 1912.

34. Quoted in [23], p. 468.

35. [238], October 2, 3, and 9, 1912.

36. [155], p. 98.

37. [88], II, 157. The *Min-li pao*'s reports do not clearly indicate the day of Huang's departure from Peking.

38. [238], October 13, 1912.

39. *Ibid.*, October 12, 1912.

40. For example, see Huang Hsing's speech delivered in the Kuomintang reception of September 15, 1912, Peking; in [240], September 21, 1912, p. 235.

41. [131], pp. 50–51; also [238], October 28, 1912.

42. It is not clear whether Huang Hsing had ever secretly returned home during the interval.

43. Huang Te-hua, the youngest daughter of Huang Hsing, is married to the author. She had an elder sister, Wen-hua, who was married to Huang Ling-shuang, later known as Huang Wen-shan. It is said that Wen-hua's mother was a Japanese, but Huang Chen-hua, the oldest daughter of Huang Hsing, maintains that her father adopted the Japanese girl to cover up his revolutionary activities. Neither of the two versions can be verified. Huang Wen-hua was born in 1910, divorced her husband in the 1930's, and lived in Malaya in World War II.

44. [238], December 20, 1912.

45. *Ibid.*, November 30, 1912.

46. *Ibid.*, December 18, 1912.

47. [245], Vol. I, No. 44 (February 1, 1913), p. 1756; also the telegram of Li Yüan-hung to Yüan Shih-k'ai, dated January 14, 1913. Li argued for Huang Hsing against the Ministry of Communications, which attempted to restrict Huang's power as the Director-General of the railway; see [116], XVI, 10.

48. Huang Hsing's speech delivered in the Shanghai Kuomintang welcoming meeting of January 26, 1913; in [238], January 28, 1913.

49. [80], p. 56.

50. [178], pp. 48–49. It is interesting to note that the T'ung Meng Hui members were now explicitly forbidden by the Constitution (Article 10) to "affiliate themselves with any other secret society." For the English translation of the Constitution of the T'ung Meng Hui, see [54], 1913, pp. 663–66.

51. For the declaration proposing the formation of the Kuomintang, dated August 13, 1912, see [164], I, 126–28.

52. [146], IV, 222.

53. *Cf.* [164], I, 128–36, and [75], I, Part I, pp. 1–15.

54. [178], p. 59. The list of Kuomintang officers in [164], I, 141, is slightly different from the one in Yang's book.

55. [152], p. 121. Annoyed by the press, which talked a great deal of "Sun's faction," "Huang's faction," and "Sung's faction," Sung Chiao-jen denied the existence of any cleavage between Huang Hsing and himself. He was quoted as saying that no one in the Kuomintang who had a high regard for him did not also admire Huang. [88], II, 151–52.

56. In an article dated October 5, 1912, Huang Yüan-sheng wrote: "In the eyes of this reporter, Huang Hsing is a man of sincerity, frankness, and earnestness. His advocacy of a citizens' contribution fund and an unlimited issue of inconvertible paper currency clearly indicates that his political ideas are not applicable to China today. Although he may not have as clear and

logical a mind as Sung Chiao-jen, he is different from [Sun Yat-sen], who speaks in an empty and boastful manner." [88], II, 153. For Huang Yüan-sheng's four press dispatches on his impression of Sun Yat-sen, published by the current newspapers on September 5, 6, 8, and 10 (1912), respectively, during Sun's visit in Peking, see *ibid.*, pp. 115–31.

57. [80], pp. 57–58.

58. [88], II, 154–55.

59. See, for example, Sun Yat-sen's speech delivered in the Shanghai Kuomintang meeting of January 10, 1913, in [238], January 12, 1913. In [146], III, 106–8, the speech is dated January 12, 1913.

60. See the letter from Sun Yat-sen to Chang Chien, dated January 5, 1912; the exchange of letters and telegrams between Chang Chien and Sun Yat-sen relating to Chang's wishes to resign from the post of Minister of Industry; and the letter from Hu Han-min to Chang Chien on the same matter. [35], pp. 170, 174–77.

61. [178], pp. 60–61.

62. Huang Yüan-sheng's article of February 4, 1913, in [88], I, 54.

63. [163], p. 419.

64. Huang Yüan-sheng's article of February 26, 1913, in [88], III, 70.

65. *Ibid.*, p. 69; and Huang Yüan-sheng's article of March 20, 1913, *ibid.*, III, 87.

66. [163], pp. 418–19.

67. For a detailed account of the assassination, see [103], VI, 3–20.

68. [163], p. 420.

69. Huang Yüan-sheng's article of April 2, 1913, in [88], III, 95.

70. [113], p. 95.

71. Report of Kiangsu Military Governor Ch'eng Te-ch'üan to Provisional President Yüan Shih-k'ai, the cabinet, and the National Assembly, dated April 25, 1913. [103], VI, 21–23, where the editor dates the telegram April 26, 1913. For an English translation of the contents of some of the telegrams and letters quoted in the report, see [110], p. 287. For the text of the judgment of the Chinese Supreme Court which sentenced Hung Shu-tsu to death on March 27, 1919, see [103], VI, 24–29.

72. [103], VI, 24.

73. [163], pp. 443–44.

74. Two articles of Huang Yüan-sheng, dated May 31, 1913, and June 14, 1913, respectively. [88], III, 123–26, 141.

75. [155], p. 108.

76. [155], pp. 105–6; and [131], p. 60.

77. For the text of the contract, see [103], VI, 30–40.

78. [163], p. 451. For the text of Huang Hsing's telegram to the Peking Government, see [238], May 2, 1913.

79. In an attempt to reconcile the cleavage between South and North, Chang Chien wrote to his friends in Peking: "I have seen Mr. Huang [Hsing] twice. Indeed he was bitter and angry when Sung's assassination was men-

tioned, but there is not the slightest indication that he plans to establish another government in the South." [27], IV, 8–12.

80. [103], VI, 40–42. For the telegram of May 9, 1913, in which Li Yüan-hung to Huang Hsing and four other Kuomintang provincial military governors urged peaceful solution of the issue, see [116], XX, 15–18.

81. [155], p. 119. For telegrams from Huang Hsing to Yüan Shih-k'ai declining to accept titles and honors, see [181], III.

82. [155], pp. 119–20; also [238], May 18, 1913. Yüan Shih-k'ai did not order the ouster of Sun Yat-sen as Director of Railroads until July 24, more than ten days after the outbreak of the "second revolution." [155], p. 131.

83. Declaration of the Kuomintang, June 1913, reprinted in [164], III, 1040–41; and [163], p. 456.

84. [113], p. 95.

85. [88], III, 123.

86. Early in 1913 Li Lieh-chün had several disputes with Yüan Shih-k'ai over the appointment of the civil governor of Kiangsi province and the buying of arms from a foreign country. For the exchange of telegrams on these disputes during late January and early February of 1913, see [116], XVI, 16–21, and XVII, 1–8.

87. [24], p. 360.

88. [151], p. 14.

89. For the recollections of Kuo Chi-sheng, see [90], I, 96–97; also [151], pp. 71–72.

90. For details of the plots and later campaigns, see [106], IV, Nos. 3–4, pp. 615–69 and 819–50. For Li Lieh-chün's reminiscences of the "second revolution," see [102], pp. 89–90.

91. Wu Chih-hui's note on Huang Hsing's letter addressed to Hsü Tsung-han, in [9], Part II, pp. 52–53.

92. [103], VI, 45.

93. See, for example, [65], I, 23.

94. [245], Vol. II, No. 17 (July 26, 1913), p. 666.

95. The editorial of the *New York Times* of July 26, 1913: ". . . it is doubtful if all China can produce another statesman with the gift of organization and the personal influence of Yuan Shih-kai. He is charged with high-handed methods, but the country has been in a very unsettled state and the Chinese are not yet ripe for perfect self-government; . . . [therefore] his way may be wiser and safer. . . . In the circumstances the victory of Yuan Shih-kai seems to be desirable for the peace of the world."

96. Quoted in [131], pp. 77–79.

97. [242], August 1, 1913, p. 3. Huang Hsing's abrupt departure from Nanking has been criticized by some historians and defended by others; see [142], p. 117. [151], p. 74, states that Huang was tricked out of the city by his wavering staff, who falsely reported news from the front so that the city seemed in imminent danger.

98. The author has the original copy of this letter. In commenting on the

politics of the early days of the Republic, Ch'en Ch'i-mei argued that the failure of the Republic was caused by the failure of the Kuomintang members to follow the leadership of Sun Yat-sen. He expressed Sun's view so fully that Sun had it included in his own *Sun Wen hsüeh-shuo* (Philosophy of Sun Yat-sen) as an appendix. For the complete text of the letter, see [146], II, 66–72; an English translation is available in [172], pp. 147–66.

99. [146], V, 193.

100. [88], III, 170. The Peking authorities accurately predicted at the end of August that the war would be over in two weeks. *Ibid.*, p. 179.

101. According to [175], pp. 403–6, the Mitsui executive Mori Kaku wired his agent in Nanking during the "second revolution" of 1913, suggesting that Sun Yat-sen be offered twenty million *yen* and equipment for two divisions in return for the cession of Manchuria. It was alleged that Sun agreed after discussing the proposition with Huang Hsing. But Sun told the agent that he was unable to leave China and that he would designate Huang as his alternate to go to Japan to discuss the details. The story is retold in [92], pp. 165–66. There are at least two points in this story that merit attention. First, the agent was not present when Huang Hsing supposedly gave his consent to the proposition. Second, why was Sun unable to leave China at that time while Huang, who was in charge of the revolt, was allegedly free to go? The whole story cannot be verified from Chinese sources. In this connection it may be mentioned that according to Ch'en Ch'i-mei's letter to Huang Hsing dated February 4, 1915, Sun Yat-sen attempted to go to Japan personally before the outbreak of the "second revolution" in order to "make an alliance" with Japan to fight Yüan Shih-k'ai, but was obliged to give up the trip because Huang Hsing and other comrades were not in favor of the plan. The details, however, are not known. Ch'en's letter is in [146], II, 68.

CHAPTER TEN

1. [51], II, 67. An English weekly in Shanghai, *The National Review* [240], published the following news in its issue of August 16, 1913, p. 162: "After repeated rumours, it now appears certain that Chozo Imamura, alias Hwang Hsin, who described himself as the Japanese Secretary of the Chinese Legation, arrived on board the Unkai Maru at Mutsuri Island bound for Moji. There a launch which was waiting took him off and conveyed him secretly to Wakamatsu, where he is hiding in the house of a merchant named Yasukawa, who is known to sympathize with Hwang Hsin." When Huang Hsing left Nanking, his first destination seemed to be Canton, where Sun Yat-sen was to join him. While on the way Sun learned (on August 3) that the revolt in Canton had been defeated. Consequently, Sun proceeded to Taiwan and then to Japan. [95], pp. 202–3; *cf.* [105], I, 364–65. The *New York Times* of August 9, 1913, published a dispatch from Moji, Japan (dated August 8), reporting his arrival.

2. [51], II, 67.

3. For the English translation of the Presidential Mandate, see [245], Vol. II, No. 19 (August 9, 1913), p. 786. The date of the order is based on [54], 1914, p. 546.

4. [245], Vol. II, No. 19 (August 9, 1913), p. 760.

5. [155], p. 131.

6. On July 31, 1913, Yüan Shih-k'ai offered $100,000 "for the capture and handing over dead or alive" of Huang Hsing. The proclamation was reproduced in facsimile in [87], pp. 4–5. Sun Yat-sen was not named on the list.

7. [163], pp. 426–27.

8. [98], p. 152.

9. For the text of the order, see [192], pp. 116–17.

10. [98], p. 158.

11. [92], p. 170.

12. Letter from Sun Yat-sen to the comrades in Malaya, February 4, 1914. [146], V, 169–70.

13. "Manifesto of the Chinese Revolutionary Party, Sept. 1, 1914," in [103], V, 2–3.

14. [103], V, 3–5.

15. In commenting on the organization of the Chinese Revolutionary Party, Tsou Lu writes: "The character of the Leader [Sun Yat-sen] cannot be better revealed than by the Charter of the Chinese Revolutionary Party: the Leader was responsible for the Party, which rules the country. Those who say that the reorganization of the Kuomintang in 1924 followed the Russian pattern fail to understand that actually the Leader used the Russian method to fulfill his own personal wishes." See [164], Introduction to the first edition, February 2, 1929.

16. [146], V, 171–72. 17. [140].

18. [95], p. 204. 19. [58], pp. 82–83.

20. [9], Part II, p. 51. According to Huang Hsing's oldest son, I-ou, this letter of historical significance was lost after World War II. It had been kept by Huang Wen-shan, from whom Huang I-ou took it back at Chungking during the war.

21. [58], p. 86.

22. Letter from Wang Ching-wei to his friends, dated July 18, [1914 or 1915], reproduced in facsimile in [190]. Wang was then in Singapore in an attempt to reconcile the differences between the two groups.

23. [58], p. 86.

24. "Manifesto of the Chinese Revolutionary Party," [103], V, 2.

25. For an account of the welcome given Huang Hsing by the overseas Chinese in Honolulu and San Francisco, see [236].

26. Letter from Huang Chen-hua to the author. It is not clear when and where Hsü Tsung-han joined Huang Hsing in America. It was probably later in Media, Pennsylvania. Huang I-mei was born in Shanghai on May 4, 1913.

He was graduated from Chaoyang College of Law, Peiping, in 1932, and did postgraduate study in France. He was married to a daughter of Chang Chi and died in Shanghai in the spring of 1949.

27. [246], July 16, 1914, p. 1.

28. [241], p. 7.

29. [242], August 1, 1914, p. 10.

30. [246], August 1, 1914, p. 5.

31. [9], Part I, pp. 116–17.

32. For the text of his speech, see [246], August 16, 1914, p. 37.

33. [247], September 23 and 28, 1914.

34. [223], p. 3.

35. [118], pp. 272–77.

36. [242], October 4, 1914, p. 1; [247], October 12, 1914; and [9], Part I, p. 118.

37. For the accounts of receptions given to Huang Hsing by the Chinese communities in San Francisco, Los Angeles, Salt Lake City, Chicago, and New York, see [247], July 15 to October 20, 1914, *passim*.

38. [242], October 4, 1914, Section VIII, p. 1. One of the editors of the *New York Times* confused Yüan Shih-k'ai with Sun Yat-sen, and published the interview with a subtitle: "He [Huang Hsing] Predicts the Downfall of Dr. Sun Yat Sen, Who, He Says, Is a Despot."

39. Letter from Huang Hsing to Kayano Nagatomo, November 11 [1914], in [9], Part I, pp. 119–20.

40. [82], III, 615–18. The text of the telegram is also available in [247], April 1–2, 1915.

41. [70], III, 399–401.   42. [24], p. 421.

43. Huang Hsing moved out of New York in the middle of November 1914; see his letter to comrades in New York, November 16, 1914, in [247], November 25, 1914. He had probably been living at Media, Pa., since then.

44. [70], III, 399–400. Sun Yat-sen was eager to win Japanese support in his fight against Yüan. For an interesting account of the concessions Sun was willing to give to the Japanese in order to obtain their support, see [92], pp. 188–93. However, in this account, Jansen, in citing Japanese newspaper reports that Yüan Shih-k'ai had offered pardon and money to the revolutionists who would return to China to help resist Japanese aggression, gives the impression that Huang was one of those who "were taking advantage of the offer" and that Huang had returned to China by March 13, 1915. *Ibid.,* pp. 190–91. In point of fact, Huang Hsing did not return to China until the summer of 1916, after the death of Yüan Shih-k'ai. It should be mentioned, however, that Jansen's statement implies that those who ceased to oppose Yüan at a time of foreign aggression were the more patriotic.

45. [70], III, 399–401.   46. [121], p. 40.

47. [70], III, 397; also [164], I, 275. Sun Yat-sen's attitude toward Huang

Hsing is reflected in his letter to James Deitrick, dated August 14, 1914 (although Sun gave a different reason for Huang's not joining the party) : "I did not admit him [Huang Hsing] in the next movement, for his last flight from Nanking during the Second Revolution disappointed me bitterly. But as a friend and an old revolutionist, for he did a good deal during and before the First Revolution, I still regard him friendly so I ordered my followers in America to give him welcome, and I hope you will do the same if you should happen to meet him." [147], p. 9. There are reasons to believe that the enthusiastic receptions given to Huang Hsing by the Chinese communities in the United States were also spontaneous.

48. [103], VI, 58. 49. [103], VI, 56–60.

50. For a Chinese translation of this letter, see *Hu-kuo chün chi-shih*, in [233], No. 2 (April 1916), pp. 3–13.

51. Letter from Li Hung-lun, dated May 1943, to the Committee for the Compilation of Materials on the Party History of the Central Executive Committee of the Kuomintang; and Chou Chung-yo's speech delivered at a meeting commemorating the revolt, held in Chungking on December 25, 1944. For the text of the speech, see [103], VI, 92–98. The account given by Li Lieh-chün in his *Tzu-chuan* (Autobiography) (Chungking, 1944) can be found in [103], VI, 87–92.

52. [103], VI, 83.

53. Li Lieh-chün arrived in Yunnan from Singapore two days before Ts'ai O. Each then led a newly organized army in attacks on the neighboring provinces, whose authorities were loyal to the regime of Yüan Shih-k'ai. T'ang Chi-yao remained in Yunnan as its Military Governor.

54. [9], Part I, pp. 124–25.

55. When Po Wen-wei was reported to have arrived in Shantung, Sun instructed Chu to ask Po "in front of the Japanese whether Po would be willing to obey my orders. If not, ask Kayano to find a way to get rid of him." [146], V, 223–24.

56. Telegram from Sun Yat-sen to Chü Cheng, May 23, 1916, in [146], IV, 259.

57. [242], April 8, 1916, p. 16; April 9, 1916, Section 1, p. 15; and April 11, 1916, p. 10.

58. [247], April 23, 1916.

59. *Ibid.,* May 14, 1916. This report was based on the articles in Japanese newspapers in Honolulu.

60. *Ibid.,* May 11, 12, and 30, 1916. The stories were based on current Japanese newspaper reports in Tokyo.

61. Letter from Huang Hsing to Chü Cheng, May 19, 1916, in [9], Part I, pp. 126–28. [121], p. 41, states that Huang returned to Japan on June 3, 1916. Lo Chia-lun, in his "introduction" to [9], p. xi, states that it was after the death of Yüan Shih-k'ai (June 6, 1916) that Huang arrived in Tokyo. These are obvious errors.

62. [146], IV, 256.

63. Letter from Huang Hsing to Chü Cheng, May 19, 1916, in [9], Part I, pp. 126–28.

64. Telegram from Huang Hsing to T'an Jen-feng, in [103], V, 85; the statement referred to in the telegram was probably the statement made by Sun Yat-sen on May 9, 1916, which may be found in [146], IV, 16–19.

65. Telegram from Sun Yat-sen to Huang Hsing, May 21, 1916, and Huang Hsing's reply to Sun the next day; in [7].

66. Telegram from Huang Hsing to the leaders of the military council, June 12, 1916, in [208], chap. iv, pp. 48–49.

67. [7].

68. Telegram from Sun Yat-sen to Huang Hsing, July 13, 1916, in [146], IV, 263.

69. Telegram from Huang Hsing to Sun Yat-sen, June 14, 1916, in [247], July 7, 1916.

70. *Ibid.*, June 24, 1916.

71. *Cf.* [141], p. 191: "On May 9th [1916] a dispatch from Tokyo reported the arrival of Huang Hsing from the United States. He hastened to Canton to take part in the revolt there, but fell ill and died." Sharman's account was probably based on [152], p. 129.

72. 24, p. 241.

73. *Hsin-wen pao* (Shanghai), July 26, 1916; reprinted in [247], August 25, 1916. The Chung-hua Ko-ming Tang was formally reorganized into the Chung-kuo Kuo Min Tang (Nationalist Party of China, or Kuomintang) on October 10, 1919, the title which it still bears. In reality, the Kuomintang (Kuo Min Tang, as distinguished from Chung-kuo Kuo Min Tang), rather than the Chung-hua Ko-ming Tang, existed from 1916 to 1919. In any event, political circumstances in 1919 made the reorganization possible without complications.

74. [7]. Chang Chi had resigned both from the presidency of the Senate and from membership in the National Assembly prior to its dissolution.

75. Letter from Huang Hsing to Ho Ch'eng-chün, September 4, 1916; in [9], Part I, pp. 136–38.

76. *Ibid.*, p. 134.

77. *Ibid.*, Part II, p. 82.

78. Letter from Huang Hsing to Ho Ch'eng-chün, September 19, 1916; *ibid.*, Part I, p. 140. For Sun Yat-sen's view of the national scene after the death of Yüan Shih-k'ai, see his letter to James Deitrick, July 5, 1916, in [147], pp. 45–50.

79. Five days before Huang Hsing's death, a son, I-ch'iu, was born to Hsü Tsung-han. Two and a half months after Huang's death, another son, I-huan, was born to his Hunanese wife. Educated in Germany and the United States, Huang I-ch'iu is married to a daughter of General Ch'eng Ch'ien, Governor of Hunan province. Huang I-huan was educated in Japan; he is known as Huang Nai.

80. [146], V, 238–39. Instead of following the custom of the family announcing a death, the announcement was made by Sun Yat-sen alone. This was considered by Lo Chia-lun a "most significant point heretofore overlooked by historians. It demonstrated the everlasting comradeship between the two great revolutionary leaders who founded the Republic." [9], Introduction, pp. xvi–xvii.

CHAPTER ELEVEN

1. [152], p. 56.   2. [146], II, 68.

BIBLIOGRAPHY

This is a selected bibliography of sources pertaining to this study. Works in English and Japanese are listed only if they are cited in the Notes. Chinese works known to exist but inaccessible to this writer are not listed. Asterisks (*) have been used to indicate names for which Chinese characters are given in the Glossary, pp. 247-51.

BIBLIOGRAPHIES

[1] Ch'ai Te-keng and Chang Tz'u-ch'i, comps. "Cheng-yin shu-mu yü ts'an-k'ao shu-mu" (Bibliography and reference works), in Chung-kuo Shih-hsüeh Hui (Chinese Historical Association), Hsin-hai ko-ming (The revolution of 1911). VII, 611-74. Chung-kuo chin-tai shih tzu-liao ts'ung-kan (Modern Chinese historical materials series). Shang-hai, 1957.—In addition to the annotated bibliography (pp. 611-44) listing 177 works in which the materials of the 8-volume Hsin-hai ko-ming [62] are collected, this list includes another annotated bibliography of 133 works (pp. 644-74).

[2] Chang Tz'u-ch'i, comp. Chi-shih hsin-hai ko-ming shih-chi shu-lu (A bibliography on the revolution of 1911), pp. 185-250 of Chang Ching-lu, ed., Chung-kuo ch'u-pan shih-liao pu-pien (Source materials on publications in China: a supplement). Peking, 1957.—An excellent annotated bibliography of 170 books, pamphlets, and periodicals. In addition, it lists 54 articles published in various magazines and reprints 85 out of 128 items in the bibliography published in issue No. 7 of the Ko-ming wen-hsien ts'ung-k'an (September 1947). It excludes the works that have been included in Chang Yü-ying's bibliography listed below.

[3] Chang Yü-ying, comp. "Hsin-hai ko-ming shu-cheng" (A bibliography of the revolution of 1911), in Hsüeh-lin, No. 6 (Shanghai, April 1931), pp. 179-204.—An annotated bibliography of 206 items, classified in six categories. Included are books, pamphlets, and periodicals published at the end of the Ch'ing Dynasty and in the early years of the Chinese Republic; newspapers are excluded. Reprinted in Chang Ching-lu, ed., Chung-kuo chin-tai ch'u-pan shih-liao, I (Shanghai, 1953), 97-103 and 140-83.

[4] Chung-kuo K'o-hsüeh Yüan Li-shih Yen-chiu So, comp. Chung-kuo shih-hsüeh lun-wen so-yin (Index to articles on Chinese history).

Vol. I. Peking, 1957.—Published by the Institute of History of the Academy of Sciences of China and the Department of History of Peking University, this two-volume index lists more than thirty thousand articles from 1,300-odd Chinese periodicals published between 1900 and July 1937. Volume I (pp. 163–69) lists 139 articles on the Revolution of 1911 and the Republic to 1916. In addition, there are about 60 entries (pp. 290–329) on personalities prominent in the same period.

[5] "Hsin-hai kuang-fu shih-liao shu-mu" (A bibliography on the revolution of 1911), in *Ko-ming wen-hsien ts'ung-k'an* (Serial publications of the collected documents on the revolution). Vol. I, No. 7 (September 1947), pp. 18–20.—This bibliography lists 128 manuscripts, books, and articles on the Revolution of 1911 from the Kuomintang archives.

[6] Kuomintang, Committee for the Compilation of Materials on the Party History of the Central Executive Committee, comp. Tang-shih shih-liao mu-lu hui-k'an (A check list of the party archives), n. p., n. d., mimeo.—Only Volume IV (chi) is available.

HUANG HSING'S WORKS

[7] Huang Hsing.* Unpublished Private Papers.—Copies of 124 unpublished telegrams sent by Huang Hsing to his friends and to the civil and military leaders of China from May to October 22, 1916. In addition, the private papers contain a copy of a telegram from Sun Yat-sen dated May 21, 1916, which is not included in any of Sun's Collected Works published by the Kuomintang. There is also a copy of a telegram dated June 8, 1916, sent to Huang Hsing by his friends, reporting the affairs of state two days after the death of Yüan Shih-k'ai.

[8] ———. Huang K'o-ch'iang hsien-sheng yen-shuo tz'u hui-pien (The speeches of Huang Hsing). San Francisco, 1914.—A collection of three speeches delivered by Huang in San Francisco and Oakland in July 1914.

[9] ———. Huang K'o-ch'iang hsien-sheng shu-han mo-chi (Correspondence and calligraphy of Huang Hsing). Edited by the Committee for the Compilation of Materials on the Party History of the Central Executive Committee of the Kuomintang. Taiwan, 1956.—Published by the Kuomintang in commemoration of the forty-fifth anniversary of Huang Hsing's inauguration as the Commander-in-Chief of the Revolutionary Army after the outbreak of the Wuchang Revolution, this book includes 41 letters written by Huang to Sun Yat-sen and other comrades from 1906 to 1916 and some of his literary works, such as poems, *tz'u*, couplets, etc. All these writings and letters are reproduced in facsimile in the first part of the book and are followed by full texts with editor's notes.

[10] ———. Huang Liu-shou shu-tu (Letters and communications of Resident-General Huang). Edited by Wu Yen-yün. Shanghai, 1912.

—A collection of Huang Hsing's letters and communications written between April and June of 1912, when he was the Nanking Resident-General. A handwritten manuscript copied from the book was consulted.

[11] ———. "San-yüeh erh-chiu ko-ming chih ch'ien-yin hou-kuo" (The causes and the effects of the Revolution of March 29), in *Ko-ming wen-hsien ts'ung-k'an* (Serial publications of the collected documents on the revolution). Vol. I, No. 5 (March 1947), pp. 7–8.—A speech delivered by Huang Hsing at a meeting in 1912 commemorating the first anniversary of the Canton Revolution.

[12] ———. Wei-jen Huang Hsing cheng-chien shu (The political opinions of Huang Hsing). Edited by Liao Yün-hsiang. San Francisco, 1916.—In addition to four speeches delivered by Huang in Shanghai during July 1916, this pamphlet includes a letter he wrote to his friends and a long telegram he sent to Li Yüan-hung.

OFFICIAL DOCUMENTS

The Ch'ing Government

[13] Yü che hui-ts'un (Memorials and imperial decrees). [Peking?] January 30, 1892 to November 5, 1907.

[14] Cheng-chi kuan-pao (Government gazettes). Nos. 1–1370. Peking, October 26, 1907 to August 23, 1911.

[15] Nei-ko kuan-pao (Cabinet gazettes). Nos. 1–173. Peking, August 24, 1911 to February 12, 1912.

[16] Chin Yü-fu, ed. Hsüan-t'ung cheng-chi (Official documents of the Hsüan-t'ung reign). 43 vols. [Dairen?] 1934.

The Nanking Provisional Government

[17] Lin-shih cheng-fu kung-pao (The provisional government gazette). Nos. 1–58. Nanking, January 29, 1912 to April 5, 1912.

The Peking Government

[18] Lin-shih kung-pao (Provisional gazette). Peking, February 13, 1892 to April 16, 1912.

[19] Cheng-fu kung-pao (The government gazette). Peking, May 1, 1912 to 1916.

[20] Ts'an-i yüan hui-i su-chi lu (The record of the provisional parliament), n.p., n.d.—The 1st meeting (May 4, 1912) to the 100th meeting (October 28, 1912), and the 121st meeting (December 18, 1912) to the 131st meeting (April 7, 1913).

[21] Ts'an-i yüan i-chüeh an hui-pien (Collection of the resolutions of the provisional parliament). 2 vols., n.p., December 1913.—Resolutions passed between April and December 1913.

[22] Ts'an-i yüan i-shih lu (Proceedings of the provisional parliament), September 2, 1912 to April 7, 1913. n.p., n.d.

BOOKS, PAMPHLETS, AND ARTICLES

[23] Bland, J. O. P. Recent Events and Present Policies in China. Philadelphia: J. B. Lippincott, 1912.

[24] Chang Chi.* Chang P'u-ch'üan hsien-sheng ch'üan-chi (Collected works of Chang Chi). Edited by the Committee for the Compilation of Materials on the Party History of the Central Reorganization Committee of the Kuomintang. Taiwan, 1951.—Chang was a member of Huang Hsing's Hua Hsing Hui, took part in Huang's first revolutionary attempt in 1904, and escaped with him to Changsha after its failure. His memoirs contain information on Huang Hsing's early revolutionary activities.

[25] ———. Chang P'u-ch'üan hsien-sheng ch'üan-chi pu-pien (Collected works of Chang Chi: a supplement). Edited by the Committee for the Compilation of Materials on the Party History of the Central Reorganization Committee of the Kuomintang. Taiwan, 1952.

[26] Chang Ch'i-yün. Chung-hua min-kuo ch'uang-li shih (A History of the founding of the Republic of China). Taiwan, 1952.—An orthodox Kuomintang presentation of the revolutionary history.

[27] Chang Chien.* Chang Chi-tzu chiu-lu (Nine records of Chang Chien). Edited by Chang Hsiao-jo. 31 vols. Shanghai, 1932.—Records of a prominent gentry-industrialist who held Cabinet posts in the early years of the Republic, containing several letters to Huang Hsing on current affairs.

[28] Chang Chih-tung.* Chang Wen-hsiang kung kung-tu kao (A collection of the official correspondence of Chang Chih-tung). Compiled by Hsü T'ung-hsin. 28 vols. China, n.d.—A collection of Chang's official correspondence from 1882 to 1907. With an interruption of about three years, Chang was the Governor-General of Hunan and Hupeh from 1889 to 1907. The compiler's preface is dated 1920.

[29] ———. Chang Wen-hsiang kung tien-kao (A collection of the telegraphic correspondence of Chang Chih-tung). Compiled by Hsü T'ung-hsin. 66 vols. China, n.d.—A collection of Chang's telegrams from 1884 to 1907. The compiler's preface is dated 1929.

[30] ———. Chang Wen-hsiang kung tsou-kao (A collection of Chang Chih-tung's memorials to the throne). Compiled by Hsü T'ung-hsin. 26 vols. China, n.d.—A collection of memorials submitted between 1879 and 1909. The compiler's preface is dated 1920.

[31] Chang Ching-lu. Chung-kuo chin-tai ch'u-pan shih-liao (Source materials on publications in modern China). 2 vols. Shanghai, 1953–54.

[32] ———. Chung-kuo ch'u-pan shih-liao pu-pien (Source materials on publications in China: a supplement). Peking, 1957.

[33] Chang Ch'un-t'ing. Chang Wen-hsiang kung chih-O chi (Chang Chih-tung's rule in Hupeh). Wuchang, 1947.—A record of Chang Chih-tung's administration in Hupeh, where Chang's educational reforms had a bearing upon Huang Hsing's education.

[34] Chang Hsiang-wen. Nan-yüan ts'ung-kao (Collected works). Vols. VII and VIII. Peking, 1929.—These two volumes contain an account of the Canton Revolution of 1911.

[35] Chang Hsiao-jo. Nan-t'ung Chang Chi-chih hsien-sheng chuan-chi (A biography of Chang Chien). Shanghai, 1931.—Chapter I of Part III of this book deals with the establishment of the Nanking Provisional Government and the assistance Chang Chien gave to Huang Hsing.

[36] Chang Huang-ch'i. "Kuang Fu Hui ling-hsiu T'ao Ch'eng-chang ko-ming shih" (Revolutionary activities of T'ao Ch'eng-chang, leader of the Restoration Party), in Chung-kuo Shih-hsüeh Hui, Hsin-hai ko-ming, Vol. 1.

[37] ———. "Su-pao an shih-lu" (A factual record of the Su-pao case), in Chung-kuo Shih-hsüeh Hui, Hsin-hai ko-ming, Vol. I.

[38] Chang Kuo-kan. Hsin-hai ko-ming shih-liao (Source materials on the revolution of 1911). Shanghai, 1958.—A documentary study by an author who was a member of the delegation sent by Yüan Shih-k'ai to negotiate peace with the South at the end of 1911.

[39] Chang Nan and Wang Jen-chih, ed. Hsin-hai ko-ming ch'ien shih-nien chien shih-lun hsüan-chi (Selected essays on current events written during the ten years prior to the revolution of 1911). 2 vols. Peking, 1960.

[40] Chang Nan-hsien.* Hu-pei ko-ming chih-chih lu (An account of the revolutionary movement in Hupeh). Chungking, 1945.—Based on the personal experience and careful research of the author, who was the Governor of Chekiang in 1931.

[41] Chang Ping-lin.* "Chiao Ta-feng chuan" (Biographical sketch of Chiao Ta-feng), in Chang-shih ts'ung-shu. China, 1919.

[42] ———. "Ch'in Li-shan chuan" (Biographical sketch of Ch'in Li-shan), in Chang-shih ts'ung-shu.

[43] Chang Yü-k'un.* Wen-hsüeh She Wu-ch'ang shou-i chi-shih (A factual account of the Wuchang revolution initiated by the Literary Society). Peking, 1952.—Written by a member of the Literary Society, which had a direct hand in the Wuchang Revolution, this book deals with the revolutionary movement in Hupeh from 1904 to 1912. It is substantially the same as the 1944 edition. The author's preface is dated 1936.

[44] Che-yin-sheng (pseud.). O-luan hui-lu ch'u-p'ien (Record of the Hupeh uprising), n.p., October 1911.—A collection of newspaper reports, comments, and some documents relating to the Wuchang Revolution. The tone is sympathetic to the revolution.

[45] Chen, Stephen, and Robert Payne. Sun Yat-sen. New York: John Day, 1946.

[46] [Ch'en Ch'iung-ming].* Ch'en Ching-ts'un hsien-sheng nien-p'u (A chronological biography of Ch'en Ch'iung-ming). Hong Kong, n.d.—Twice in 1911–13, Ch'en was the Military Governor of Kwangtung.

[47] Ch'en Hsü-lu. Hsin-hai ko-ming (The revolution of 1911). Shanghai, 1955.

[48] Ch'en Po-ta. Ch'ieh-kuo ta-tao Yüan Shih-k'ai (Yüan Shih-k'ai, the traitor). Peking, 1949.—Written by a noted Chinese Communist writer, this book is based on well-known secondary sources. The preface is dated 1945.

[49] Ch'en T'ien-hua.* Ch'en T'ien-hua chi (Selected works). Shanghai, 1946.—A collection of eighteen essays written by a noted young Hunanese propagandist who was a member of Huang Hsing's Hua Hsing Hui.

[50] Chiang Wei-ch'iao. "Chung-kuo Chiao-yü Hui chih hui-i" (Reminiscences of the Chinese Educational Society), in Chung-kuo Shih-hsüeh Hui, Hsin-hai ko-ming, Vol. I.

[51] Chieh-pei i-shou (pseud.). Kuei-ch'ou huo-luan chi-lüeh (A brief record of the insurrections of 1913). 2 vols. Shanghai, 1913.—An account of the war against Yüan Shih-k'ai, based on contemporary newspapers. The author was critical of Huang Hsing and the other revolutionary leaders.

[52] Ch'ien Chi-po. "Hsin-hai chiang-nan kuang-fu shih-lu" (A factual account of the revolution of Shanghai and Nanking), in Chung-kuo Shih-hsüeh Hui, Hsin-hai ko-ming, Vol. VII.

[53] ———. "Hsin-hai nan-pei i-ho pieh-chi" (The unofficial story of the peace negotiations), in Chung-kuo Shih-hsüeh Hui, Hsin-hai ko-ming, Vol. VIII.

[54] China Year Book, The (London). 1912–1914 and 1916.

[55] Ch'ing-shih kao (Draft history of the Ch'ing Dynasty). Edited by Chao Erh-sun and others. 132 vols. China, 1927.

[56] Chu Ho-chung.* "Ou-chou T'ung Meng Hui chi-shih" (The history of the European branch of the T'ung Meng Hui), in Kuomintang, Ko-ming wen-hsien, Vol. II.

[57] Chu Te-shang. Liu K'uei-i. N.p., June 1912.—A biographical sketch.

[58] Chü Cheng.* "Chung-hua Ko-ming Tang shih-tai ti hui-i" (Reminiscences of the Chinese Revolutionary Party), in Kuomintang, Ko-ming wen-hsien, Vol. V.

[59] ———. Hsin-hai ta-chi mei-ch'uan jih-chi ho-k'an (Diary and random notes of 1911, published in one volume). Reprint. Taipei, 1956. —The author played a leading role in the Hupeh revolutionary movement in 1911 and was Vice-Minister of the Interior in the Nanking Provisional Government in 1912.

[60] ———. Mei-ch'uan p'u-chieh (Autobiography in verse). Taiwan, n.d.; the preface is dated 1949.

[61] Chung-kuo K'o-hsüeh Yüan Li-shih Yen-chiu So (Institute of History of the Academy of Sciences of China), ed. Yün-nan Kuei-chou hsin-hai ko-ming tzu-liao (Source materials on the revolution of 1911 in Yunnan and Kweichow). Peking, 1959.

[62] Chung-kuo Shih-hsüeh Hui (Chinese Historical Association). Hsin-hai ko-ming (The revolution of 1911). 8 vols. Edited by Ch'ai Te-keng and others. Chung-kuo chin-tai shih tzu-liao ts'ung-k'an (Modern Chinese historical materials series). Shanghai, 1957.—Materials included in these volumes cover the period from 1894 to 1912 and include many official documents from the Ch'ing archives.

[63] Dingle, Edwin J. China's Revolution, 1911–1912. New York: McBride, Nast & Co., 1912.

[64] Farjenel, Fernand. Through the Chinese Revolution. Translated by Margaret Vivian. New York: Frederick A. Stokes, 1916.

[65] Feng Jen-ch'üan, comp. Erh-tz'u ko-ming lun pai-pien (One hundred essays on the second revolution). 2 vols., n.p., n.d. [1914?]—A collection of newspaper articles hostile to the "second revolution" of 1913. Some official documents are also included.

[66] Feng-kang chi-men-ti-tzu, comp. San-shui Liang Yen-sun hsien-sheng nien-p'u (Chronological biography of Liang Shih-i). 2 vols. 2d ed., n.p., 1946 (1st ed., 1939).—Liang Shih-i was appointed by Yüan Shih-k'ai as the Secretary-General of the President's Office on March 2, 1912.

[67] Feng Tzu-yu.* Chung-hua min-kuo k'ai-kuo ch'ien ko-ming shih (Revolutionary history prior to the founding of the Republic of China). 3 vols. Vol. I, Shanghai, 1928; Vols. II and III [Chungking], 1944.—A chronological account of the revolutionary movement from 1894 to 1911. The 1944 wartime edition of Volume I and the post-war editions of these volumes are not used. The author was one of the most authoritative historians of the Republican Revolution. However, his writings were based on his own recollections as well as on research, and discrepancies and repetitions are frequent.

[68] ———. Chung-hua min-kuo k'ai-kuo ch'ien ko-ming shih hsü-pien (Supplement to the revolutionary history prior to the founding of the Republic of China). Vol. I. Shanghai, 1946.

[69] ———. Chung-kuo ko-ming yün-tung erh-shih-liu nien tsu-chih shih (Twenty-six years' organizational history of the Chinese revolutionary movement). Shanghai, 1948.—This book lists hundreds of organizations, overseas and in China, which were connected with the revolutionary movement. A brief description of each organization is given.

[70] ———. Ko-ming i-shih (Fragments of revolutionary history). 5 vols. Vol. I, Changsha, 1939; Vol. II, Chungking, 1943; Vol. III, Chungking, 1945; Vol. IV, Shanghai, 1946; Vol. V, Shanghai, 1947.—The Changsha (1939) edition of Volume I is better than any other subsequent editions of the same volume, because it contains pictures and facsimile reproductions of documents. Some of the letters written by Huang Hsing to Feng are of great historical significance.

[71] Hackett, Roger F. "Chinese Students in Japan, 1900–1910," Harvard University Regional Studies, Papers on China, III (May 1949), 134–69. Mimeo.

[72] Han-jen (pseud.). T'ai-wan ko-ming shih (The revolutionary history of Taiwan). Taiwan, n.d.

[73] Ho Po-yen. Huang K'o-ch'iang (Huang Hsing). Nanking, 1946.—A biography based on secondary sources.

[74] Hsiung Ping-k'un.* "Wu-ch'ang ch'i-i t'an" (On the outbreak of the Wuchang revolution), in Chung-kuo Shih-hsüeh Hui, *Hsin-hai ko-ming,* Vol. V.

[75] Hsü Hsüeh-erh *et al.* Sung Yü-fu (Sung Chiao-jen). Shanghai, 1913.

[76] Hsü, Leonard S. Sun Yat-sen: His Political and Social Ideals. Los Angeles: University of Southern California Press, 1933.

[77] Hsü Shih-shen. Kuo-fu ko-ming yüan-ch'i hsiang-chu (Detailed explanatory notes to Sun Yat-sen's autobiography). Shanghai, 1947.—Well-documented.

[78] Hsü T'ung-hsin. Chang Wen-hsiang kung nien-p'u (A chronological biography of Chang Chih-tung). 2d ed. Shanghai, 1947.—Well-documented.

[79] Hsüeh-shu (Blood Book). 3 vols. China, n.d.—A collection of revolutionary documents issued between October and December 1911. Volume III contains a biographical sketch of Huang Hsing. The unknown compiler's preface is dated 1911.

[80] Hu Han-min.* "Tzu-chuan" (Autobiography), in Committee for the Compilation of Materials on the Party History of the Central Executive Committee of the Kuomintang, ed., *Ko-ming wen-hsien* (Documents of the revolution), Vol. III. Taiwan, 1953.—This posthumous publication contains valuable information on the Republican Revolution.

[81] Hu O-kung. Hsin-hai ko-ming pei-fang shih-lu (A factual account of the revolution in North China). Shanghai, 1948.—A personal account written by a section chief of the Hupeh Military Government. The author was sent by Li Yüan-hung to Tientsin shortly after the outbreak of the Wuchang Revolution for the purpose of instigating revolution in the north.

[82] Hu Shih. Liu-hsüeh jih-chi (Diary of a student in the United States). Shanghai, 1947.

[83] Hu Tsu-shun.* Liu-shih t'an-wang (Reminiscences at Sixty). [Chungking, 1944].—A personal account of the Wuchang Revolution. The author was a local revolutionary leader, took an active part in the revolution, and became an officer in the Hupeh Military Government.

[84] ———. Wu-ch'ang k'ai-kuo shih-lu (A factual account of the founding of the Republic in Wuchang). 2 vols. Wuchang, 1948.—Based on original sources as well as the author's own experience.

[85] Hu Yüan-t'an.* "Ti Huang K'o-ch'iang hsien-sheng i-mo" (Comments on Huang Hsing's calligraphy), in Huang Hsing, *Huang K'o-ch'iang hsien-sheng shu-han mo-chi.*

[86] Huang Kuang-hsüeh. Kuo-fu ko-ming i-shih (Revolutionary

anecdotes of Sun Yat-sen). Taipei, 1952.—A collection of well-known anecdotes from secondary sources.

[87] Huang Ying-pai hsien-sheng ku-chiu kan-i lu (Reminiscences of Huang Fu by his friends). Shanghai, 1937.

[88] Huang Yüan-sheng. Yüan-sheng i-chu (Selected works of Huang Yüan-sheng). 4 vols. 2d ed. Shanghai, 1924.—A collection of articles written by a well-informed Chinese journalist in Peking during the first few years of the Republic. The author was assassinated in San Francisco in 1915.

[89] Hummel, Arthur W., ed. Eminent Chinese of the Ch'ing Period. 2 vols. Washington: U.S. Government Printing Office, 1943–44.

[90] Hupeh Committee of the Chinese People's Political Consultative Conference, ed. Hsin-hai shou-i hui-i lu (A collection of reminiscences of the revolution of 1911). 2 vols. Wuchang, 1957.—The first volume contains the record of a symposium and twenty articles; the second volume has eight articles. All were written by former Hupeh New Army soldiers who took part in the revolution of October 10, 1911, including the man who reputedly fired the first shot. Carefully edited, although the editor errs on the founding date of the T'ung Meng Hui.

[91] Ike Kyōkichi.* Shina kakumei jikkenki (An eyewitness' account of the Chinese revolution). Tokyo, 1911.—This book also contains some letters and calligraphy by Huang Hsing and a photograph of him taken in March 1907.

[92] Jansen, Marius B. The Japanese and Sun Yat-sen. Cambridge, Mass.: Harvard University Press, 1954.

[93] Jung Meng-yüan, ed. Chung-kuo chin-tai shih tzu-liao hsüan-chi (Selected source materials on the modern history of China). Peking, 1954.

[94] ———. "O-kuo i-chiu-ling-wu nien ko-ming tui Chung-kuo ti ying-hsiang" (The impact of the Russian revolution of 1905 on China), in Li-shih yen-chiu (Historical studies), Vol. I, No. 2 (Peking, 1954), pp. 53–69.

[95] Kayano Nagatomo.* Chūka minkoku kakumei hikyū (Private sources on the Chinese Republican revolution). Tokyo, 1940.

[96] Ko Kung-chen. Chung-kuo pao-hsüeh shih (A history of Chinese journalism). Peking, 1955.—This book contains a list of newspapers and periodicals published in the Ch'ing and early Republican periods. It appears to be unchanged from its earlier editions (Shanghai, 1927, 1928, and 1935) except for the deletion of the author's introduction and some illustrations.

[97] Ko-ming hsien-lieh wen-i chi (Selected works of the revolutionary martyrs). Vol. I. [Shanghai, 1930].—This book contains some of Huang Hsing's literary work and letters. The unknown editor's preface is dated September 1, 1930.

[98] Ku Chung-hsiu. Chung-hua min-kuo k'ai-kuo shih (A history

of the founding of the Chinese Republic). 2d ed. Shanghai, 1917.—This book, which has been widely used by Chinese historians, traces political events from October 1911 to January 1914. The author was a provincial representative and later a Kuomintang member of the National Assembly, but he did not really belong to the hard core of the party. He was one of the constitutionalists who went over to the revolutionary camp after the success of the revolution.

[99] Kuan-tu-lu (pseud. of Wu Ting-fang*), ed. Kung-ho kuan-chien lu (A record of the peace negotiations that were crucial to the Republic). Shanghai, 1912.—A collection of documents on the peace negotiations between the South and the North, which led to the abdication of the Ch'ing emperor. It was edited by the chief representative of the revolutionary government in the negotiations.

[100] Kung I-hsing. "Kuang-fu chün chi" (Records of the Restoration Army), in Chung-kuo Shih-hsüeh Hui, Hsin-hai ko-ming, Vol. I.

[101] Kuo Hsiao-ch'eng. Chung-hua ko-ming chi-shih pen-mo (A complete record of the Chinese revolution). Shanghai, 1912.—An account of the revolution in various provinces from October 10, 1911 to April 1, 1912, compiled from current newspaper reports and government sources.

[102] Kuomintang, Committee for the Compilation of Materials on the Party History of the Central Executive Committee, ed. Chung-kuo Kuo-min-tang wu-shih chou-nien chi-nien t'e-k'an (Special commemoration issue on the fiftieth anniversary of the founding of the Kuomintang). Chungking, 1944.—A collection of reminiscences by Kuomintang leaders on the Republican Revolution. It contains valuable firsthand information.

[103] ———. Ko-ming wen-hsien (Documents of the revolution). Vols. I–VI. Taiwan, 1953–56.—The first six volumes of this collection cover the period from 1894 to 1916 and contain source materials published for the first time.

[104] ———. Kuo-fu hua-chuan (The pictorial biography of Sun Yat-sen). Taiwan, 1954.

[105] ———. Kuo-fu nien-p'u ch'u-kao (Chronological biography of Sun Yat-sen: a preliminary draft). 2 vols. Taiwan, 1958.—The most comprehensive chronological biographical data on the life of Sun Yat-sen ever published by the Kuomintang.

[106] Kuo Pin-chia. "Min-kuo erh-tz'u ko-ming shih" (A history of the second revolution of the Republic), Kuo-li Wu-han ta-hsüeh wen-che chi-k'an (Quarterly journal of liberal arts, Wuhan University), Vol. IV, Nos. 3–4 (Wuchang, 1935), pp. 615–69 and 819–50.—A detailed account of politics and war against Yüan Shih-k'ai in 1913.

[107] Kuo-shih hsin-wen, ed. Pei-ching ping-pien shih-mo chi (An account of the soldiers' riots in Peking). Peking, 1912.—Compiled shortly after the riots that gave Yüan Shih-k'ai an excuse for remaining in Peking.

[108] Li Chieh-ju. Yüeh-tung chün-pien chi (Record of the Kwang-tung army uprising). [Canton, 1910].—A collection of official documents and newspaper reports by an army man who was an eyewitness to the Canton army uprising in 1910.

[109] Li Chien-nung.* Chung-kuo chin-pai-nien cheng-chi shih (The political history of China in the last one hundred years). Shanghai, 1947.

[110] ——. The Political History of China, 1840–1928. Translated and edited by Ssu-yu Teng and Jeremy Ingalls. Princeton: D. Van Nostrand, 1956.—A translation of the book listed above, but based on the Chinese edition of 1948.

[111] Li Hung-lun. A letter, dated May 1943, to the Committee for the Compilation of Materials on the Party History of the Central Executive Committee of the Kuomintang.—A high-ranking army officer's personal account of the Yunnan revolt against Yüan Shih-k'ai, which criticizes the Kuomintang party line that has generally credited Ts'ai O alone with leading the revolt.

[112] Li Lien-fang.* Hsin-hai Wu-ch'ang shou-i chi (An account of the Wuchang revolution of 1911). Wuchang, 1947.—An objective account of the revolution, based on the author's firsthand information and careful research. The author was a fellow student of Huang Hsing's in Japan; both belonged to the same small anti-Manchu group prior to the formation of the T'ung Meng Hui. The author was the chief secretary of the Hupeh Military Government for seven days after the outbreak of the Wuchang Revolution.

[113] Li Nai-han. Hsin-hai ko-ming yü Yüan Shih-k'ai (Yüan Shih-k'ai and the revolution of 1911). 3d ed. Peking, 1950.—Well-written.

[114] Li Shih-yüeh. Hsin-hai ko-ming shih-ch'i liang-hu ti-ch'ü ti ko-ming yün-tung (The revolutionary movement in the Hunan and Hupeh areas in the period of the Republican revolution). Peking, 1957. —Secondary sources with special emphasis on the political and social background of the Revolution of 1911 in Hunan and Hupeh provinces.

[115] Li Shu. "I-chiu-ling-wu nien O-kuo ko-ming ho Chung-kuo" (The Russian Revolution of 1905 and China), Li-shih yen-chiu (Historical studies), Vol. II, No. 1 (Peking, 1955), pp. 1–17.

[116] Li Yüan-hung.* Li fu-tsung-t'ung cheng-shu (Official correspondence of vice-president Li Yüan-hung). 34 vols. Wuchang, 1914. —Primarily a collection of Li Yüan-hung's telegrams sent out between October 15, 1911 (five days after the outbreak of the Wuchang Revolution) and December 9, 1913 (when he left Hupeh for Peking).

[117] Liao Shao-yu. Hsin Chung-kuo wu-chuang chieh-chüeh ho-ping chi (An account of the peaceful solution in new China). Nanking, 1912.—This diary (December 5, 1911 to February 15, 1912) was kept by the author while he conducted secret negotiations with the revolutionaries for the North. It was published by the Ministry of War of the

Provisional Government in Nanking in June 1912. The book itself was not available for use in the present study, but a 108-page handwritten manuscript copied from the book has been consulted.

[118] Linebarger, Paul. Sun Yat-sen and the Chinese Republic. New York: The Century Co., 1925.—The chapter entitled "Sun and Hwang" is one of the very few accounts written by Westerners which points out the dual leadership of Sun Yat-sen and Huang Hsing.

[119] Liu Ch'eng-yü.* "Hsien tsung-li chiu-te lu" (My reminiscences of Sun Yat-sen), Kuo-shih kuan kuan-k'an (Publications of the National Historical Bureau), Vol. I, No. 1. (December 1947).—Firsthand information recorded by a veteran revolutionist.

[120] Liu Hou-sheng. Chang Chien chuan-chi (A biography of Chang Chien). Shanghai, 1958.—Well written by a close friend and colleague of Chang Chien's, the bulk of the book discusses the political figures, social conditions, and national and international affairs of Chang Chien's time.

[121] Liu K'uei-i.* Huang Hsing chuan-chi (A biography of Huang Hsing). Taipei, 1952.—First published in 1929, this book has been a basic source for Chinese historians on the revolutionary activities of Huang Hsing. The author was Huang's close associate in the Hua Hsing Hui and the T'ung Meng Hui. In 1912–13 he was Minister of Industry and Commerce.

[122] Lo Chia-lun, ed. Huang-hua-kang ko-ming lieh-shih hua-shih (Pictorial history of the martyrs of the Canton revolution of 1911). Taiwan, 1952.—This book contains reproductions of pictures of 43 of the more than 86 revolutionaries who died in the famous revolt, with a brief biographical sketch of each.

[123] Lu Tan-lin. Ko-ming shih-t'an (Anecdotes of the revolution). Chungking, 1945.

[124] Lung Yü-chün. Lin-chao lu (My reminiscences). Chungking, 1945.—The author saw Huang Hsing quite often in Japan in 1902–3. He was of the Lung family that helped Huang to escape after the abortive Changsha revolt in 1904. For more than fifteen years after 1930, he was a "reporter" for the Committee for the Compilation of Materials on the Party History of the Central Executive Committee of the Kuomintang.

[125] Ma Ta-chung. Ta Chung-hua min-kuo shih (A history of the Republic of China). Peking, 1929.

[126] McCormick, Frederick. The Flowery Republic. London: John Murray, 1913.

[127] Man-hua* (pseud. of T'ang Tseng-pi*). "T'ung Meng Hui shih-tai Min-pao shih-mo chi" (The People's Journal during the period of the T'ung Meng Hui), in Kuomintang, Ko-ming wen-hsien, Vol. II.

[128] Martin, Bernard. Strange Vigour: A Biography of Sun Yat-sen. London, 1944.

[129] Min-kuo ching-shih wen-pien (Essays on the national affairs

of the Republic). Compiled by the Editorial Department of the Ching-shi wen-she. 40 vols. Shanghai, 1914.—A collection of articles written by prominent figures in the first few years of the Republic. Volume XI contains a letter from Yang Tu to Huang Hsing discussing the Kuomintang policy.

[130] Miyazaki Tōten (Torazō).* Shina kakumei-gundan (Episodes of the Chinese revolutionary army). Tokyo, 1912.

[131] Mullowney, John J. A Revelation of the Chinese Revolution. New York: Fleming H. Revell, 1914.—This is probably the only English biography of Huang Hsing, who was called by the author the "real leader" of the revolution.

[132] Ou-yang Jui-hua. "Wu-ch'ang K'o-hsüeh Pu-hsi So ko-ming yün-tung shih-mo chi" (An account of the revolutionary activities of the Science Study Group in Wuchang), in Chung-kuo Shih-hsüeh Hui, Hsin-hai ko-ming, Vol. I.

[133] Pai Chiao. Yüan Shih-k'ai yü Chung-hua min-kuo (Yüan Shih-k'ai and the Republic of China). Shanghai, 1936.—This book, based primarily on newspaper files, contains many original documents. The author's analysis of Yüan Shih-k'ai is excellent.

[134] P'an Kung-chan. Ch'en Ch'i-mei.* Taiwan, 1954.—First published in 1946, this biography was written by a one-time Minister of Propaganda of the Kuomintang.

[135] Po-k'uei. "T'ung-meng chiu-kan lu" (Reminiscences), Chien-kuo yüeh-k'an, Vol. IX, No. 5 (November 1933).

[136] "Saggitarius" (pseud.). The Strange Apotheosis of Sun Yat-sen. London: Heath Cranton, 1939.

[137] Schiffrin, Harold. "Sun Yat-sen's Early Land Policy," Journal of Asian Studies, Vol. XVI, No. 4 (August 1957), 549–64.

[138] Shang Ping-ho. Hsin-jen ch'un-ch'iu (Annals of the years 1911 and 1912). n.p., [1924?].—A detailed account of the events in each of the provinces in the years 1911 and 1912. The author was critical of Huang Hsing and other revolutionary leaders.

[139] Shao Yüan-ch'ung. Ch'en Ying-shih hsien-sheng ko-ming hsiao-shih (Biographical sketch of Ch'en Ch'i-mei). Shanghai, [1925].—A sympathetic account containing no new material except a letter from Ch'en to his brother from Japan, reprinted in facsimile.

[140] ———. "Chung-hua Ko-ming Tang lüeh-shih" (A brief history of the Chinese Revolutionary Party), Chien-kuo yüeh-k'an, Vol. I, No. 1 (June 15, 1929).

[141] Sharman, Lyon. Sun Yat-sen: His Life and Its Meaning. New York: John Day, 1934.

[142] Shen Yün-lung. Hsien-tai cheng-chih jen-wu shu-p'ing (Political figures of modern China). Hong Kong, 1959.

[143] Shu Hsin-ch'eng. Chin-tai Chung-kuo liu-hsüeh shih (A history of Chinese students studying abroad). Shanghai, 1927.—A study of Chinese students studying abroad between 1870 and 1926, based on primary sources.

[144] Su-min (pseud. of Yang Tun-i), ed. Man-i hua-hsia shih-mo chi (A record of the Manchus' treacherous deeds in China). 12 vols. [Shanghai, 1912].—A collection of anti-Manchu writings, including a biographical sketch of Huang Hsing.

[145] Sun Yao. Chung-hua min-kuo shih-liao (Historical materials on the Republic of China). 3 vols. Shanghai, 1929.—Volume I and the first part of Volume II contain documents covering the period 1911–16.

[146] Sun Yat-sen. Kuo-fu ch'üan-chi (Collected works of Sun Yat-sen). Compiled and edited by the Committee for the Compilation of Materials on the Party History of the Central Executive Committee of the Kuomintang. 6 vols. Revised ed. Taiwan, 1957.—The most comprehensive collected works of Sun Yat-sen.

[147] ———. 10 Letters of Sun Yat-sen. Stanford, California: Stanford University Libraries, 1942.—These English letters, addressed to James Deitrick, are reproduced in facsimile. It appears that only one or two of them are in Sun's own handwriting.

[148] Sung Chiao-jen.* Wo chih li-shih (Diary). Hunan, 1920.— A posthumous publication of Sung's diary, which covers the period from the autumn of 1904 to the spring of 1907. Sung was a member of Huang Hsing's Hua Hsing Hui and of the T'ung Meng Hui. His diary contains valuable information on the revolutionary movement in general and on Huang Hsing in particular. Few of the Chinese historians who have used the book have realized that prior to Sung's arrival in Japan, the dates recorded in the diary are given in old style, while the dates given after his arrival in Japan (December 1904) are in Western style.

[149] Sung Chiao-jen and Tai Chi-t'ao. Sung Yü-fu Tai T'ien-ch'ou wen-chi ho-k'an (Works of Sung Chiao-jen and Tai Chi-t'ao). Shanghai, 1921.—A collection of essays and editorials written by Sung and Tai for Chinese newspapers in Shanghai in 1911–12. With a few exceptions, it is difficult to ascertain the authorship of the works collected in this volume.

[150] Sung Yüeh-lun. Tsung-li tsai Jih-pen chih ko-ming huo-tung (The revolutionary activities of Sun Yat-sen in Japan). Taipei, 1953.— A fragmentary account based on Chinese and Japanese sources.

[151] T'an Jen-feng.* Shih-shou p'ai-tz'u hsü-lu (Reminiscences), reprinted in Chin-tai shih tzu-liao (Source materials on modern history) No. 10 (August 1956), pp. 26–76.—The author, who was a close friend of Huang Hsing's, played a leading role in the revolutionary movement.

[152] T'ang Leang-li. The Inner History of the Chinese Revolution. London, 1930.

[153]. ———. Wang Ching-wei. Tientsin, 1931 (written in English).

[154] T'ao Ch'eng-chang.* Che-an chi-lüeh (A brief account of the revolts in Chekiang), n.p., 1916.—An authoritative account written in 1908–10 by a leader of the Restoration Society (Kuang Fu Hui) and later of the T'ung Meng Hui.

[155] T'ao Ch'ü-yin. Liu chün-tzu chuan (Biographies of the "six gentlemen"). Shanghai, 1946.

[156] Teng Mu-han. "T'ung Meng Hui ch'eng-li shih-jih k'ao" (A study on the date of the founding of the T'ung Meng Hui), in Kuomintang, Ko-ming wen-hsien, Vol. II.

[157] Teng Wen-hui. "Kung Chin Hui ti yüan-ch'i chi jo-kan chih-tu" (The origin of the Common Advancement Society and its various regulations), Chin-tai shih tzu-liao, No. 10 (August 1956).

[158] T'ien-ku. Nan-pei ch'un-ch'iu (The annals of the North and South). Shanghai, n.d.—A record of daily events arranged in chronological order from the outbreak of the Wuchang Revolution to the abdication of the Manchu emperor.

[159] T'ien T'ung.* "T'ung Meng Hui ch'eng-li chi" (An account of the founding of the T'ung Meng Hui), in Kuomintang, Ko-ming wen-hsien, Vol. II.

[160] Ts'ai Chi-min and Wu Hsing-han. "Wu-han shou-i shih-lu" (A factual account of the Wuchang revolution), in Kuomintang, Ko-ming wen-hsien, Vol. IV.

[161] Ts'ai Chi-ou. O-chou hsüeh-shih (The bloody history of Hupeh). Shanghai, 1958.—This posthumous publication deals with the Hupeh revolutionary movement from 1900 to 1913. The author, who was a journalist in Wuhan area in 1911, adopted a judicial attitude toward the personalities involved.

[162] Ts'ao Ya-po.* Wu-ch'ang ko-ming chen-shih (The true history of the Wuchang revolution). 3 vols. Shanghai, 1930.—Called a "goldmine for modern students of the revolution of 1911," this book was immediately suppressed by the Kuomintang after its publication. The author was a veteran revolutionary who helped Huang Hsing to escape in 1904 and was among the first to join the T'ung Meng Hui in 1905; but he was not a "participant in the preparation of the Wuchang revolt." Volume I is based partly on the author's firsthand information about events between 1904 and 1911. Volumes II and III, which cover the period from October 1911 to May 1912, are reportedly based on the private papers of Wu Ch'ao-lun, Assistant Chief of Staff of the Hupeh Military Government in 1911. Discrepancies of dates and events are, however, many.

[163] Tsou Lu.* Ch'eng-lu wen-hsüan (Selected works of Tsou Lu). Shanghai, 1948.—The author was a Kuomintang member of the National Assembly in 1913. His article "My Reminiscences of 1913," written in the winter of that year and reprinted in this book (pp. 415–58), is a useful aid toward an understanding of the Kuomintang policy toward Yüan Shih-k'ai in 1913.

[164] ———. Chung-kuo Kuo-min-tang tang-shih kao (Draft history of the Kuomintang). 4 vols. 3d ed. Chungking, 1944.—This book is heavily packed with documents and is familiar to Western historians. It should be noted, however, that Tsou did not take any significant part

in the revolutionary movement prior to the establishment of the Republic. He knew Sun Yat-sen well only in the last years of Sun's life and he became an ardent advocate of the cult of Sun Yat-sen.

[165] ———. Kuang-chou san-yüeh erh-shih-chiu ko-ming shih (History of the Canton revolution of March 29, 1911). Shanghai, 1926. —A well-documented and comprehensive study.

[166] Tsou Yung-ch'eng. "Tsou Yung-ch'eng hui-i lu" (Reminiscences of Tsou Yung-ch'eng), *Chin-tai shih tzu-liao,* No. 10 (August 1956).

[167] Tu Ch'eng-hsiang. Tsou Jung chuan (A biography of Tsou Jung). 2d ed. Taipei, 1953.—A well-written biography of a famous revolutionary pamphleteer.

[168] Tu-li ts'ang-mang tzu (pseud.). "Tung-ching hsüeh-chieh kung-fen shih-mo kao hsiang-jen fu-lao hsing-hsüeh shu" (A report on the public protest of Chinese students in Tokyo, with a suggestion to the village elders to establish schools), in Chung-kuo Shih-hsüeh Hui, *Hsin-hai ko-ming,* Vol. II.

[169] Tzu-hsü-tzu (pseud.). Hsiang-shih chi (Hunan affairs). 2 vols. Peking, 1914.—A record of political events that took place in Hunan province from October 1911 to the fall of 1913. The author was pro-Yüan Shih-k'ai.

[170] Wang Ching-wei.* Wang Ching-wei wen-ts'un (Collected essays of Wang Ching-wei). Vol. I. Canton, 1926.—A collection of Wang's writings in 1905–11, which appeared originally in the *Min-pao (People's Journal).*

[171] Wang Hsing-jui. "Ch'ing-chi Fu-jen Wen-she yü ko-ming yün-tung ti kuan-hsi" (The Fu-jen Literary Society and the revolutionary movement in the Ch'ing period), *Shih-hsüeh tsa-chih* (Historical Magazine), Vol. I, No. 1 (Chungking, December 5, 1945), pp. 35–45.— A study of the personalities and the nature of the organization that cooperated with Sun Yat-sen in the revolutionary attempt of 1895.

[172] Wei Yung. The Cult of Dr. Sun. Shanghai: The Independent Weekly, 1931.

[173] Wu Chih-hui.* Wu Chih-hui ch'üan-chi (Collected works). Shanghai, 1927.

[174] Wu Hsing-han. "Wu-ch'ang ch'i-i san-jih chi" (An account of the first three days after the outbreak of the Wuchang revolution), in Chung-kuo Shih-hsüeh Hui, *Hsin-hai ko-ming,* Vol. V.

[175] Yamaura Kanichi.* Mori Kaku* (A biography of Mori Kaku). Tokyo, 1940.

[176] Yang Shih-chi. Hsin-hai ko-ming ch'ien-hou Hu-nan shih-shih (The revolutionary movement in Hunan before and after the revolution of 1911). Changsha, 1958.—Based on primary and secondary sources as well as interviews of the participants.

[177] Yang Shou-jen.* Hsin Hu-nan (New Hunan). [Tokyo, 1903?].—Written by Huang Hsing's close friend under the pseudonym

Hu-nan jen chih Hu-nan (Hunanese of Hunan), this book presents the author's idea of Hunanese responsibility in the country's critical era.

[178] Yang Yu-ch'iung. Chung-kuo cheng-tang shih (A history of Chinese political parties). Shanghai, 1936.

[179] Yang Yü-ju.* Hsin-hai ko-ming hsien-chu chi (The decisive steps of the revolution of 1911). Peking, 1958.—Written by a local revolutionary leader in Hupeh, this book contains firsthand information on the developments of the Hupeh revolutionary movement that led to the outbreak of the Wuchang Revolution. The title of the book is derived from a poem by Huang Hsing.

[180] Yü Han-ying, ed. Chih-yüan Chüeh-ssu T'uan shih-mo chi (A complete record of the Dare-to-Die Corps). Wuchang, 1912.—A record of the Dare-to-Die Corps, which was set up in Shanghai after the outbreak of the Wuchang Revolution.

[181] Yüan Shih-k'ai.* Yüan ta-tsung-t'ung shu-tu hui-pien (A collection of President Yüan's correspondence). Compiled by Hsü Yu-p'eng. 2d ed. Shanghai, 1935 (1st ed., 1914).—A collection of the correspondence of Yüan Shih-k'ai in the first few years of the Republic, including some telegrams exchanged between Yüan and Huang Hsing.

[182] Yün Tai-ying. Chung-kuo min-tsu ko-ming yün-tung shih (A history of the Chinese revolutionary movement). China, n.d.—A noted Chinese Communist's lectures, probably delivered in the fall of 1926.

[183] Yung-tsan (pseud. of Kung Hsia-ch'u). "Wu-ch'ang liang-jih chi" (An account of events in Wuchang on October 9–10, 1911), in Chung-kuo Shih-hsüeh Hui, Hsin-hai ko-ming, Vol. V.

OVERSEAS CHINESE AND THE REVOLUTION

[184] Chang Yung-fu.* Nan-yang yü ch'uang-li min-kuo (Nanyang and the founding of the Republic). Shanghai, 1933.—Written by the chairman of the Singapore Branch of the T'ung Meng Hui, this book is an account of Sun Yat-sen's activities in Singapore up to 1908. One letter written by Huang Hsing and a number of Sun Yat-sen's letters are reproduced in facsimile. An appendix contains Hu Han-min's speech, "Southeast Asia and the Chinese Revolution."

[185] Chung-kuo Kuo-min-tang chu Mei-kuo Tsung-chih-pu li-nien tang-wu kai-yao (Party activities of the American Bureau of the Kuomintang). [San Francisco, 1933].—Published by the Chinese Nationalist League (American Bureau of the Kuomintang), this pamphlet contains brief information on the early revolutionary movement in the United States, especially in San Francisco.

[186] Feng Tzu-yu.* Hua-ch'iao ko-ming k'ai-kuo shih (The overseas Chinese, the revolution, and the establishment of the Republic). Shanghai, 1946.

[187] ———. Hua-ch'iao ko-ming tsu-chih shih-hua (History of overseas Chinese revolutionary organizations). Taipei, 1954.

BIBLIOGRAPHY

[188] Hsü Shih-yin. Mien-tien Chung-kuo T'ung Meng Hui k'ai-kuo ko-ming shih (The revolutionary history of the Burma branch of the T'ung Meng Hui). 2 vols. [Rangoon, 1931?].—Volume I is a source book on the Chinese revolutionary movement in Burma from 1908 to 1912, but it contains no information on Huang Hsing's sojourn in that country. Volume II was not available for use in this study.

[189] Hu Han-min.* "Nan-yang yü Chung-kuo ko-ming" (Southeast Asia and the Chinese revolution), in Feng Tzu-yu, Ko-ming i-shih, V (Shanghai, 1947), 206–40.—This speech was published in the Shanghai Hsin Ya-hsi-ya (New Asia), Vol. I, Nos. 5–6 (February 1 to March 1, 1931). Because issue No. 5 is not available, the text found in Feng's book is used. Obviously, it was not delivered in 1936 as Feng stated.

[190] Huang Ching-wan, ed. Nan-yang P'i-li hua-ch'iao ko-ming shih-chi (Revolutionary historical materials on the overseas Chinese in Perak). Shanghai, 1933.—A valuable collection of documents and letters reproduced in facsimile. The letters were written by Huang Hsing, Sun Yat-sen, Hu Han-min, Wang Ching-wei, and other revolutionary leaders to their comrades in Perak, Malaya.

[191] Huang San-te. Hung-meng ko-ming shih (The revolutionary history of the Hung League). [San Francisco or Los Angeles], 1936.—A critical account of Sun Yat-sen's activities in the United States, written by an old friend of his who was the leader of the Hung League in California and assisted him in the revolution.

[192] Teng Tse-ju.* Chung-kuo Kuo-min-tang erh-shih nien shih-chi. (Twenty years' historical materials of the Kuomintang). Shanghai, 1948.—This book contains twelve letters written by Huang Hsing to the author in 1911 in connection with Huang's fund-raising campaign in Malaya for the Canton revolution.

[193] Wang Tun-ken. Wu P'ing-i (Ch'eng-yü) chi-nien ts'e (In commemoration of Wu P'ing-i). Shanghai, 1932.—This pamphlet contains two letters written by Huang Hsing, one of which is reproduced in facsimile.

HSING CHUNG HUI

[194] Ch'en Ch'un-sheng. "Keng-tzu Hui-chou ch'i-i chi" (An account of the Waichow revolt of 1900), Chien-kuo yüeh-k'an, Vol. V, No. 3 (July 1931).

[195] Ch'en Hsi-ch'i. T'ung Meng Hui ch'eng-li ch'ien ti Sun Chung-shan (Sun Yat-sen prior to the founding of the T'ung Meng Hui). Canton, 1957.—Based on primary and secondary sources.

[196] Ch'en Shao-pai.* Hsing Chung Hui ko-ming shih-yao (A brief revolutionary history of the Hsing Chung Hui). Taipei, 1956.—The author was Sun Yat-sen's closest comrade during the Hsing Chung Hui period but sank into oblivion after the founding of the T'ung Meng Hui. His writings appeared at first in the Shanghai Chien-kuo yüeh-

242

k'an, Vol. I, No. 3 through Vol. III, No. 1 (July 15, 1929 to May 1930) ; they were published in book form in 1935.

[197] Ch'en Te-yün, ed. Ch'en Shao-pai hsien-sheng ai-ssu lu (An obituary record of Ch'en Shao-pai). [Canton, 1934?].—This book includes a biographical sketch of Ch'en Shao-pai.

[198] Duncan, Chesney. Tse Tsan Tai. London, 1917.

[199] Hsüeh, Chün-tu.* "Sun Yat-sen, Yang Ch'ü-yün, and the Early Revolutionary Movement in China," *Journal of Asian Studies,* Vol. XIX, No. 3 (May 1960), pp. 307–18.

[200] Lo Chia-lun. Chung-shan hsien-sheng lun-tun pei-nan shih-liao k'ao-ting (A critical study of the official documents concerning Sun Yat-sen's *Kidnapped in London*). Shanghai, 1930.

[201] Lo Hsiang-lin. Kuo-fu yü Ou-Mei chih yu-hao (Sun Yat-sen and his European and American friends). Taipei, 1951.

[202] Miyazaki Torazō.* Sanjūsannen no yume (The thirty-three years' dream). Tokyo, 1926.

[203] Shun-te Wang Lieh hsien-sheng pa-shih k'ai-i jung-shou cheng-wen ch'i-shih (An announcement for the contribution of articles in commemoration of the eighty-first birthday of Wang Lieh). Hong Kong, 1935.—Contains a dubious version of the early history of the Hsing Chung Hui. Many phrases are identical with those in the *Yang Ch'ü-yün lüeh-shih,* listed below.

[204] Sun Yat-sen. Kidnapped in London. Bristol: J. W. Arrowsmith, [1897].

[205] Tse Tsan Tai.* The Chinese Republic: Secret History of the Revolution. Hong Kong: *South China Morning Post,* 1924.

[206] Yang Ch'ü-yün lüeh-shih (Biographical sketch of Yang Ch'ü-yün). [Hong Kong], 1927.—The unknown author appears to have known Yang personally, although dubious facts are presented.

THE MONARCHICAL MOVEMENT
OF NINETEEN-FIFTEEN

[207] Chün-hsien wen-t'i wen-tien hui-pien (A collection of letters and telegrams concerning constitutional monarchy). Peking, [1915].

[208] Chün-wu Yüan k'ao-shih: fu Liang-Kuang Tu-ssu-ling-pu k'ao-shih (Authentic records of the Council of Military Affairs: supplemented by records of the Office of the Commander-in-Chief of Kwangtung and Kwangsi). Edited by the Office of the General Staff, the Headquarters of the Commander-in-Chief of Kwangtung and Kwangsi. Shanghai, 1916.—A collection of documents concerning the anti-Yüan Shih-k'ai campaigns conducted by the Council of Military Affairs. It contains some telegrams exchanged between Huang Hsing and the leaders of the Council, which was established on May 8, 1916 and was abolished on July 14 of the same year.

[209] Hou I. Hung-hsien chiu-wen (The story of the Hung-hsien reign). China, 1928.

[210] Huang I. Yüan-shih tao-kuo chi (The record of Yüan Shih-k'ai's betrayal of the Republic). 2d ed. [Hong Kong?], 1916.—A source book on the monarchical movement.

[211] Kao Lao. Ti-chih yün-tung shih-mo chi (The monarchical movement in China in 1915). Shanghai, 1923.

[212] Liang Ch'i-ch'ao.* Tun-pi chi (Works written in the army). 2 vols. 9th ed. Shanghai, 1926 (1st ed., 1916).—A collection of telegrams, letters, and essays written during the war against Yüan Shih-k'ai in 1916.

[213] Liu Ch'eng-yü.* Hung-hsien chi-shih shih pen-shih pu-chu (Poems recording historical events of the reign of Hung-hsien, with annotations). China, n.d.; Sun Yat-sen's preface is dated 1922.

[214] [T'ang Chi-yao].* Hui-tse shou-i wen-tu (A collection of T'ang Chi-yao's telegrams, letters, and documents relating to the campaigns against Yüan Shih-k'ai). 2 vols. Yunnan, 1917.—T'ang was the Military Governor of Yunnan province.

[215] Ts'ai O.* Ts'ai Sung-p'o hsien-sheng i-chi (Works of Ts'ai O). Hunan, 1933. 13 vols.

[216] Wang Chien-chung. Hung-hsien tsan-shih (A grievous story of the Hung-hsien period). Peking, 1925.—The author was one of those arrested for opposing Yüan Shih-k'ai.

[217] Yu Hui-yüan. Chung-hua min-kuo tsai-tsao shih (The reestablishment of the Chinese Republic). Shanghai, 1917.—Based on primary sources.

[218] Yüan Shih-k'ai wei-tsao min-i chi-shih (An exposure of the political intrigues at Peking against the Republic of China). [Yunnan, 1916].

NEWSPAPERS AND PERIODICALS

[219] *Ai-kuo pao.* Peking, Nos. 824 (March 22, 1909)–1139 [February 1910].

[220] *Ch'ang-yen pao.* Shanghai, Nos. 1 (August 17, 1898)–10 (November 19, 1898).

[221] *Che-chiang ch'ao* (The Tide of Chekiang). 10 nos. Tokyo, 1903.—A Chinese monthly published by the Chekiang students in Japan.

[222] *Chia-yin* (The Tiger). Tokyo, Nos. 1 (May 10, 1914)–10 (October 10, 1915). A scholarly monthly edited by Chang Shih-chao. Anti–Yüan Shih-k'ai.

[223] *Chicago Herald.* September 30, 1914.

[224] *Chien-kuo yüeh-k'an.* (The Reconstruction Monthly). Shanghai and Nanking, Vol. I, No. 1 (May 15, 1929)–Vol. XV, No. 1 (July 20, 1936).—This monthly is an important source for the study of the Republican Revolution. It was published in Nanking from Vol. IV, No. 5 (March 1931).

[225] *Chin-tai shih tzu-liao* (Source materials on modern history). Peking, 1954—.

[226] *Ching-hua pao.* Peking, Nos. 1–4 (1901).

[227] *Ch'ing-i pao ch'üan-pien.* 6 vols. Yokohama, n.d.—An accumulative edition of the *Ch'ing-i pao* published from 1898 to 1901 totaling one hundred issues.

[228] *Hsiang-hsüeh pao.* Changsha, [1897?]—The first issue contains a curriculum of the Academy of Hunan and Hupeh (Liang-hu Shuyüan).

[229] *Hsin-min ts'ung-pao.* Yokohama, Nos. 1 (1902)–96 (1907).

[230] *Hsin shih-chi (Le Siècle Nouveau).* Paris, June 22, 1907 to May 21, 1910. Reprinted in 4 vols. Shanghai, 1947.—A Chinese weekly published by Wu Chih-hui and others in Paris. The French title, *Le Siècle Nouveau,* was adopted after January 23, 1909.

Hu-kuo chün chi-shih. See *Kung-ho chün chi-shih.*

[231] *Hu-nan li-shih tzu-liao* [quarterly] (Historical source materials on Hunan). Hunan, No. 1 (March 30, 1959).

[232] *Ko-ming wen-hsien ts'ung-k'an* (Serial publications of the collected documents on the revolution). Vol. I, Nos. 5–7 (March to September 1947).—See also *Tang-shih shih-liao ts'ung-k'an.*

[233] *Kung-ho chün chi-shih* (Annals of the Republican Army). Shanghai, Nos. 1–3 and 5 (April to December 1916).—This monthly contains articles, documents, and accounts of the army's opposition to Yüan Shih-k'ai in the civil war of 1915–16. It was also issued under the title *Hu-kuo chün chi-shih.*

[234] *Kuo-feng pao.* Shanghai, Nos. 1–17 (1910–11).

[235] *Kuo-shih Kuan kuan-k'an* (Publications of the National Historical Bureau). Nanking, Vol. I, Nos. 1–4, and Vol. II, No. 1 (1947–49).—A quarterly published by the government bureau of official history, containing valuable source materials on the Republican Revolution.

[236] *Min-k'ou tsa-chih* (Public Opinion Magazine). San Francisco, No. 6 (1914).—This issue of the monthly contains an account of Huang Hsing's visit and his speeches at Honolulu and San Francisco.

[237] *Min-kuo.* Tokyo, Nos. 1 (May 10, 1914)–4 (August 10, 1914).

[238] *Min-li pao.** Shanghai, October 11, 1910, to September 4, 1913.—This complete file of the revolutionary newspaper in Shanghai is probably the most important source on Huang Hsing's political ideas and activities in the first two years of the Republic.

[239] *Min-pao** (People's Journal). 26 nos. Tokyo, 1905–10. Photolithographed by the Institute of History of the Chinese Academy of Sciences in 4 vols. Peking, 1957.—Official organ of the T'ung Meng Hui.

[240] *National Review.* Shanghai, 1912–13.

[241] *New York Daily Tribune.* July 20, 1914.

[242] *New York Times.* 1913–16.

[243] *Pei-ching hsin-wen hui-pao.* Peking, Nos. 1 (April 25, 1901) -12 (June 6, 1901).

[244] *Pu-jen.* Shanghai, Nos. 1 (February 1913)-9/10 (December 1917).—K'ang Yu-wei's publication.

[245] *Republican Advocate.* Shanghai, April 1912 to November 1913.

[246] *San Francisco Examiner.* July–August 1914.

[247] *Shao-nien Chung-kuo ch'en-pao** (The Young China). San Francisco, July 1914 to December 1916.—This revolutionary newspaper began publication in 1910. It is one of the most important sources on Huang Hsing's visit in the United States.

[248] *Shih-wu pao.* Shanghai, Nos. 1 (April 9, 1896)-69 (August 8, 1898).

[249] *Tang-pao.* Tokyo, Nos. 1 (April 20, 1913)-4 (July 20, 1913). —An organ of the Chinese Republican Party (Kung Ho Tang, later called the Progressive Party) in Japan with articles on Chinese politics and finance. It also contains government regulations, presidential decrees, official documents. The "National Affairs" column of the first issue contains a text of Huang Hsing's telegram to Yüan Shih-k'ai dated March 21 [1913], reporting the assassination of Sung Chiao-jen.

[250] *Tang-shih shih-liao ts'ung-k'an* (Serial publications of the collected materials on the party history). Chungking, Nos. 1 [1942?]– 4 (November 1945).—Published irregularly by the Committee for the Compilation of Materials on the Party History of the Central Executive Committee of the Kuomintang, the first few issues of this periodical contain writings of Huang Hsing. Issues Nos. 1 and 2 are undated. The title of the publication was subsequently changed to the *Ko-ming wen-hsien ts'ung-k'an.*

[251] *Tu-li chou-pao* (The Independent). Shanghai, Nos. 6 (October 27, 1912)-35 (June 1, 1913).—This weekly was edited by Chang Shih-chao after he had left the *Min-li pao.*

[252] *Tung-fang tsa-chih* (The Eastern Miscellany). Shanghai, 1904–16.—A well-known Chinese magazine that contains reports on the current events in the nation, as well as other articles. It ceased publication in December 1948.

[253] *Yu-hsüeh i-pien** (Translations by Hunan students abroad). 12 nos. Tokyo, 1902–3.—A Chinese monthly published by Huang Hsing and other Hunanese students in Japan.

[254] *Yün-nan tsa-chih hsüan-chi* (Selections from the Yunnan magazine). Peking, 1958.—Reprints from a monthly originally published in Tokyo by Yunnan students. The magazine put out 23 issues and one supplement. The first issue was published on October 15, 1906, and publication ceased after the outbreak of the Revolution of 1911. The reprint lacks Nos. 17, 21–23.

[255] *Yung-yen* (The Justice). Tientsin, Vol. I, No. 1 (December 1, 1912)-Vol. II, No. 6 (June 5, 1914).—Edited by Huang Yüan-yung after January 1914.

GLOSSARY

This list provides Chinese characters for some of the personal, geographical and institutional names occurring in the text, as well as for newspaper and periodical titles therein.

Akasaka, 赤坂

Aoyama, 靑山

Chang Cheng-wu, 張振武

Chang Chi, 張繼

Chang Chien, 張謇

Chang Chih-tung, 張之洞

Chang Jen-chieh, 張人傑

Chang Nan-hsien, 張難先

Chang Ping-lin, 章炳麟

Chang Shao-ts'eng, 張紹曾

Chang Shih-chao, 章士釗

Chang Yü-k'un, 章裕昆

Chang Yung-fu, 張永福

Chao Ping-chün, 趙秉鈞

Chao Sheng, 趙聲

Chaochow, 潮州

Ch'en Ch'i-mei, 陳其美

Ch'en Chin-t'ao, 陳錦濤

Ch'en Ch'iung-ming, 陳炯明

Ch'en Fan, 陳範

Ch'en Shao-pai, 陳少白

Ch'en T'ien-hua, 陳天華

Ch'en Wei-lun, 陳維綸

Cheng Shih-liang, 鄭士良

Ch'eng Ch'ien, 程潛

Ch'eng Te-ch'üan, 程德全

Ch'eng-wu Hsüeh-she, 振武學社

Chengnankuan, 鎭南關

Chiang I-wu, 蔣翊武

Chiao Ta-feng, 焦達峯

Ch'in-hsüeh She, 勤學舍

Ch'in Li-shan, 秦力山

Ch'iu Chin, 秋瑾

Chinchow, 欽州

ching, 井

Chinuhu, 七女湖

Chou Chung-yo, 周鐘嶽

Chu Ho-chung, 朱和中

Chü Cheng, 居正

Chün Kuo-min Chiao-yü Hui, 軍國民教育會

Ch'ün-chih Hsüeh-hui, 羣治學會

Chung-hua Ko-ming Tang, 中華革命黨

247

Chung-kuo Ko-ming T'ung-meng Hui, 中國革命同盟會

Chungshan, 中山

Erh-shih shih-chi chih chih-na, 二十世紀之支那

En Ming, 恩銘

Fang Wei, 方維

Fangcheng, 防城

Feng Kuo-chang, 馮國璋

Feng-lo Yüan, 鳳樂園

Feng Shan, 鳳山

Feng Tzu-yu, 馮自由

Fu-jen Wen-she, 輔仁文社

Fuji, 富士

Fukuzumi, 福住

Furukawa, 古川

Ginza, 銀座

Haiphong, 海防

Hakone, 箱根

Hasegawa Yoshimichi, 長谷川好道

Hirayama Shū, 平山周

Ho Ch'eng-chün, 何成濬

Ho Hai-ming, 何海鳴

Ho Kai (Ho Chi), 何啓

Hokow, 河口

Hsing Chung Hui (Revive China Society), 興中會

Hsiangtan, 湘潭

Hsin-wen pao, 新聞報

Hsiu-ts'ai, 秀才

Hsiung Ch'eng-chi, 熊成基

Hsiung Hsi-ling, 熊希齡

Hsiung Ping-k'un, 熊秉坤

Hsü Hsi-lin, 徐錫麟

Hsü Tsung-han, 徐宗漢

Hsüeh Chün-tu, 薛君度

Hu Han-min, 胡漢民

Hu Lin-i, 胡林翼

Hu-nan Pien-i She, 湖南編譯社

Hu-pei hsüeh-sheng chieh, 湖北學生界

Hu Tsu-shun, 胡祖舜

Hu Ying, 胡瑛

Hu Yüan-t'an, 胡元倓

Hua Hsing Hui (Society for the Revival of China), 華興會

Huang Chen, 黃軫

Huang Chen-hua, 黃振華

Huang Chi-t'ing, 黃吉亭

Huang Chin-wu, 黃厪午

Huang Fu, 黃郛

Huang Fu-sheng, 黃復生

Huang Hsiao-ts'un, 黃筱村

Huang Hsing, 黃興

Huang I-ch'iu, 黃一球

Huang I-chung, 黃一中

Huang I-huan, 黃一寰

Huang I-mei, 黃一美

Huang I-ou, 黃一歐

Huang K'o-ch'iang, 黃克強

Huang Ling-shuang, 黃凌霜

Huang Nai, 黃鼐

Huang Te-hua, 黃德華

Huang Ti, 黃帝

Huang Wen-hua, 黃文華

Huang Wen-shan, 黃文山

Huang Yü-ying, 黃毓英

Huang Yung-shang, 黃詠商

Huanghuakang, 黃花崗

Huangkang, 黃岡

Hung Shu-tsu, 洪述祖

Hungchiang, 洪江

I-shu hui-pien, 譯書彙編

I Tzu-ju, 易自如

I Ying-tien, 倪映典

Ike Kyōkichi, 池亨吉

Inukai Tsuyoshi, 犬養毅

Ipoh, 怡保

Jih Chih Hui, 日知會

Jui Cheng, 瑞徵

Kagura-zaka, 神樂坂

K'ai-chih lu, 開智錄

Kakumei Hyōron, 革命評論

K'ang Yu-wei, 康有為

Kayano Nagatomo (Chōchi), 萱野長知

Ko-ming chün, 革命軍

K'o-hsüeh Pu-hsi So, 科學補習所

K'o-lao, 克老

Kōbun Institute, 弘(宏)文學院

Kodama Yūji, 兒玉右二

Kōjimachi, 麴町

Kozu, 國府津

Ku Chung-ch'en, 顧忠琛

Kuang Fu Hui, 光復會

Kuang-hsü, 光緒

Kung Chin Hui, 共進會

Kung Ho Tang, 共和黨

Kung Pao-ch'ün, 龔寶銓

Kuo Jen-chang, 郭人漳

Kuo-min pao, 國民報

Kuo-t'ing, 過庭

Kwangchowwan, 廣州灣

Lan T'ien-wei, 藍天蔚

Laokai, 老街

Li Chien-nung, 李劍農

Li Chih Hui, 勵志會

Li Hsieh-ho, 李燮和

Li Hung-chang, 李鴻章

Li Lieh-chün, 李烈鈞

Li Lien-fang, 李廉方

Li Liu-ju, 李六如

Li Shu-ch'eng, 李書城

Li Yüan-hung, 黎元洪

Liang Ch'i-ch'ao, 梁啟超

Liang-Hu Shu-yüan, 兩湖書院

Liang Pi, 良弼

Liang Shih-i, 梁士詒

Liang Ting-fen, 梁鼎芬

Liao Hsing-fang, 廖星舫

Liao Tan-ju, 廖淡如

Lienchow, 廉州

Liling, 醴陵

Lin Kuei, 林圭

Lingshan, 靈山

Liu Ch'eng-yü, 劉成禺

Liu K'uei-i, 劉揆一

Liu Kung, 劉公

Liu-shou, 留守

Liu Tao-i, 劉道一

Liuyang, 瀏陽

Lo Fu-hsing, 羅福星

Lu Cheng-hsiang, 陸徵祥

Lu Hao-tung, 陸皓東

Lü Chih-i, 呂志伊

Luanchow, 灤州

Lung Hua Hui, 龍華會

Lungchow, 龍州

Lungpan, 龍邦

Ma Chün-wu, 馬君武

Ma Fu-i, 馬福益

Man-hua, 曼華

Mengtsz, 蒙自

Min-li pao, 民立報

Min-pao (People's Journal), 民報

Ming-te, 明德

Mitsui, 三井

Miyazaki Tamizō, 宮崎民藏

Miyazaki Torazō (Tōten), 宮崎寅藏 (滔天)

Momowara, 桃原

Mori Kaku, 森恪

Niu Yung-chien, 鈕永鍵

Ōmori, 大森

Pai Ch'u-hsiang, 白楚香

Paoan, 寶安

Pi Yung-nien, 畢永年

Pingsiang, 萍鄉

Po Wen-wei, 柏文蔚

Pu Yi (P'u-i), 溥儀

Sa Chen-ping, 薩鎮冰

Sakamoto Kinya, 阪本金彌

Seremban, 芙蓉

Shanhua, 善化

Shao-nien Chung-kuo ch'en-pao, 少年中國晨報

Sheng Hsüan-huai, 盛宣懷

Shih Chien-ju, 史堅如

Shu-wu, 庶務

Su-pao, 蘇報

Su Tung-p'o, 蘇東坡

Suenaga Setsu, 末永節

Sun Chia-nai, 孫家鼐

Sun Chu-tan, 孫竹丹

Sun Pao-ch'i, 孫寶琦

Sun Yü-yün, 孫毓筠

Sun Wu, 孫武

Sung Chiao-jen, 宋教仁

Sung Yü-lin, 宋玉琳

T'an Jen-feng, 譚人鳳

T'an Ssu-t'ung, 譚嗣同

T'an Yen-k'ai, 譚延闓

T'ang Chi-yao, 唐繼堯

T'ang Shao-i, 唐紹儀

T'ang Shou-ch'ien, 湯壽潛

T'ang Ts'ai-ch'ang, 唐才常

T'ang Tseng-pi, 湯增璧

T'ao Ch'eng-chang, 陶成章

Te Shou, 德壽

Teng Tse-ju, 鄧澤如

Terauchi Masatake, 寺內正毅

T'ien T'ung, 田桐

Tsai Feng, 載灃

Ts'ai Chün, 蔡鈞

Ts'ai O, 蔡鍔

Ts'ai Yüan-p'ei, 蔡元培

Ts'ao Ya-po, 曹亞伯

Tse Tsan Tai (Hsieh Tsuan-t'ai), 謝纘泰

Ts'en Ch'un-hsüan, 岑春煊

Tseng Chi-tse, 曾紀澤

Tseng Kuo-fan, 曾國藩

Tso Tsung-t'ang, 左宗棠

Tsou Jung, 鄒容

Tu-tsung, 都總

Tuan Ch'i-jui, 段祺瑞

T'ung Ch'ou Hui, 同仇會

T'ung Meng Hui (The United League), 同盟會

Tung-ya Wan-kuo T'ung-meng Hui, 東亞萬國同盟會

Tunghsing, 東興

Tunghua, 通化

tz'u, 詞

Uchida Ryōhei, 內田良平

Waichow, 惠州

Wan Fu-hua, 萬福華,

Wan-kuo kung-pao, 萬國公報

Wang Chih-ch'un, 王之春

Wang Chih-hsiang, 王芝祥

Wang Ching-wei, 汪精衛

Wang Ch'ung-hui, 王寵惠

Wang Fu-chih, 王夫之

Wang K'ang-nien, 汪康年

Wang T'ao, 王韜

Wei Yüan, 魏源

Wen Hsüeh Hui, 文學會

Wen P'u-t'ung Hsüeh-t'ang, 文普通學堂

Wu Chao-lin, 吳兆麟

Wu Chih-hui, 吳稚暉

Wu Lu-chen, 吳祿貞

Wu Shih-ying, 武士英

Wu Ting-fang, 伍廷芳

Wu Yüeh, 吳樾

Yamaura Kanichi, 山浦貫一

Yang Chao-jung, 楊兆蓉

Yang Ch'ü-yün, 楊衢雲

Yang Jui, 楊銳

Yang Shou-jen, 楊守仁

Yang Shu-k'an, 楊庶堪

Yang Tu, 楊度

Yang Yü-ju, 楊玉如

Ying Ch'ang, 蔭昌

Ying Kuei-hsing, 應桂馨

Yo-lo Mountain, 嶽麓山

Yokosuka, 橫須賀

Yu-hsüeh i-pien, 游學譯編

Yü Lien-san, 俞廉三

Yüan Shih-k'ai, 袁世凱

INDEX

Academy of Current Affairs (Changsha), 3, 7
Academy of Hunan and Hupeh, 3–5, 16
American Revolution, 9, 18, 120
Anking: revolt of 1907, 46, 62; of 1908, 72
Assassinations, as revolutionary scheme, 75
Association for European Studies, 177–78, 180
Association for Universal Military Education, 10–12, 14, 39, 46

Beard, Charles A., 173
Berlin: Chinese students in, 36, 37; T'ung Meng Hui in, 47
Black Dragon Society, 42
Blake, Sir Henry A., 33
Border provinces, revolutionary activity in, 56–57. *See also* Ten unsuccessful revolutionary attempts
Boxer uprising, 6, 10, 16, 32, 94
Brussels: Chinese students in, 36, 37; T'ung Meng Hui in, 47

Canada: T'ung Meng Hui in, 48; contributions of Chinese in, 86. *See also* Overseas Chinese
Cantlie, James, 196
Canton: attempted coup of 1895, 30–31, 51, 56, 196; attempted army coup of 1910, 76–77, 78; revolution of March 29, 1911, 56, 78–86 *passim*, 87–93, 206
Chang Cheng-wu, 139 f., 142
Chang Chi, 39 f., 53 f., 63, 128, 149, 199; early revolutionary career, 8, 14, 16, 193; quoted, 17; and at-

tempted Changsha revolt, 22 ff.; and founding of T'ung Meng Hui, 44; editor of *People's Journal*, 48–49, 200 f.; on early days of Provisional Government, 130–31; opposes Yüan Shih-k'ai, 162, 164; in National Assembly, 183, 222
Chang Chien, 119, 130 ff., 150 f.; quoted, 217
Chang Chih-tung, 3–4, 62
Chang Jen-chieh, 127
Chang, Nan-hsien, 108, 110
Chang Ping-lin, 75, 127, 135; early revolutionary activities, 8, 13, 14–15, 35, 193, 199; in T'ung Meng Hui, 54, 60, 63 f.; editor of *People's Journal*, 49, 52–53, 73, 201
Chang Shao-ts'eng, 133
Chang Shih-chao, 13 f., 157, 193; and attempted Changsha revolt, 19, 23–24
Chang Yü-k'un, 207
Chang Yung-fu, quoted, 58
Changsha: attempted revolt in (1904), 19–25, 31, 41, 46, 95, 198, 202; rice riot in, 94, 96
Chao Ping-chün, 144, 146, 153
Chao Sheng, 65 f., 78, 82, 100; and attempted Canton army coup (1910), 76 f.; role of, in Canton Revolution (1911), 83 f., 86, 88, 90–91, 92, 206
Ch'en Ch'i-mei, 100, 152, 160, 168, 211; role of, in Wuchang Revolution, 119 f.; political role in Republic, 127, 137; opposes Yüan Shih-k'ai, 162, 180; on politics of Republic, 218
Ch'en Chin-t'ao, 130 f.
Ch'en Ch'iung-ming, 86, 162, 168, 174, 177 f., 200

Hupeh New Army, 20, 102, 111–12
Hupeh province, revolutionary organ-
izations in, 95–103
Hupeh Students' Circle, 9

I Tzu-ju, 2
I Ying-tien, 76 f.
Ike Kyōkichi, 67
Imperial armies, and revolutionary
cause, 57, 80–81. *See also* Canton;
Chao Sheng; Kuo Jen-chang
Intellectuals, 45; Sun Yat-sen and, 35–
37. *See also* Chinese students; Hua
Hsing Hui; *People's Journal*; Res-
toration Society; T'ung Meng Hui
Inukai Tsuyoshi, 162

Japan: Chinese students in, 6–12, 38–
39, 59–60, 198; reform movement
in, 31; war with Russia, 39; threats
against China, 177. *See also* Huang
Hsing; Sun Yat-sen; T'ung Meng
Hui
Jenks, Jeremiah W., 173
Jiu Cheng, 108

K'ang Yu-wei, 3, 5, 7, 14, 33, 37
Kayano Nagatomo, 53, 65, 81, 115,
164, 170; on meeting of Sun Yat-
sen and Huang Hsing (1910), 82–
83
Kiangsu Journal, 13, 14–15
Kōbun Institute (Tokyo), 9, 12, 199
Kodama Yūji, 79
Ku Chung-ch'en, 134
Ku Chung-hsiu, 211–12
Kuang Fu Hui, *see* Restoration So-
ciety
Kung Hsia-ch'u, 209
Kung Pao-ch'üan, 46
Kuo Chih-sheng, 156
Kuo Jen-chang, 24, 57, 68–69; and
fifth revolutionary attempt, 65 f.
Kuo-min pao, 7 f., 192
Kuo Sung-tao, 1
Kuomintang, 42, 95, 114, 140 f., 146 f.,
159, 161, 172, 177 f., 182, 185, 188;
early struggles with Yüan Shih-
k'ai, 144–45; purposes of, 148–49;
victory of, in elections of 1912–13,
151–52; deterioration of relations
with Yüan, 154–56; growing dis-

unity and loss of power, 162–64;
reorganization of, as Chinese Revolutionary Party, 164–69; revived
(1916), 183, 222. *See also* Chinese
Revolutionary Party; T'ung Meng
Hui
Kwangtung Independent Association,
35

Lan T'ien-wei, 10, 133, 212–13
Lea, Homer, 79
Lea, Mrs. Homer, 171
Li Chien-nung, 138; on political situation following Wuchang Revolu-
tion, 123–24
Li Hsieh-ho, 54 f., 119
Li Hung-chang, 26, 33
Li Lieh-chün, 155–56, 160, 162, 168,
174, 177–80 *passim*, 217, 221
Li Lien-fang, 108, 113; quoted, 118–19
Li Shu-ch'eng, 210 f.
Li Yüan-hung, 125, 134, 139, 142, 145,
147 f., 154, 182; role of, in Wu-
chang Revolution, 109–14 *passim*,
military governor of Hupeh, 118–
23, 209; Generalissimo, 124; vice-
president of Provisional Govern-
ment, 129; succeeds to presidency
of Republic (1916), 181
Liang Ch'i-ch'ao, 3, 5, 7, 34, 37, 39, 50
Liang Pi, 135
Liang Shih-i, 141
Liang Ting-fen, 5
Liao Hsing-fang, 2
Liao Shao-yu, 134
Liao Tan-ju, 2
Lin Kuei, 34
Linebarger, Paul, quoted, 171
Literary Society (in Hupeh), 95, 96–
97, 99, 102–3, 207, 209
Literati, *see* Intellectuals
Liu Ch'eng-yü, 8, 36, 197
Liu K'uei-i, 6, 17, 81, 97, 110, 153–54;
early revolutionary activities of, 18–
19, 24–25, 41, 61, 194; quoted, 54–
55
Liu Kung, 102, 108 f.
Liu Tao-i, 61 f.
Lo Fu-hsing, 209
Los Angeles, Huang Hsing in, 171
Lu Cheng-hsiang, 139
Lü Chih-i, 83, 97, 103–4, 128, 208